FOUNDATIONS OF SOFTWARE TESTING

ISTQB CERTIFICATION

FOURTH EDITION

Dorothy Graham

Rex Black

Erik van Veenendaal

Australia • Brazil • Mexico • Singapore • United Kingdom • United States

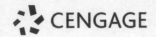

Foundations of Software Testing:
ISTQB Certification, **4th Edition**
Dorothy Graham, Rex Black, Erik van Veenendaal

Publisher: Annabel Ainscow

List Manager: Virginia Thorp

Marketing Manager: Anna Reading

Senior Content Project Manager:
   Melissa Beavis

Manufacturing Buyer: Elaine Bevan

Typesetter: SPi Global

Text Design: SPi Global

Cover Design: Jonathan Bargus

Cover Image(s): © dem10/iStock/Getty
   Images

For product information and technology assistance,
contact us at **emea.info@cengage.com.**

For permission to use material from this text or product
and for permission queries,
email **emea.permissions@cengage.com.**

British Library Cataloguing-in-Publication Data
A catalogue record for this book is available from the British Library.

ISBN: 978-1-4737-6479-8

Cengage Learning, EMEA
Cheriton House, North Way,
Andover, Hampshire, SP10 5BE
United Kingdom

Cengage Learning is a leading provider of customized learning solutions with employees residing in nearly 40 different countries and sales in more than 125 countries around the world. Find your local representative at: **www.cengage.co.uk.**

Cengage Learning products are represented in Canada by Nelson Education, Ltd.

To learn more about Cengage platforms and services, register or access your online learning solution, or purchase materials for your course, visit **www.cengage.com.**

Printed in the United Kingdom by CPI, Antony Rowe
Print Number: 07   Print Year: 2023

CONTENTS

FIGURES AND TABLES

ACKNOWLEDGEMENTS

The materials in this book are based on the ISTQB Foundation Syllabus 2018. The Foundation Syllabus is copyrighted to the ISTQB (International Software Testing Qualification Board). Permission has been granted by the ISTQB to the authors to use these materials as the basis of a book, provided that recognition of authorship and copyright of the Syllabus itself is given.

The ISTQB Glossary of Testing Terms, released as version 3.2 by the ISTQB in 2018 is used as the source of definitions in this book.

The co-authors would like to thank Dorothy Graham for her effort in updating this book to be fully aligned with the 2018 version of the ISTQB Foundation Syllabus and version 3.2 of the ISTQB Glossary.

Be aware that there are some defects in this book! The Syllabus, Glossary and this book were written by people – and people make mistakes. Just as with testing, we have applied reviews and tried to identify as many defects as we could, but we also needed to release the manuscript to the publisher. Please let us know of defects that you find in our book so that we can correct them in future printings.

The authors wish to acknowledge the contribution of Isabel Evans to a previous edition of this book. We also acknowledge contributions to this edition from Gerard Bargh, Mark Fewster, Graham Freeburn, Tim Fretwell, Gary Rueda Sandoval, Melissa Tondi, Nathalie van Delft, Seretta Gamba, and Tebogo Makaba.

Dorothy Graham, Macclesfield, UK
Rex Black, Texas, USA
Erik van Veenendaal, Hato, Bonaire
2019

PREFACE

The purpose of this book is to support the ISTQB Foundation Syllabus 2018, which is the basis for the International Foundation Certificate in Software Testing. The authors have been involved in helping to establish this qualification, donating their time and energy to the Syllabus, terminology Glossary and the International Software Testing Qualifications Board (ISTQB).

The authors of this book are all passionate about software testing. All have been involved in this area for most or all of their working lives, and have contributed to the field through practical work, training courses and books. They have written this book to help to promote the discipline of software testing.

The initial idea for this collaboration came from Erik van Veenendaal, author of *The Testing Practitioner*, a book to support the ISEB Software Testing Practitioner Certificate. The other authors agreed to work together as equals on this book. Please note that the order of the authors' names does not indicate any seniority of authorship, but simply which author was the last to update the book as the Foundation Syllabus evolved.

We intend that this book will increase your chances of passing the Foundation Certificate exam. If you are taking a course (or class) to prepare for the exam, this book will give you detailed and additional background about the topics you have covered. If you are studying for the exam on your own, this book will help you be more prepared. This book will give you information about the topics covered in the Syllabus, as well as worked exercises and practice exam questions (including a full 40-question mock exam paper in Chapter 7).

This book is a useful reference work about software testing in general, even if you are not interested in the exam. The Foundation Certificate represents a distilling of the essential aspects of software testing at the time of writing (2019), and this book will give you a good grounding in software testing.

ISTQB AND CERTIFICATION

ISTQB stands for International Software Testing Qualifications Board and is an organization consisting of software testing professionals from each of the countries who are members of the ISTQB. Each representative is a member of a Software Testing Board in their own country. The purpose of the ISTQB is to provide internationally accepted and consistent qualifications in software testing. ISTQB sets the Syllabus and gives guidelines for each member country to implement the qualification in their own country. The Foundation Certificate is the first internationally accepted qualification in software testing and its Syllabus forms the basis of this book.

From the first qualification in 1998 until the end of 2018, around 700,000 people have taken the Foundation Certificate exam administered by a National Board of the ISTQB, or by an Exam Board contracted to a National Board. This represents 86% of all ISTQB certifications. All ISTQB National Boards and Exam Boards recognize each other's Foundation Certificates as valid.

The ISTQB qualification is independent of any individual training provider. Any training organization can offer a course based on this publicly available Syllabus. However, the National Boards associated with ISTQB give special approval to organizations that meet their requirements for the quality of the training. Such organizations are accredited and are allowed to have an invigilator or proctor from an authorized National Board or Exam Board to give the exam as part of the accredited course. The exam is also available independently from accrediting organizations or National Boards.

Why is certification of testers important? The objectives of the qualification are listed in the Syllabus. They include:

● Recognition for testing as an essential and professional software engineering specialization.

● Enabling professionally qualified testers to be recognized by employers, customers and peers.

● Raising the profile of testers.

● Promoting consistent and good testing practices within all software engineering disciplines internationally, for reasons of opportunity, communication and sharing of knowledge and resources internationally.

FINDING YOUR WAY AROUND THIS BOOK

This book is divided into seven chapters. The first six chapters of the book each cover one chapter of the Syllabus, and each has some practice exam questions.

Chapter 1 is the start of understanding. We'll look at some fundamental questions: what is testing and why is it necessary? We'll examine why testing is not just running tests. We'll also look at why testing can damage relationships and how bridges between colleagues can be rebuilt.

In Chapter 2, we'll concentrate on testing in relation to the common software development models, including iterative and waterfall models. We'll see that different types of testing are used at different stages in the software development life cycle.

In Chapter 3, we'll concentrate on test techniques that can be used early in the software development life cycle. These include reviews and static analysis: tests done before compiling the code.

Chapter 4 covers test techniques. We'll show you techniques including equivalence partitioning, boundary value analysis, decision tables, state transition testing, use case testing, statement and decision coverage and experience-based techniques. This chapter is about how to become a better tester in terms of designing tests. There are exercises for the most significant techniques included in this chapter.

Chapter 5 is about the management and control of testing, including estimation, risk assessment, defect management and reporting. Writing a good defect report is a key skill for a good tester, so we have an exercise for that too.

In Chapter 6, we'll show you how tools support all the activities in the test process, and how to select and implement tools for the greatest benefit.

Chapter 7 contains general advice about taking the exam and has the full 40-question mock paper. This is a key learning aid to help you pass the real exam.

The appendices of the book include a full list of references and a copy of the ISTQB testing terminology Glossary, as well as the answers to all the practice exam questions.

TO HELP YOU USE THE BOOK

1 **Get a copy of the Syllabus:** You should download the Syllabus from the ISTQB website so that you have the current version, and so that you can check off the Syllabus objectives as you learn. This is available at https://www.istqb.org/downloads/syllabi/foundation-level-syllabus.html

2 **Understand what is meant by learning objectives and knowledge levels:** In the Syllabus, you will see learning objectives and knowledge (or cognitive) levels at the start of each section of each chapter. These indicate what you need to know and the depth of knowledge required for the exam. We have used the timings in the Syllabus and knowledge levels to guide the space allocated in the book, both for the text and for the exercises. You will see the learning objectives and knowledge levels at the start of each section within each chapter. The knowledge levels expected by the Syllabus are:

- **K1: remember, recognize, recall:** you will recognize, remember and recall a term or concept. For example, you could recognize one definition of failure as 'Non-delivery of service to an end user or any other stakeholder'.
- **K2: understand, explain, give reasons, compare, classify, summarize:** you can select the reasons or explanations for statements related to the topic, and can summarize, compare, classify and give examples for the testing concept. For example, you could explain that one reason why tests should be designed as early as possible is to find defects when they are cheaper to remove.
- **K3: apply:** you can select the correct application of a concept or technique and apply it to a given context. For example, you could identify boundary values for valid and invalid partitions, and you could select test cases from a given state transition diagram in order to cover all transitions.

Remember, as you go through the book, if a topic has a learning objective marked K1 you just need to recognize it. If it has a learning objective of K3 you will be expected to apply your knowledge in the exam, for example.

3 **Use the Glossary of terms:** Each chapter of the Syllabus has a number of terms listed in it. You are expected to remember these terms at least at K1 level, even if they are not explicitly mentioned in the learning objectives. You will see a number of **definitions** throughout this book, as in the sidebar.

Definition A description of the meaning of a word.

All definitions of software testing terms (called keywords in the chapters) are taken from the *ISTQB Glossary* (version 3.2), which is available online at www.glossary.istqb.org. A copy of this Glossary is also at the back of the book. All the terms that are specifically mentioned in the Syllabus, that is, the ones you need to learn for the exam, are mentioned in each section of this book.

You will notice that some terms in the Glossary at the back of this book are underlined. These are terms that are mentioned specifically as keywords in the Syllabus. These are the terms that you need to be familiar with for the exam.

4 **Use the references sensibly:** We have referenced all the books used by the Syllabus authors when they constructed the Syllabus. You will see these underlined in the list at the end of the book. We also added references to some other books, papers and websites that we thought useful or which we referred to when writing. You do not need to read all referenced books for the exam! However, you may find some of them useful for further reading to increase your knowledge after the exam, and to help you apply some of the ideas you will come across in this book.

5 **Do the practice exams:** When you get to the end of a chapter (for Chapters 1 to 6), answer the exam questions, and then turn to 'Answers to the Sample Exam Questions' to check if your answers were correct. After you have completed all of the six chapters, then take the full mock exam in Chapter 7. If you would like the most realistic exam conditions, then allow yourself just an hour to take the exam in Chapter 7. Also take the free sample exams from the ISTQB web site. You can download both the exam and the answers including justifications for the correct (and wrong) answers.

CENGAGE

Teaching & Learning Support Resources

Cengage's peer reviewed content for higher and further education courses is accompanied by a range of digital teaching and learning support resources. The resources are carefully tailored to the specific needs of the instructor, student and the course.

 A password protected area for instructors.

 An open-access area for students.

Lecturers: to discover the dedicated teaching digital support resources accompanying this textbook please register here for access:
cengage.com/dashboard/#login

Students: to discover the dedicated Learning digital support resources accompanying this textbook, please search for Foundations of Software Testing: ISTQB Certification, Fourth Edition on: **cengage.com**

BE UNSTOPPABLE!

Learn more at **cengage.com**

CHAPTER ONE
Fundamentals of testing

In this chapter, we will introduce you to the fundamentals of testing: what software testing is and why testing is needed, including its limitations, objectives and purpose; the principles behind testing; the process that testers follow, including activities, tasks and work products; and some of the psychological factors that testers must consider in their work. By reading this chapter you will gain an understanding of the fundamentals of testing and be able to describe those fundamentals.

Note that the learning objectives start with 'FL' rather than 'LO' to show that they are learning objectives for the Foundation Level qualification.

1.1 WHAT IS TESTING?

SYLLABUS LEARNING OBJECTIVES FOR 1.1 WHAT IS TESTING? (K2)

FL-1.1.1   Identify typical objectives of testing (K1)

FL-1.1.2   Differentiate testing from debugging (K2)

In this section, we will kick off the book by looking at what testing is, some misconceptions about testing, the typical objectives of testing and the difference between testing and debugging.

Within each section of this book, there are terms that are important – they are used in the section (and may be used elsewhere as well). They are listed in the Syllabus as keywords, which means that you need to know the definition of the term and it could appear in an exam question. We will give the definition of the relevant keyword terms in the margin of the text, and they can also be found in the Glossary (including the ISTQB online Glossary). We also show the keyword in **bold** within the section or subsection where it is defined and discussed.

In this section, the relevant keyword terms are **debugging**, **test object**, **test objective**, **testing**, **validation** and **verification**.

Software is everywhere

The last 100 years have seen an amazing human triumph of technology. Diseases that once killed and paralyzed are routinely treated or prevented – or even eradicated entirely, as with smallpox. Some children who stood amazed as they watched the first gasoline-powered automobile in their town are alive today, having seen people walk on the moon, an event that happened before a large percentage of today's workforce was even born.

Perhaps the most dramatic advances in technology have occurred in the arena of information technology. Software systems, in the sense that we know them, are a recent innovation, less than 70 years old, but have already transformed daily life around the world. Thomas Watson, the one-time head of IBM, famously predicted that only about five computers would be needed in the whole world. This vastly inaccurate prediction was based on the idea that information technology was useful only for business and government applications, such as banking, insurance and conducting a census. (The Hollerith punch-cards used by computers at the time Watson made his prediction were developed for the United States census.) Now, everyone who drives a car is using a machine not only designed with the help of computers, but which also contains more computing power than the computers used by NASA to get Apollo missions to and from the Moon. Mobile phones are now essentially handheld computers that get smarter with every new model. The Internet of Things (IoT) now gives us the ability to see who is at our door or turn on the lights when we are nowhere near our home.

However, in the software world, the technological triumph has not been perfect. Almost every living person has been touched by information technology, and most of us have dealt with the frustration and wasted time that occurs when software fails and exhibits unexpected behaviours. Some unfortunate individuals and companies have experienced financial loss or damage to their personal or business reputations as a result of defective software. A highly unlucky few have even been injured or killed by software failures, including by self-driving cars.

One way to help overcome such problems is software testing, when it is done well. Testing covers activities throughout the life cycle and can have a number of different objectives, as we will see in Section 1.1.1.

Testing is more than running tests

Testing The process consisting of all life cycle activities, both static and dynamic, concerned with planning, preparation and evaluation of software products and related work products to determine that they satisfy specified requirements, to demonstrate that they are fit for purpose and to detect defects.

An ongoing misperception, although less common these days, about **testing** is that it only involves running tests. Specifically, some people think that testing involves nothing beyond carrying out some sequence of actions on the system under test, submitting various inputs along the way and evaluating the observed results. Certainly, these activities are one element of testing – specifically, these activities make up the bulk of the test execution activities – but there are many other activities involved in the test process.

We will discuss the test process in more detail later in this chapter (in Section 1.4), but testing also includes (in addition to test execution): test planning, analyzing, designing and implementing tests, reporting test progress and results, and reporting defects. As you can see, there is a lot more to it than just running tests.

Notice that there are major test activities both before and after test execution. In addition, in the ISTQB definition of software testing, you will see that testing includes both static and dynamic testing. Static testing is any evaluation of the software or related work products (such as requirements specifications or user stories) that occurs without executing the software itself. Dynamic testing is an evaluation of that software or related work products that does involve executing the software. As such, the ISTQB definition of testing not only includes a number of pre-execution and post-execution activities that non-testers often do not consider 'testing', but also includes software quality activities (for example, requirements reviews and static analysis of code) that non-testers (and even sometimes testers) often do not consider 'testing' either.

The reason for this broad definition is that both dynamic testing (at whatever level) and static testing (of whatever type) often enable the achievement of similar project objectives. Dynamic testing and static testing also generate information that can help achieve an important process objective – that of understanding and improving the software development and testing processes. Dynamic testing and static testing are complementary activities, each able to generate information that the other cannot.

Testing is more than verification

Another common misconception about testing is that it is only about checking correctness; that is, that the system corresponds to its requirements, user stories or other specifications. Checking against a specification (called **verification**) is certainly part of testing, where we are asking the question, 'Have we built the system correctly?' Note the emphasis in the definition on 'specified requirements'.

But just conforming to a specification is not sufficient testing, as we will see in Section 1.3.7 (Absence-of-errors is a fallacy). We also need to test to see if the delivered software and system will meet user and stakeholder needs and expectations in its operational environment. Often it is the tester who becomes the advocate for the end-user in this kind of testing, which is called **validation**. Here we are asking the question, 'Have we built the right system?' Note the emphasis in the definition on 'intended use'.

In every development life cycle, a part of testing is focused on verification testing and a part is focused on validation testing. Verification is concerned with evaluating a work product, component or system to determine whether it meets the requirements set. In fact, verification focuses on the question, 'Is the deliverable built according to the specification?' Validation is concerned with evaluating a work product, component or system to determine whether it meets the user needs and requirements. Validation focuses on the question, 'Is the deliverable fit for purpose; for example, does it provide a solution to the problem?'

Verification Confirmation by examination and through provision of objective evidence that specified requirements have been fulfilled.

Validation Confirmation by examination and through provision of objective evidence that the requirements for a specific intended use or application have been fulfilled.

1.1.1 Typical objectives of testing

The following are some **test objectives** given in the Foundation Syllabus:

- To evaluate work products such as requirements, user stories, design and code by using static testing techniques, such as reviews.
- To verify whether all specified requirements have been fulfilled, for example, in the resulting system.
- To validate whether the test object is complete and works as the users and other stakeholders expect – for example, together with user or stakeholder groups.
- To build confidence in the level of quality of the test object, such as when those tests considered highest risk pass, and when the failures that are observed in the other tests are considered acceptable.
- To prevent defects, such as when early test activities (for example, requirements reviews or early test design) identify defects in requirements specifications that are removed before they cause defects in the design specifications and subsequently the code itself. Both reviews and test design serve as a verification and validation of these test basis documents that will reveal problems that otherwise would not surface until test execution, potentially much later in the project.

Test objective A reason or purpose for designing and executing a test.

- To find failures and defects; this is typically a prime focus for software testing.

- To provide sufficient information to stakeholders to allow them to make informed decisions, especially regarding the level of quality of the **test object** – for example, by the satisfaction of entry or exit criteria.

- To reduce the level of risk of inadequate software quality (e.g. previously undetected failures occurring in operation).

- To comply with contractual, legal or regulatory requirements or standards, and/or to verify the test object's compliance with such requirements or standards.

Test object The component or system to be tested.

These objectives are not universal. Different test viewpoints, test levels and test stakeholders can have different objectives. While many levels of testing, such as component, integration and system testing, focus on discovering as many failures as possible in order to find and remove defects, in acceptance testing the main objective is confirmation of correct system operation (at least under normal conditions), together with building confidence that the system meets its requirements. The context of the test object and the software development life cycle will also affect what test objectives are appropriate. Let's look at some examples to illustrate this.

When evaluating a software package that might be purchased or integrated into a larger software system, the main objective of testing might be the assessment of the quality of the software. Defects found may not be fixed, but rather might support a conclusion that the software be rejected.

During component testing, one objective at this level may be to achieve a given level of code coverage by the component tests – that is, to assess how much of the code has actually been exercised by a set of tests and to add additional tests to exercise parts of the code that have not yet been covered/tested. Another objective may be to find as many failures as possible so that the underlying defects are identified and fixed as early as possible.

During user acceptance testing, one objective may be to confirm that the system works as expected (validation) and satisfies requirements (verification). Another objective of testing here is to focus on providing stakeholders with an evaluation of the risk of releasing the system at a given time. Evaluating risk can be part of a mix of objectives, or it can be an objective of a separate level of testing, as when testing a safety-critical system, for example.

During maintenance testing, our objectives often include checking whether developers have introduced any regressions (new defects not present in the previous version) while making changes. Some forms of testing, such as operational testing, focus on assessing quality characteristics such as reliability, security, performance or availability.

1.1.2 Testing and debugging

Let's end this section by saying what testing is not, but is often thought to be. Testing is not **debugging**. While dynamic testing often locates failures which are caused by defects, and static testing often locates defects themselves, testing does not fix defects. It is during debugging, a development activity, that a member of the project team finds, analyzes and removes the defect, the underlying cause of the failure. After debugging, there is a further testing activity associated with the defect, which is called confirmation testing. This activity ensures that the fix does indeed resolve the failure.

Debugging The process of finding, analyzing and removing the causes of failures in software.

In terms of roles, dynamic testing is a testing role, debugging is a development role and confirmation testing is again a testing role. However, in Agile teams, this distinction may be blurred, as testers may be involved in debugging and component testing.

Further information about software testing concepts can be found in the ISO standard ISO/IEC/IEEE 29119-1 [2013].

1.2 WHY IS TESTING NECESSARY?

> ### SYLLABUS LEARNING OBJECTIVES FOR 1.2 WHY IS TESTING NECESSARY? (K2)
>
> **FL-1.2.1**   Give examples of why testing is necessary (K2)
>
> **FL-1.2.2**   Describe the relationship between testing and quality assurance and give examples of how testing contributes to higher quality (K2)
>
> **FL-1.2.3**   Distinguish between error, defect and failure (K2)
>
> **FL-1.2.4**   Distinguish between the root cause of a defect and its effects (K2)

In this section, we discuss how testing contributes to success and the relationship between testing and quality assurance. We will describe the difference between errors, defects and failures and illustrate how software defects or bugs can cause problems for people, the environment or a company. We will draw important distinctions between defects, their root causes and their effects.

As we go through this section, watch for the Syllabus terms **defect**, **error**, **failure**, **quality**, **quality assurance** and **root cause**.

Testing can help to reduce the risk of failures occurring during operation, provided it is carried out in a rigorous way, including reviews of documents and other work products. Testing both verifies that a system is correctly built and validates that it will meet users' and stakeholders' needs, even though no testing is ever exhaustive (see Principle 2 in Section 1.3, Exhaustive testing is impossible). In some situations, testing may not only be helpful, but may be necessary to meet contractual or legal requirements or to conform to industry-specific standards, such as automotive or safety-critical systems.

1.2.1 Testing's contributions to success

As we mentioned in Section 1.1, all of us have experienced software problems; for example, an app fails in the middle of doing something, a website freezes while taking your payment (did it go through or not?) or inconsistent prices for exactly the same flights on travel sites. Failures like these are annoying, but failures in safety-critical software can be life-threatening, such as in medical devices or self-driving cars.

The use of appropriate test techniques, applied with the right level of test expertise at the appropriate test levels and points in the software development life cycle, can be of significant help in identifying problems so that they can be fixed before the software or system is released into use. Here are some examples where testing could contribute to more successful systems:

- Having testers involved in requirements reviews or user story refinement could detect defects in these work products before any design or coding is done for the functionality described. Identifying and removing defects at this stage reduces the risk of the wrong software (incorrect or untestable) being developed.

- Having testers work closely with system designers while the system is being designed can increase each party's understanding of the design and how to test it. Since misunderstandings are often the cause for defects in software, having a better understanding at this stage can reduce the risk of design defects. A bonus is that tests can be identified from the design – thinking about how to test the system at this stage often results in better design.

- Having testers work closely with developers while the code is under development can increase each party's understanding of the code and how to test it. As with design, this increased understanding, and the knowledge of how the code will be tested, can reduce the risk of defects in the code (and in the tests).

- Having testers verify and validate the software prior to release can detect failures that might otherwise have been missed – this is traditionally where the focus of testing has been. As we see with the previous examples, if we leave it until release, we will not be nearly as efficient as we would have been if we had caught these defects earlier. However, it is still necessary to test just before release, and testers can also help to support debugging activities, for example, by running confirmation and regression tests. Thus, testing can help the software meet stakeholder needs and satisfy requirements.

In addition to these examples, achieving the defined test objectives (see Section 1.1.1) also contributes to the overall success of software development and maintenance.

1.2.2 Quality assurance and testing

Is quality assurance (QA) the same as testing? Many people refer to 'doing QA' when they are actually doing testing, and some job titles refer to QA when they really mean testing. The two are not the same. Quality assurance is actually one part of a larger concept, quality management, which refers to all activities that direct and control an organization with regard to quality in all aspects. Quality affects not only software development but also human resources (HR) procedures, delivery processes and even the way people answer the company's telephones.

Quality management consists of a number of activities, including **quality assurance** and quality control (as well as setting quality objectives, quality planning and quality improvement). Quality assurance is associated with ensuring that a company's standard ways of performing various tasks are carried out correctly. Such procedures may be written in a quality handbook that everyone is supposed to follow. The idea is that if processes are carried out correctly, then the products produced will be of higher **quality**. Root cause analysis and retrospectives are used to help to improve processes for more effective quality assurance. If they are following a recognized quality management standard, companies may be audited to ensure that they do actually follow their prescribed processes (say what you do, and do what you say).

Quality assurance
Part of quality management focused on providing confidence that quality requirements will be fulfilled.

Quality The degree to which a component, system or process meets specified requirements and/or user/customer needs and expectations.

Quality control is concerned with the quality of products rather than processes, to ensure that they have achieved the desired level of quality. Testing is looking at work products, including software, so it is actually a quality control activity rather than a quality assurance activity, despite common usage. However, testing also has processes that should be followed correctly, so quality assurance does support good testing in this way. Sections 1.1.1 and 1.2.1 describe how testing contributes to the achievement of quality.

So, we see that testing plays an essential supporting role in delivering quality software. However, testing by itself is not sufficient. Testing should be integrated into a complete, team-wide and development process-wide set of activities for quality assurance. Proper application of standards, training of staff, the use of retrospectives to learn lessons from defects and other important elements of previous projects, rigorous and appropriate software testing: all of these activities and more should be deployed by organizations to ensure acceptable levels of quality and quality risk upon release.

1.2.3 Errors, defects and failures

Why does software fail? Part of the problem is that, ironically, while computerization has allowed dramatic automation of many professions, software engineering remains a human-intensive activity. And humans are fallible beings. So, software is fallible because humans are fallible.

The precise chain of events goes something like this. A developer makes an **error** (or mistake), such as forgetting about the possibility of inputting an excessively long string into a field on a screen. The developer thus puts a **defect** (or fault or bug) into the program, such as omitting a check on input strings for length prior to processing them. When the program is executed, if the right conditions exist (or the wrong conditions, depending on how you look at it), the defect may result in unexpected behaviour; that is, the system exhibits a **failure**, such as accepting an over-long input that it should reject, with subsequent corruption of other data.

Other sequences of events can result in eventual failures, too. A business analyst can introduce a defect into a requirement, which can escape into the design of the system and further escape into the code. For example, a business analyst might say that an e-commerce system should support 100 simultaneous users, but actually peak load should be 1,000 users. If that defect is not detected in a requirements review (see Chapter 3), it could escape from the requirements phase into the design and implementation of the system. Once the load exceeds 100 users, resource utilization may eventually spike to dangerous levels, leading to reduced response time and reliability problems.

A technical writer can introduce a defect into the online help screens. For example, suppose that an accounting system is supposed to multiply two numbers together, but the help screens say that the two numbers should be added. In some cases, the system will appear to work properly, such as when the two numbers are both 0 or both 2. However, most frequently the program will exhibit unexpected results (at least based on the help screens).

So, human beings are fallible and thus, when they work, they sometimes introduce defects. It is important to point out that the introduction of defects is not a purely random accident, though some defects may be introduced randomly, such as when a phone rings and distracts a systems engineer in the middle of a complex series of design decisions. The rate at which people make errors increases when they are under time pressure, when they are working with complex systems, interfaces or code, and when they are dealing with changing technologies or highly interconnected systems.

Error (mistake) A human action that produces an incorrect result.

Defect (bug, fault) An imperfection or deficiency in a work product where it does not meet its requirements or specifications.

Failure An event in which a component or system does not perform a required function within specified limits.

While we commonly think of failures being the result of 'bugs in the code', a significant number of defects are introduced in work products such as requirements specifications and design specifications. Capers Jones reports that about 20% of defects are introduced in requirements, and about 25% in design. The remaining 55% are introduced during implementation or repair of the code, metadata or documentation [Jones 2008]. Other experts and researchers have reached similar conclusions, with one organization finding that as many as 75% of defects originate in requirements and design. Figure 1.1 shows four typical scenarios, the upper stream being correct requirements, design and implementation, the lower three streams showing defect introduction at some phase in the software life cycle.

Ideally, defects are removed in the same phase of the life cycle in which they are introduced. (Well, ideally defects are not introduced at all, but this is not possible because, as discussed before, people are fallible.) The extent to which defects are removed in the phase of introduction is called phase containment. Phase containment is important because the cost of finding and removing a defect increases each time that defect escapes to a later life cycle phase. Multiplicative increases in cost, of the sort seen in Figure 1.2, are not unusual. The specific increases vary considerably, with Boehm reporting cost increases of 1:5 (from requirements to after release) for simple systems, to as high as 1:100 for complex systems [Boehm 1986]. If you are curious about the economics of software testing and other quality-related activities, you can see Gilb [1993], Black [2004] or Black [2009].

Defects may result in failures, or they may not, depending on inputs and other conditions. In some cases, a defect can exist that will never cause a failure in actual use, because the conditions that could cause the failure can never arise. In other cases, a defect can exist that will not cause a failure during testing, but which always results in failures in production. This can happen with security, reliability and performance defects, especially if the test environments do not closely replicate the production environment(s).

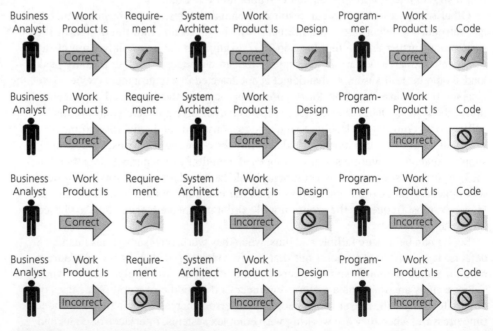

FIGURE 1.1   Four typical scenarios

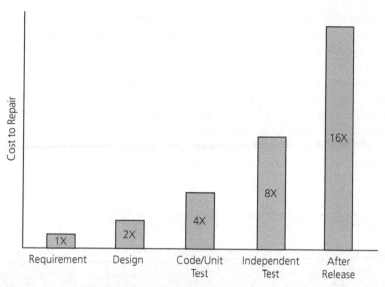

FIGURE 1.2   Multiplicative increases in cost

It can also happen that expected and actual results do not match for reasons other than a defect. In some cases, environmental conditions can lead to unexpected results that do not relate to a software defect. Radiation, magnetism, electronic fields and pollution can damage hardware or firmware, or simply change the conditions of the hardware or firmware temporarily in a way that causes the software to fail.

1.2.4 Defects, root causes and effects

Testing also provides a learning opportunity that allows for improved quality if lessons are learned from each project. If root cause analysis is carried out for the defects found on each project, the team can improve its software development processes to avoid the introduction of similar defects in future systems. Through this simple process of learning from past mistakes, organizations can continuously improve the quality of their processes and their software. A **root cause** is generally an organizational issue, whereas a cause for a defect is an individual action. So, for example, if a developer puts a 'less than' instead of 'greater than' symbol, this error may have been made through carelessness, but the carelessness may have been made worse because of intense time pressure to complete the module quickly. With more time for checking his or her work, or with better review processes, the defect would not have got through to the final product. It is human nature to blame individuals when in fact organizational pressure makes errors almost inevitable.

> **Root cause** A source of a defect such that if it is removed, the occurrence of the defect type is decreased or removed.

The Syllabus gives a good example of the difference between defects, root causes and effects: suppose that incorrect interest payments result in customer complaints. There is just a single line of code that is incorrect. The code was written for a user story that was ambiguous, so the developer interpreted it in a way that they thought was sensible (but it was wrong). How did the user story come to be ambiguous? In this example, the product owner misunderstood how interest was to be calculated, so was unable to clearly specify what the interest calculation should have been. This misunderstanding could lead to a lot of similar defects, due to ambiguities in other user stories as well.

The failure here is the incorrect interest calculations for customers. The defect is the wrong calculation in the code. The root cause was the product owner's lack of knowledge about how interest should be calculated, and the effect was customer complaints.

The root cause can be addressed by providing additional training in interest rate calculations to the product owner, and possibly additional reviews of user stories by interest calculation experts. If this is done, then incorrect interest calculations due to ambiguous user stories should be a thing of the past.

Root cause analysis is covered in more detail in two other ISTQB qualifications: Expert Level Test Management, and Expert Level Improving the Test Process.

1.3 SEVEN TESTING PRINCIPLES

> **SYLLABUS LEARNING OBJECTIVES FOR 1.3 SEVEN TESTING PRINCIPLES (K2)**
>
> **FL-1.3.1   Explain the seven testing principles (K2)**

In this section, we will review seven fundamental principles of testing that have been observed over the last 40+ years. These principles, while not always understood or noticed, are in action on most if not all projects. Knowing how to spot these principles, and how to take advantage of them, will make you a better tester.

In addition to the descriptions of each principle below, you can refer to Table 1.1 for a quick reference of the principles and their text as written in the Syllabus.

Principle 1. Testing shows the presence of defects, not their absence

As mentioned in the previous section, a typical objective of many testing efforts is to find defects. Many testing organizations that the authors have worked with are quite effective at doing so. One of our exceptional clients consistently finds, on average, 99.5% of the defects in the software it tests. In addition, the defects left undiscovered are less important and unlikely to happen frequently in production. Sometimes, it turns out that this test team has indeed found 100% of the defects that would matter to customers, as no previously unreported defects are reported after release. Unfortunately, this level of effectiveness is not common.

However, no test team, test technique or test strategy can guarantee to achieve 100% defect-detection percentage (DDP) – or even 95%, which is considered excellent. Thus, it is important to understand that, while testing can show that defects are present, it cannot prove that there are no defects left undiscovered. Of course, as testing continues, we reduce the likelihood of defects that remain undiscovered, but eventually a form of Zeno's paradox takes hold: each additional test run may cut the risk of a remaining defect in half, but only an infinite number of tests can cut the risk down to zero.

That said, testers should not despair or let the perfect be the enemy of the good. While testing can never prove that the software works, it can reduce the remaining level of risk to product quality to an acceptable level, as mentioned before. In any endeavour worth doing, there is some risk. Software projects – and software testing – are endeavours worth doing.

TABLE 1.1   Testing principles

Principle 1:	**Testing shows the presence of defects, not their absence**	Testing can show that defects are present, but cannot prove that there are no defects. Testing reduces the probability of undiscovered defects remaining in the software but, even if no defects are found, testing is not a proof of correctness.
Principle 2:	**Exhaustive testing is impossible**	Testing everything (all combinations of inputs and preconditions) is not feasible except for trivial cases. Rather than attempting to test exhaustively, risk analysis, test techniques and priorities should be used to focus test efforts.
Principle 3:	**Early testing saves time and money**	To find defects early, both static and dynamic test activities should be started as early as possible in the software development life cycle. Early testing is sometimes referred to as 'shift left'. Testing early in the software development life cycle helps reduce or eliminate costly changes (see Chapter 3, Section 3.1).
Principle 4:	**Defects cluster together**	A small number of modules usually contains most of the defects discovered during pre-release testing, or they are responsible for most of the operational failures. Predicted defect clusters, and the actual observed defect clusters in test or operation, are an important input into a risk analysis used to focus the test effort (as mentioned in Principle 2).
Principle 5:	**Beware of the pesticide paradox**	If the same tests are repeated over and over again, eventually these tests no longer find any new defects. To detect new defects, existing tests and test data are changed and new tests need to be written. (Tests are no longer effective at finding defects, just as pesticides are no longer effective at killing insects after a while.) In some cases, such as automated regression testing, the pesticide paradox has a beneficial outcome, which is the relatively low number of regression defects.
Principle 6:	**Testing is context dependent**	Testing is done differently in different contexts. For example, safety-critical software is tested differently from an e-commerce mobile app. As another example, testing in an Agile project is done differently to testing in a sequential life cycle project (see Chapter 2, Section 2.1).
Principle 7:	**Absence-of-errors is a fallacy**	Some organizations expect that testers can run all possible tests and find all possible defects, but Principles 2 and 1, respectively, tell us that this is impossible. Further, it is a fallacy to expect that *just* finding and fixing a large number of defects will ensure the success of a system. For example, thoroughly testing all specified requirements and fixing all defects found could still produce a system that is difficult to use, that does not fulfil the users' needs and expectations or that is inferior compared to other competing systems.

Principle 2. Exhaustive testing is impossible

This principle is closely related to the previous principle. For any real-sized system (anything beyond the trivial software constructed in first-year software engineering courses), the number of possible test cases is either infinite or so close to infinite as to be practically innumerable.

Infinity is a tough concept for the human brain to comprehend or accept, so let's use an example. One of our clients mentioned that they had calculated the number of possible internal data value combinations in the Unix operating system as greater than the number of known molecules in the universe by four orders of magnitude. They further calculated that, even with their fastest automated tests, just to test all of these internal state combinations would require more time than the current age of the universe. Even that would not be a complete test of the operating system; it would only cover all the possible data value combinations.

So, we are confronted with a big, infinite cloud of possible tests; we must select a subset from it. One way to select tests is to wander aimlessly in the cloud of tests, selecting at random until we run out of time. While there is a place for automated random testing, by itself it is a poor strategy. We'll discuss testing strategies further in Chapter 5, but for the moment let's look at two.

One strategy for selecting tests is risk-based testing. In risk-based testing, we have a cross-functional team of project and product stakeholders perform a special type of risk analysis. In this analysis, stakeholders identify risks to the quality of the system, and assess the level of risk (often using likelihood and impact) associated with each risk item. We focus the test effort based on the level of risk, using the level of risk to determine the appropriate number of test cases for each risk item, and also to sequence the test cases.

Another strategy for selecting tests is requirements-based testing. In requirements-based testing, testers analyze the requirements specification (which would be user stories in Agile projects) to identify test conditions. These test conditions inherit the priority of the requirement or user story they derive from. We focus the test effort based on the priority to determine the appropriate number of test cases for each aspect, and also to sequence the test cases.

Principle 3. Early testing saves time and money

This principle tells us that we should start testing as early as possible in order to find as many defects as possible. In addition, since the cost of finding and removing a defect increases the longer that defect is in the system, early testing also means we are likely to minimize the cost of removing defects.

So, the first principle tells us that we cannot find all the bugs, but rather can only find some percentage of them. The second principle tells us that we cannot run every possible test. The third principle tells us to start testing early. What can we conclude when we put these three principles together?

Imagine that you have a system with 1,000 defects. Suppose we wait until the very end of the project and run one level of testing, system test. You find and fix 90% of the defects. That still leaves 100 defects, which presumably will escape to the customers or users.

Instead, suppose that you start testing early and continue throughout the life cycle. You perform requirements reviews, design reviews and code reviews. You perform unit testing, integration testing and system testing. Suppose that, during each test activity, you find and remove only 45% of the defects – half as effective as the previous system test level. Nevertheless, at the end of the process, fewer than 30 defects remain. Even though each test activity was only 45% effective at finding defects, the overall sequence of activities was 97% effective. Note that now we are doing both static testing (the reviews) and dynamic testing (the running of tests at the different test levels). This approach of starting test activities as early as possible is also called 'shift left' because the test activities are no longer all done on the right-hand side of a sequential life cycle diagram, but on the left-hand side at the beginning of development. Although unit test execution is of course on the right side of a sequential life cycle diagram, improving and spending more effort on unit testing early on is a very important part of the shift left paradigm.

In addition, defects removed early cost less to remove. Further, since much of the cost in software engineering is associated with human effort, and since the size of a project team is relatively inflexible once that project is underway, reduced cost of defects also means reduced duration of the project. That situation is shown graphically in Figure 1.3.

Now, this type of cumulative and highly efficient defect removal only works if each of the test activities in the sequence is focused on different, defined objectives. If we simply test the same test conditions over and over, we will not achieve the cumulative effect, for reasons we will discuss in a moment.

FIGURE 1.3 Time savings of early defect removal

Principle 4. Defects cluster together

This principle relates to something we discussed previously, that relying entirely on the testing strategy of a random walk in the infinite cloud of possible tests is relatively weak. Defects are not randomly and uniformly distributed throughout the software under test. Rather, defects tend to be found in clusters, with 20% (or fewer) of the modules accounting for 80% (or more) of the defects. In other words, the defect density of modules varies considerably. While controversy exists about why defect clustering happens, the reality of defect clustering is well established. It was first demonstrated in studies performed by IBM in the 1960s [Jones 2008], and is mentioned in Myers [2011]. We continue to see evidence of defect clustering in our work with clients.

Defect clustering is helpful to us as testers, because it provides a useful guide. If we focus our test effort (at least in part) based on the expected (and ultimately observed) likelihood of finding a defect in a certain area, we can make our testing more effective and efficient, at least in terms of our objective of finding defects. Knowledge of and predictions about defect clusters are important inputs to the risk-based testing strategy discussed earlier. In a metaphorical way, we can imagine that bugs are social creatures who like to hang out together in the dark corners of the software.

Principle 5. Beware of the pesticide paradox

This principle was coined by Boris Beizer [Beizer 1990]. He observed that, just as a pesticide repeatedly sprayed on a field will kill fewer and fewer bugs each time it is used, so too a given set of tests will eventually stop finding new defects when re-run against a system under development or maintenance. If the tests do not provide adequate coverage, this slowdown in defect finding will result in a false level of confidence and excessive optimism among the project team. However, the air will be let out of the balloon once the system is released to customers and users.

Using the right test strategies is the first step towards achieving adequate coverage. However, no strategy is perfect. You should plan to regularly review the test results during the project, and revise the tests based on your findings. In some cases, you need to write new and different tests to exercise different parts of the software or system. These new tests can lead to discovery of previously unknown defect clusters, which is a good reason not to wait until the end of the test effort to review your test results and evaluate the adequacy of test coverage.

The pesticide paradox is important when implementing the multilevel testing discussed previously in regards to the principle of early testing. Simply repeating our tests of the same conditions over and over will not result in good cumulative defect detection. However, when used properly, each type and level of testing has its own strengths and weaknesses in terms of defect detection, and collectively we can assemble a very effective sequence of defect filters from them. After such a sequence of complementary test activities, we can be confident that the coverage is adequate, and that the remaining level of risk is acceptable.

Sometimes the pesticide paradox can work in our favour, if it is not *new* defects that we are looking for. When we run automated regression tests, we are ensuring that the software that we are testing is still working as it was before; that is, there are no new unexpected side-effect defects that have appeared as a result of a change elsewhere. In this case, we are pleased that we have not found any new defects.

Principle 6. Testing is context dependent

Our safety-critical clients test with a great deal of rigour and care – and cost. When lives are at stake, we must be extremely careful to minimize the risk of undetected defects. Our clients who release software on the web, such as e-commerce sites, or who develop mobile apps, can take advantage of the possibility to quickly change the software when necessary, leading to a different set of testing challenges – and opportunities. If you tried to apply safety-critical approaches to a mobile app, you might put the company out of business; if you tried to apply e-commerce approaches to safety-critical software, you could put lives in danger. So, the context of the testing influences how much testing we do and how the testing is done.

Another example is the way that testing is done in an Agile project as opposed to a sequential life cycle project. Every sprint in an Agile project includes testing of the functionality developed in that sprint; the testing is done by everyone on the Agile team (ideally) and the testing is done continually over the whole of development. In sequential life cycle projects, testing may be done more formally, documented in more detail and may be focused towards the end of the project.

Principle 7. Absence-of-errors is a fallacy

Throughout this section we have expounded the idea that a sequence of test activities, started early and targeting specific and diverse objectives and areas of the system, can effectively and efficiently find – and help a project team to remove – a large percentage of the defects. Surely that is all that is required to achieve project success?

Sadly, it is not. Many systems have been built that failed in user acceptance testing or in the marketplace, such as the initial launch of the US healthcare.gov website, which suffered from serious performance and web access problems.

Consider desktop computer operating systems. In the 1990s, as competition peaked for dominance of the PC operating system market, Unix and its variants had higher levels of quality than DOS and Windows. However, 25 years on, Windows dominates the desktop marketplace. One major reason is that Unix and its variants were too difficult for most users in the early 1990s.

Consider a system that perfectly conforms to its requirements (if that were possible), which has been tested thoroughly and all defects found have been fixed. Surely this would be a success, right? Wrong! If the requirements were flawed, we now have a perfectly working wrong system. Perhaps it is hard to use, as in the previous example. Perhaps the requirements missed some major features that users were expecting or needed to have. Perhaps this system is quite OK, but a competitor has come out with a competing system that is easier to use, includes the expected features and is cheaper. Our 'perfect' system is not looking so good after all, even though it has effectively 'no defects' in terms of 'conformance to requirements'.

1.4 TEST PROCESS

SYLLABUS LEARNING OBJECTIVES FOR 1.4 TEST PROCESS (K2)

FL-1.4.1   **Explain the impact of context on the test process (K2)**

FL-1.4.2   **Describe the test activities and respective tasks within the test process (K2)**

FL-1.4.3   **Differentiate the work products that support the test process (K2)**

FL-1.4.4   **Explain the value of maintaining traceability between the test basis and test work products (K2)**

In this section, we will describe the test process: tasks, activities and work products. We will talk about the influence of context on the test process and the importance of traceability.

In this section, there are a large number of Glossary keywords (19 in all): **coverage, test analysis, test basis, test case, test completion, test condition, test control, test data, test design, test execution, test execution schedule, test implementation, test monitoring, test oracle, test planning, test procedure, test suite, testware** and **traceability**.

In Section 1.1, we looked at the definition of testing, and identified misperceptions about testing, including that testing is not just test execution. Certainly, test execution is the most visible testing activity. However, effective and efficient testing requires test approaches that are properly planned and carried out, with tests designed and implemented to cover the proper areas of the system, executed in the right sequence and with their results reviewed regularly. This is a process, with tasks and activities that can be identified and need to be done, sometimes formally and other times very informally. In this section, we will look at the test process in detail.

There is no 'one size fits all' test process, but testing does need to include common sets of activities, or it may not achieve its objectives. An organization may have a test strategy where the test activities are specified, including how they are implemented and when they occur within the life cycle. Another organization may have a test strategy where test activities are not formally specified, but expertise about test activities is shared among team members informally. The 'right' test process for you is one that achieves your test objectives in the most efficient way. The best test process for you would not be the best for another organization (and vice versa).

Simply having a defined test strategy is not enough. One of our clients recently was a law firm that sued a company for a serious software failure. It turned out that while the company had a written test strategy, this strategy was not aligned with the testing best practices described in this book or the Syllabus. Further, upon close examination of their test work products, it was clear that they had not even carried out the strategy properly or completely. The company ended up paying a substantial penalty for their lack of quality. So, you must consider whether your actual test activities and tasks are sufficient.

1.4.1 Test process in context

As mentioned above, there is no one right test process that applies to everyone; each organization needs to adapt their test process depending on their context. The factors that influence the particular test process include the following (this list is not exhaustive):

- Software development life cycle model and project methodologies being used. An Agile project developing mobile apps will have quite a different test process to an organization producing medical devices such as pacemakers.
- Test levels and test types being considered; for example, a large complex project may have several types of integration testing, with a test process reflecting that complexity.
- Product and project risks (the lower the risks, the less formal the process needs to be, and vice versa).

- Business domain (e.g. mobile apps versus medical devices).
- Operational constraints, including:
  - budgets and resources
  - timescales
  - complexity
  - contractual and regulatory requirements.

- Organizational policies and practices.
- Required internal and external standards.

In the following sections, we will look in detail at the following topics:

- Test activities and tasks – the various things that testers do.
- Test work products – the things produced by and used by testers.
- Traceability between the test basis and test work products and why this is important.

First, one aspect to consider is **coverage**. Coverage is a partial measure of the thoroughness of testing. When examining the **test basis**, which is whatever the tests are being derived from (such as a requirement, user story, design or even code), a number of things can be identified as coverage items (we can tell whether or not we have tested them). For example, system level testing may want to ensure that every user story has been tested at least once; integration level testing may want to ensure that every communication path has been tested at least once; and, in component testing, developers may want to ensure that every code module, branch or statement has been tested at least once. When a test exercises the coverage item (user story, communication path or code element), then that item has been covered. Coverage is the percentage of coverage items that were exercised in a given test run.

It is useful to know what you want to cover with your testing right from the start; coverage can act as a Key Performance Indicator (KPI) and help to measure the achievement of test objectives (if they are related to coverage).

In addition to the coverage items relating to specifications or code, we may also have environmental aspects that we want to cover. For example, tests for mobile apps may need to be tested on a number of mobile devices and configurations – these are also coverage items or coverage criteria. We could also consider coverage items of user personas, stakeholders or user success criteria. Measuring and reporting the coverage of these aspects can also give confidence to stakeholders that failures in operation would be less likely.

There is more about coverage in Section 4.3. Test processes are described in more detail in ISO/IEC/IEEE 29119-2 [2013].

> **Coverage** The degree to which specified coverage items have been determined to have been exercised by a test suite expressed as a percentage.
>
> **Test basis** The body of knowledge used as the basis for test analysis and design.

1.4.2 Test activities and tasks

A test process consists of the following main groups of activities:

- Test planning.
- Test monitoring and control.
- Test analysis.
- Test design.

- Test implementation.
- Test execution.
- Test completion.

These activities appear to be logically sequential, in the sense that tasks within each activity often create the preconditions or precursor work products for tasks in subsequent activities. However, in many cases, the activities in the process may overlap or take place concurrently or iteratively, provided that these dependencies are fulfilled. Each group of activities consists of many individual tasks; these will vary for different projects or releases. For example, in Agile development, we have small iterations of software design, build and test that happen continuously, and planning is also a very dynamic activity throughout. If there are multiple teams, some teams may be doing test analysis while other teams are in the middle of test implementation, for example.

Note that this is 'a' test process, not 'the' test process. We have found that most of these activities, and many of the tasks within these activities, are carried out in some form or another on most successful test efforts. However, you should expect to have to tailor your test process, its main activities and the constituent tasks based on the organizational, project, process and product needs, constraints and other contextual realities. In sequential development, there will also be overlap, combination, concurrency or even omission of some tasks; this is why a test process is tailored for each project.

Test planning

Test planning involves defining the objectives of testing and the approach for meeting those objectives within project constraints and contexts. This includes deciding on suitable test techniques to use, deciding what tasks need to be done, formulating a test schedule and other things.

Metaphorically, you can think of test planning as similar to figuring out how to get from one place to another (without using your GPS – there is no GPS for testing). For small, simple and familiar projects, finding the route merely involves taking an existing map, highlighting the route and jotting down the specific directions. For large, complex or new projects, finding the route can involve a sophisticated process of creating a new map, exploring unknown territory and blazing a fresh trail.

We will discuss test planning in more detail in Section 5.2.

Test monitoring and control

To continue our metaphor, even with the best map and the clearest directions, getting from one place to another involves careful attention, watching the dashboard, minor (and sometimes major) course corrections, talking with our companions about the journey, looking ahead for trouble, tracking progress towards the ultimate destination and coping with finding an alternate route if the road we wanted is blocked. So, in **test monitoring**, we continuously compare actual progress against the plan, check on the progress of test activities and report the test status and any necessary deviations from the plan. In **test control**, we take whatever actions are necessary to meet the mission and objectives of the project, and/or adjust the plan.

Test monitoring is the ongoing comparison of actual progress against the test plan, using any test monitoring metrics that we have defined in the test plan. Test progress against the plan is reported to stakeholders in test progress reports or stakeholder meetings. One option that is often overlooked is that if things are going very wrong,

Test planning The activity of establishing or updating a test plan.

Test plan Documentation describing the test objectives to be achieved and the means and the schedule for achieving them, organized to coordinate testing activities.

(Note that we have included the definition of test plan here, even though it is not listed in the Syllabus as a term that you need to know for this chapter; otherwise the definition of test planning is not very informative.)

Test monitoring A test management activity that involves checking the status of testing activities, identifying any variances from the planned or expected status and reporting status to stakeholders.

Test control A test management task that deals with developing and applying a set of corrective actions to get a test project on track when monitoring shows a deviation from what was planned.

it may be time to stop the testing or even stop the project completely. In our driving analogy, once you find out that you are headed in completely the wrong direction, the best option is to stop and re-evaluate, not continue driving to the wrong place.

One way we can monitor test progress is by using exit criteria, also known as 'definition of done' in Agile development. For example, the exit criteria for test execution might include:

- Checking test results and logs against specified coverage criteria (we have not finished testing until we have tested what we planned to test).
- Assessing the level of component or system quality based on test results and logs (e.g. the number of defects found or ease of use).
- Assessing product risk and determining if more tests are needed to reduce the risk to an acceptable level.

We will discuss test planning, monitoring and control tasks in more detail in Chapter 5.

Test analysis

In **test analysis**, we analyze the test basis to identify testable features and define associated **test conditions**. Test analysis determines 'what to test', including measurable coverage criteria. We can say colloquially that the test basis is everything upon which we base our tests. The test basis can include requirements, user stories, design specifications, risk analysis reports, the system design and architecture, interface specifications and user expectations.

In test analysis, we transform the more general testing objectives defined in the test plan into tangible test conditions. The way in which these are specifically documented depends on the needs of the testers, the expectations of the project team, any applicable regulations and other considerations.

Test analysis includes the following major activities and tasks:

- Analyze the test basis appropriate to the test level being considered. Examples of a test basis include:
  - Requirement specifications, for example, business requirements, functional requirements, system requirements, user stories, epics, use cases or similar work products that specify desired functional and non-functional component or system behaviour. These specifications say what the component or system should do and are the source of tests to assess functionality as well as non-functional aspects such as performance or usability.
  - Design and implementation information, such as system or software architecture diagrams or documents, design specifications, call flows, modelling diagrams (for example, UML or entity-relationship diagrams), interface specifications or similar work products that specify component or system structure. Structures for implemented systems or components can be a useful source of coverage criteria to ensure that sufficient testing has been done on those structures.
  - The implementation of the component or system itself, including code, database metadata and queries, and interfaces. Use all information about any aspect of the system to help identify what should be tested.
  - Risk analysis reports, which may consider functional, non-functional and structural aspects of the component or system. Testing should be more thorough in the areas of highest risk, so more test conditions should be identified in the highest-risk areas.

Test analysis The activity that identifies test conditions by analyzing the test basis.

Test condition (charter) An aspect of the test basis that is relevant in order to achieve specific test objectives. See also: exploratory testing.

- Evaluate the test basis and test items to identify various types of defects that might occur (typically done by reviews), such as:
  - ambiguities
  - omissions
  - inconsistencies
  - inaccuracies
  - contradictions
  - superfluous statements.

- Identify features and sets of features to be tested.

- Identify and prioritize test conditions for each feature, based on analysis of the test basis, and considering functional, non-functional and structural characteristics, other business and technical factors, and levels of risks.

- Capture bi-directional traceability between each element of the test basis and the associated test conditions. This traceability should be bi-directional (we can trace in both forward and backward directions) so that we can check which test basis elements go with which test conditions (and vice versa) and determine the degree of coverage of the test basis by the test conditions. See Sections 1.4.3 and 1.4.4 for more on traceability. Traceability is also very important for maintenance testing, as we will discuss in Chapter 2, Section 2.4.

How are the test conditions actually identified from a test basis? The test techniques, which are described in Chapter 4, are used to identify test conditions. Blackbox techniques identify functional and non-functional test conditions, white-box techniques identify structural test conditions and experience-based techniques can identify other important test conditions. Using techniques helps to reduce the likelihood of missing important conditions and helps to define more precise and accurate test conditions.

Sometimes the test conditions identified can be used as test objectives for a test charter. In exploratory testing, an experience-based technique (see Chapter 4, Section 4.4.2), test charters are used as goals for the testing that will be carried out in an exploratory way – that is, test design, execution and learning in parallel. When these test objectives are traceable to the test basis, the coverage of those test conditions can be measured.

One of the most beneficial side effects of identifying what to test in test analysis is that you will find defects; for example, inconsistencies in requirements, contradictory statements between different documents, missing requirements (such as no 'otherwise' for a selection of options) or descriptions that do not make sense. Rather than being a problem, this is a great opportunity to remove these defects before development goes any further. This verification (and validation) of specifications is particularly important if no other review processes for the test basis documents are in place.

Test analysis can also help to validate whether the requirements properly capture customer, user and other stakeholder needs. For example, techniques such as behaviour-driven development (BDD) and acceptance test-driven development (ATDD) both involve generating test conditions (and test cases) from user stories. BDD focuses on the behaviour of the system and ATDD focuses on the user view of the system, and both techniques involve defining acceptance criteria. Since these acceptance criteria are produced before coding, they also verify and validate the user stories and the acceptance criteria. More about this is found in the ISTQB Foundation Level Agile Tester Extension qualification.

Test design

Test analysis addresses 'what to test' and **test design** addresses the question 'how to test'; that is, what specific inputs and data are needed in order to exercise the software for a particular test condition. In test design, test conditions are elaborated (at a high level) in **test cases**, sets of test cases and other testware. Test analysis identifies general 'things' to test, and test design makes these general things specific for the component or system that we are testing.

Test design includes the following major activities:

- Design and prioritize test cases and sets of test cases.
- Identify the necessary **test data** to support the test conditions and test cases as they are identified and designed.
- Design the test environment, including set-up, and identify any required infrastructure and tools.
- Capture bi-directional traceability between the test basis, test conditions, test cases and test procedures (see also Section 1.4.4).

As with the identification of test conditions, test techniques are used to derive or elaborate test cases from the test conditions. These are described in Chapter 4, where test analysis and test design are discussed in more detail.

Just as in test analysis, test design can also identify defects – in the test basis and in the existing test conditions. Because test design is a deeper level of detail, some defects that were not obvious when looking at test basis at a high level, may become clear when deciding exactly what values to assign to test cases. For example, a test condition might be to check the boundary values of an input field, but when determining the exact values, we realize that a maximum value has not been specified in the test basis. Identifying defects at this point is a good thing because if they are fixed now, they will not cause problems later.

Which of these specific tasks applies to a particular project depends on various contextual issues relevant to the project, and these are discussed further in Chapter 5.

Test implementation

In **test implementation**, we specify **test procedures** (or test scripts). This involves combining the test cases in a particular order, as well as including any other information needed for test execution. Test implementation also involves setting up the test environment and anything else that needs to be done to prepare for test execution, such as creating testware. Test design asked 'how to test', and test implementation asks 'do we now have everything in place to run the tests?'

Test implementation includes the following major activities:

- Develop and prioritize the test procedures and, potentially, create automated test scripts.
- Create **test suites** from the test procedures and automated test scripts (if any). See Chapter 6 for test automation.
- Arrange the test suites within a **test execution schedule** in a way that results in efficient test execution (see Chapter 5, Section 5.2.4).
- Build the test environment (possibly including test harnesses, service virtualization, simulators and other infrastructure items) and verify that everything needed has been set up correctly.

Test design The activity of deriving and specifying test cases from test conditions.

Test case A set of preconditions, inputs, actions (where applicable), expected results and postconditions, developed based on test conditions.

Test data Data created or selected to satisfy the execution preconditions and inputs to execute one or more test cases.

Test implementation The activity that prepares the testware needed for test execution based on test analysis and design.

Test procedure A sequence of test cases in execution order, and any associated actions that may be required to set up the initial preconditions and any wrap-up activities post execution.

Test suite (test case suite, test set) A set of test cases or test procedures to be executed in a specific test cycle.

Test execution schedule A schedule for the execution of test suites within a test cycle.

● Prepare test data and ensure that it is properly loaded in the test environment (including inputs, data resident in databases and other data repositories, and system configuration data).

● Verify and update the bi-directional traceability between the test basis, test conditions, test cases, test procedures and test suites (see also Section 1.4.4).

Ideally, all of these tasks are completed before test execution begins, because otherwise precious, limited test execution time can be lost on these types of preparatory tasks. One of our clients reported losing as much as 25% of the test execution period to what they called 'environmental shakedown', which turned out to consist almost entirely of test implementation activities that could have been completed before the software was delivered.

Note that although we have discussed test design and test implementation as separate activities, in practice they are often combined and done together.

Not only are test design and implementation combined, but many test activities may be combined and carried out concurrently. For example, in exploratory testing (see Chapter 4, Section 4.4.2), test analysis, test design, test implementation and test execution are done in an interactive way throughout an exploratory test session.

Test execution

Test execution The process of running a test on the component or system under test, producing actual result(s).

Testware Work products produced during the test process for use in planning, designing, executing, evaluating and reporting on testing.

In **test execution**, the test suites that have been assembled in test implementation are run, according to the test execution schedule.

Test execution includes the following major activities:

● Record the identities and versions of all of the test items (parts of the test object to be tested), test objects (system or component to be tested), test tools and other **testware**.

● Execute the tests either manually or by using an automated test execution tool, according to the planned sequence.

● Compare actual results with expected results, observing where the actual and expected results differ. These differences may be the result of defects, but at this point we do not know, so we refer to them as anomalies.

● Analyze the anomalies in order to establish their likely causes. Failures may occur due to defects in the code or they may be false-positives. (A false-positive is where a defect is reported when there is no defect.) A failure may also be due to a test defect, such as defects in specified test data, in a test document or the test environment, or simply due to a mistake in the way the test was executed.

● Report defects based on the failures observed (see Chapter 5, Section 5.6). A failure due to a defect in the code means that we can write a defect report. Some organizations track test defects (i.e. defects in the tests themselves), while others do not.

● Log the outcome of test execution (e.g. pass, fail or blocked). This includes not only the anomalies observed and the pass/fail status of the test cases, but also the identities and versions of the software under test, test tools and testware.

- As necessary, repeat test activities when actions are taken to resolve discrepancies. For example, we might need to re-run a test that previously failed in order to confirm a fix (confirmation testing). We might need to run an updated test. We might also need to run additional, previously executed tests to see whether defects have been introduced in unchanged areas of the software or to see whether a fixed defect now makes another defect apparent (regression testing).
- Verify and update the bi-directional traceability between the test basis, test conditions, test cases, test procedures and test results.

As before, which of these specific tasks applies to a particular project depends on various contextual issues relevant to the project; these are discussed further in Chapter 5.

Test completion

Test completion activities collect data from completed test activities to consolidate experience, testware and any other relevant information. Test completion activities should occur at major project milestones. These can include when a software system is released, when a test project is completed (or cancelled), when an Agile project iteration is finished (e.g. as part of a retrospective meeting), when a test level has been completed or when a maintenance release has been completed. The specific milestones that involve test completion activities should be specified in the test plan.

> **Test completion** The activity that makes test assets available for later use, leaves test environments in a satisfactory condition and communicates the results of testing to relevant stakeholders.

Test completion includes the following major activities:

- Check whether all defect reports are closed, entering change requests or product backlog items for any defects that remain unresolved at the end of test execution.
- Create a test summary report to be communicated to stakeholders.
- Finalize and archive the test environment, the test data, the test infrastructure and other testware for later reuse.
- Hand over the testware to the maintenance teams, other project teams, and/or other stakeholders who could benefit from its use.
- Analyze lessons learned from completed test activities to determine changes needed for future iterations, releases and projects (i.e. perform a retrospective).
- Use the information gathered to improve test process maturity, especially as an input to test planning for future projects.

The degree and extent to which test completion activities occur, and which specific test completion activities do occur, depends on various contextual issues relevant to the project, which are discussed further in Chapter 5.

1.4.3 Test work products

'Work products' is the generic name given to any form of documentation, informal communication or artefact that is used in testing (or indeed in development). When testing is more formal, the majority of work products may be written documentation; when testing is very informal, the corresponding work product may just be a scrap of paper, or a note in someone's mobile phone. 'Work product' is a general term covering any type of information needed to do the work (testing or development).

Test work products are created as part of the test process, and there is significant variation in the types of work products created, in the ways they are organized and managed, and in the names used for them. The work products described in this section are in the ISTQB Glossary of terms. More information can be found in ISO/IEC/IEEE 29119-3 [2013].

Test work products can be captured, stored and managed in configuration management tools, or possibly in test management tools or defect management tools.

Test planning work products

You will not be surprised to find that test planning work products include test plans. There may be different test plans for different test levels. The test plan typically includes information about the test basis, to which all the other work products will be related via traceability information (see Section 1.4.4). Test plans also include entry and exit criteria (also known as definition of ready and definition of done) for the testing within their scope – the exit criteria are used during test monitoring and control.

Beware of what people call a 'test plan'; we have seen this name applied to any kind of test document, including test case specifications and test execution schedules. A test plan is a planning document – it contains information about what is intended to happen in the future, and is similar to a project plan. It does not contain detail of test conditions, test cases or other aspects of testing.

The test plan needs to be understandable to those who need to know the information contained in it. The two-page cryptic diagram that was called a 'test plan' at one organization would not be the right sort of work product for other organizations.

Test plans can cover a whole project, or be specific to a test level or type of testing. Test plans are covered in more detail in Chapter 5, Section 5.2.

Test monitoring and control work products

The work products associated with test monitoring and control typically include different types of test reports. Test progress reports are produced on an ongoing and/or a regular basis to keep stakeholders updated about progress, on a weekly or monthly basis, for example. Test summary reports are produced at test completion milestones, as a way of summarizing the testing for a particular unit of work or test project. Any test report needs to include details relevant to its intended audience, the date of the report and the time period covered by the report. Test reports may include test execution results once those are available, in summary form (e.g. number of tests run, failed, passed or blocked and number of defects raised of different severity), and the status compared to the exit criteria or definition of done.

Test monitoring and control work products should address project management concerns such as budget and schedule, task completion, resource allocation, usage and effort. If action needs to be taken on the basis of information reported in a test report, those actions should be summarized in the next report to ensure that the desired effect of the action has been achieved.

These work products are further explained in Chapter 5, Section 5.3.

Test analysis work products

Test analysis work products include mainly test conditions, as this is the output of the test analysis activity. Each test condition is ideally traceable to the test basis (and vice versa). In exploratory testing, a test charter may be a test analysis work product. Defect reports about defects found in the test basis as a result of test analysis can also be considered a work product from test analysis.

Here is an example: The specification for an ordering system describes a sales discount feature when customers put in large orders. The test conditions might be to test all the discount values for various order values. The discount values would be coverage items – we want to make sure we have tested each of them at least once. The work product would be the list of test conditions, that is, the discount values.

Test conditions are further discussed in Chapter 4.

Test design work products

The main work products resulting from test design are test cases and sets of test cases that exercise the test conditions identified in test analysis.

Sometimes the test cases at this stage are still rather vague and high-level, that is, without concrete values for inputs and expected results. For example, a test case for the sales discount might be to set up four existing customers, one who orders only a small amount so does not qualify for a discount, and the other three who order enough to qualify for a discount at each of the three discount levels respectively.

Having the test cases at a high level means that we can use the same test case across multiple test cycles with different specific or concrete data. For example, one application may have discounts of 2%, 5% and 10%, and another may have discounts of 10%, 20% and 25%. Our high-level test case adequately documents the scope of the test even though the details will be different in each application. The test case is traceable to and from the test condition that it is derived from.

We have seen that high-level test cases can have advantages, but there are also some aspects that you need to be aware of with high-level test cases. For example, it may be difficult to reproduce the test exactly; different testers may use different test data, so the test case is not exactly repeatable. A high-level test case is not directly automatable; the tool needs exact instructions and specific data in order to execute the test. The skill and domain knowledge of the tester is also critical; a junior new-hire with no domain knowledge may struggle to know what they are supposed to be doing, unless they are well supported by more experienced testers. These are not insurmountable problems, but they do need to be considered.

Test design work products may also include test data, the design of the test environment and the identification of infrastructure and tools. The extent and way in which these are documented may vary significantly from project to project or from one company to another.

When deriving test cases from the test conditions, we may also find defects or improvements that we could make to the test conditions, so the test conditions themselves may be further refined during test design. In our sales discount example, in test analysis we identified the three discounts as test conditions, but in test design, by looking at the test cases, we identified the 'no discount' test condition – a discount of 0%.

Test cases are further discussed in Chapter 4.

Test implementation work products

Work products for test implementation include:

- test procedures and the sequencing of those procedures.
- test suites.
- a test execution schedule.

At this point, because we are preparing for test execution, we need to further refine any high-level test cases into low-level test cases that use concrete and specific data, both for test inputs and test data. In our loyalty discount example, we would now need to specify the details of our existing customers, decide on exactly how much each order will come to and calculate the final amount they would pay, including the discount. So, for example, Mrs Smith puts in an order for $50.01. Because her order is over $50, she gets a 10% discount, so she pays $45.01. We calculate the expected result for the test using a **test oracle** – the source of what the correct answer should be (in this case simple arithmetic). We would also need to set up Mrs Smith and other customers in the database as part of the preconditions of running the test, and this would be included in the test procedure.

> **Test oracle** (oracle) A source to determine expected results to compare with the actual result of the system under test.

In exploratory testing, we may be creating work products for test design and test implementation while doing test execution; traceability may be more difficult in this case.

Test implementation may also create work products that will be used by tools, for example, test scripts for test execution tools, and sometimes work products are created *by* tools, such as a test execution schedule. Service virtualization may also create test implementation work products.

As in test design, we may further refine test conditions (and high-level test cases) during test implementation. For example, by deciding on the concrete values for our sales discount example, we realize that a test condition we omitted was to consider two different ways of clients paying between $45.01 and $50.00 (that is, with or without a discount). This may not be important to include in our tests, but it is an additional test condition.

Test execution work products

Work products for test execution include:

- documentation of the status of individual test cases or test procedures (e.g. ready to run, passed, failed, blocked, deliberately skipped, etc.)
- defect reports (see Chapter 5, Section 5.6)
- documentation about which test item(s), test object(s), test tools and testware were involved in the testing.

In test execution, we want to know what happened when the tests were run. We want to know about any problems encountered that may have blocked some tests running, for example if the network was down for a time. We want to know whether or not we were able to execute all of the tests that we planned to execute (which is not necessarily all of the tests that we have designed or implemented).

When test execution is finished (or is stopped), we should be able to report test results based on traceability, so that if a set of tests that were all related to the same requirement or user story failed, we will know about that. We also want to know which requirements have passed all of their planned tests, and any that have not yet been tested – that is, the tests are still waiting to be run. This is particularly important when test execution is stopped rather than completed.

Stakeholders are more likely to appreciate the implications of failing tests if they can be related to user stories or requirements, rather than just being told that a certain number of tests passed or failed. This is why traceability is important.

Test completion work products

The work products for test completion include the following:

- test summary reports
- action items for improvement of subsequent projects or iterations (e.g. following an Agile project retrospective)
- change requests or product backlog items
- finalized testware.

Test completion work products give closure to the whole of the test process and should provide ongoing ideas for increasing the effectiveness and efficiency of testing within the organization in the future.

1.4.4 Traceability between the test basis and test work products

We have mentioned bi-directional **traceability** for all test work products covered in Section 1.4.3. Bi-directional means that we can trace, for example, a given requirement through test conditions and test cases to the test execution results, but we can also trace the test execution results back to test cases, test cases back to test conditions, and test conditions back to requirements. No matter what the work products are called, this cross-linking gives many benefits to the test process. We saw how traceability can aid in the measurement and reporting of test coverage in order to report coverage and defects related to requirements, which is more meaningful and of more value to stakeholders.

> **Traceability** The degree to which a relationship can be established between two or more work products.

Good traceability also supports the following:

- analyzing the impact of changes, whether to requirements or to the component or system
- making testing auditable, and being able to measure coverage
- meeting IT governance criteria (where applicable)
- improving the coherence of test progress reports and test summary reports to stakeholders, as described above
- relating the technical aspects of testing to stakeholders in terms that they can understand
- providing information to assess product quality, process capability and project progress against business goals.

You may find that your test management or requirements management tool provides support for traceability of work products; if so, make use of that feature. Some organizations find that they have to build their own management systems in order to organize test work products in the way that they want and to ensure that they have bi-directional traceability. However the support is implemented, it is important to have automated support for traceability – it is not something that can be sustained without tool support.

1.5 THE PSYCHOLOGY OF TESTING

SYLLABUS LEARNING OBJECTIVES FOR 1.5 THE PSYCHOLOGY OF TESTING (K2)

FL-1.5.1   Identify the psychological factors that influence the success of testing (K1)

FL-1.5.2   Explain the difference between the mindset required for test activities and the mindset required for development activities (K2)

1.5.1 Human psychology and testing

In this section, we'll discuss the various psychological factors that influence testing and its success. We'll also contrast the mindset of a tester and a developer. For a good introduction to the psychology of testing see Weinberg [2008].

As mentioned earlier, the ISTQB definition of software testing includes both dynamic testing and static testing. Let's review the distinction again. Dynamic software testing involves actually executing the software or some part of it, such as checking an application-produced report for accuracy or checking response time to user input. Static software testing does not execute the software but uses two possible approaches: automated static analysis on the code (e.g. evaluating its complexity) or on a document (e.g. to evaluate the readability of a use case); or reviews of code or documents (e.g. to evaluate a requirement specification for consistency, ambiguity and completeness).

Finding defects

While dynamic and static testing are very different types of activities, they have in common their ability to find defects. Static testing finds defects directly, while dynamic testing finds evidence of a defect through a failure of the software to behave as expected. Either way, people carrying out static or dynamic tests must be focused on the possibility – indeed, the high likelihood in many cases – of finding defects. Indeed, finding defects is often a primary objective of static and dynamic testing activities.

Identifying defects may unfortunately be perceived by developers as a criticism, not only of the product but also of its author – and in a sense, it is. But finding defects in testing should be *constructive* criticism, where testers have the best interest of the developer in mind. One meaning of the word 'criticism' is 'an examination, interpretation, analysis or judgement about something' – this is an objective assessment. But other meanings include disapproval by pointing out faults or shortcomings and even an attack on someone or something. Testing does not want to be the latter sense of criticism, but even when intended in the first sense, it can be perceived in the other ways. Testers need to be diplomats, along with everything else.

Bias

However, there is another factor at work when we are reporting defects; the author (developer) believes that their code is correct – they obviously did not write it to be intentionally wrong. This confidence in their understanding is in some sense necessary for developers; they cannot proceed without it. But at the same time, this confidence creates confirmation bias. Confirmation bias makes it difficult to accept information that disagrees with your currently held beliefs. Simply put, the author of a work product has confidence that they have solved the requirements, design, metadata or code problem, at least in an acceptable fashion; however, strictly speaking, that is false confidence. Other biases may also be at work, and it is also human nature to blame the bearer of bad news (which defects are perceived to be).

Testers are not always aware of their biases either, and they do have biases of their own. Since those biases are different from the developers, that is a benefit, but a lack of awareness of those biases sets up potential conflict.

This reluctance to accept that their work is not perfect is why some people regard testing as a destructive activity (trying to destroy their work) rather than the constructive activity it is (trying to construct better quality software). Good testing contributes greatly to product quality and project quality, as we saw in Sections 1.1 and 1.2.

While some developers are aware of their biases when they participate in reviews and perform unit testing of their own work products, those biases act to impede their effectiveness at finding their own defects. The mental mistakes that caused them to create the defects remain in their minds in most cases. When proofreading our own work, for example, we see what we meant, not what we wrote.

Review and test your own work?

Should software work product developers – business analysts, system designers, architects, database administrators and developers – review and test their own work? They certainly should; they have a deep understanding about the system, and quality is everyone's responsibility.

However, many business analysts, system designers, architects, database administrators and developers do not know the review, static analysis and dynamic testing techniques discussed in the Foundation Syllabus and this book. While that situation is gradually changing, much of the self-testing by software work product developers is either not done or is not done as effectively as it could be. The principles and techniques in the Foundation Syllabus and this book are intended to help either testers or others to be more effective at finding defects, both their own and those of others.

Attitudes

It is a particular problem when a tester revels in being the bearer of bad news. For example, one tester made a revealing – and not very flattering – remark during an interview with one of the authors. When asked what he liked about testing, he responded, 'I like to catch the developers'. He went on to explain that, when he found a defect in someone's work, he would go and demonstrate the failure on the programmer's workstation. He said that he made sure that he found at least one defect in everyone's work on a project, and went through this process of ritually humiliating the programmer with each and every one of his colleagues. When asked why, he said, 'I want to prove to everyone that I am their intellectual equal'. This person, while possessing many of the skills and traits one would want in a tester, had exactly the wrong personality to be a truly professional tester.

Instead of seeing themselves as their colleagues' adversaries or social inferiors out to prove their equality, testers should see themselves as teammates. In their special role, testers provide essential services in the development organization. They should ask themselves, 'Who are the stakeholders in the work that I do as a tester?' Having identified these stakeholders, they should ask each stakeholder group, 'What services do you want from testing, and how well are we providing them?'

While the specific services are not always defined, it is common that mature and wise developers know that studying their mistakes and the defects they have introduced is the key to learning how to get better. Further, smart software development managers understand that finding and fixing defects during testing not only reduces the level of risk to the quality of the product, it also saves time and money when compared to finding defects in production.

Communication

Clearly defined objectives and goals for testing, combined with constructive styles of communication on the part of test professionals, will help to avoid most negative personal or group dynamics between testers and their colleagues in the development team. Whenever defects are found, true testing professionals distinguish themselves by demonstrating good interpersonal skills. True testing professionals communicate facts about defects, progress and risks in an objective and constructive way that counteracts these misperceptions as much as possible. This helps to reduce tensions and build positive relationships with colleagues, supporting the view of testing as a constructive and helpful activity. While this is not necessary, we have noticed that many consummate testing professionals have business analysts, system designers, architects, developers and other specialists with whom they work as close personal friends.

This applies not only to testers but also to test managers, and not just to defects and failures but to all communication about testing, such as test results, test progress and risks.

Having good communication skills is a complex topic, well beyond the scope of a book on fundamental testing techniques. However, we can give you some basics for good communication with your development colleagues:

- Remember to think of your colleagues as teammates, not as opponents or adversaries. The way you regard people has a profound effect on the way you treat them. You do not have to think in terms of kinship or achieving world peace, but you should keep in mind that everyone on the development team has the common goal of delivering a quality system, and everyone must work together to accomplish that. Start with collaboration, not battles.

- Make sure that you focus on and emphasize the value and benefits of testing. Remind your developer colleagues that defect information provided by testing can help them to improve their own skills and future work products. Remind managers that defects found early by testing and fixed as soon as possible will save time and money and reduce overall product quality risk. Also, be sure to respond well when developers find problems in your own test work products. Ask them to review them and thank them for their findings (just as you would like to be thanked for finding problems in their work).

- Recognize that your colleagues have pride in their work, just as you do, and as such you owe them a tactful communication about defects you have found. It is not really any harder to communicate your findings, especially the potentially embarrassing findings, in a neutral, fact-focused way. In fact, you will find that if you avoid criticizing people and their work products, but instead keep your written and verbal communications objective and factual, you will also avoid a lot of unnecessary conflict and drama with your colleagues.

- Before you communicate these potentially embarrassing findings, mentally put yourself in the position of the person who created the work product. How are they going to feel about this information? How might they react? What can you do to help them get the essential message that they need to receive without provoking a negative emotional reaction from them?

- Keep in mind the psychological element of cognitive dissonance. Cognitive dissonance is a defect – or perhaps a feature – in the human brain that makes it difficult to process unexpected information, especially bad news. So, while you might have been clear in what you said or wrote, the person on the receiving end might not have clearly understood. Cognitive dissonance is a two-way street, too, and it is quite possible that you are misunderstanding someone's reaction to your findings. So, before assuming the worst about someone and their motivations, confirm that the other person has understood what you have said and vice versa.

1.5.2 Tester's and developer's mindsets

Testers and developers actually have different thought processes and different objectives for their work. A mindset reflects an individual's assumptions and the way that they like to solve problems and make decisions.

A tester's mindset should include the following:

- Curiosity. Good testers are curious about why systems behave the way they do and how systems are built. When they see unexpected behaviour, they have a natural urge to explore further, to isolate the failure, to look for more generalized problems and to gain deeper understanding.

- Professional pessimism. Good testers expect to find defects and failures. They understand human fallibility and its implications for software development. (However, this is not to say that they are negative or adversarial, as we'll discuss in a moment.)

- A critical eye. Good testers couple this professional pessimism with a natural inclination to doubt the correctness of software work products and their behaviours as they look at them. A good tester has, as a personal slogan, 'If in doubt, it is a bug'.

- Attention to detail. Good testers notice everything, even the smallest details. Sometimes these details are cosmetic problems like font-size mismatches, but sometimes these details are subtle clues that a serious failure is about to happen. This trait is both a blessing and a curse. Some testers find that they cannot turn this trait off, so they are constantly finding defects in the real world – even when not being paid to find them.

- Experience. Good testers not only know a defect when they see one, they also know where to look for defects. Experienced testers have seen a veritable parade of bugs in their time, and they leverage this experience during all types of testing, especially experience-based testing such as error guessing (see Chapter 4).

- Good communication skills. All of these traits are essential, but, without the ability to effectively communicate their findings, testers will produce useful information that will, alas, be put to no use. Good communicators know how to explain the test results, even negative results such as serious defects and quality risks, without coming across as preachy, scolding or defeatist.

A good tester has the skills, the training, the certification and the mindset of a professional tester, and of these four skills, the most important – and perhaps the most elusive – is the mindset.

The tester's mindset is to think about what could go wrong and what is missing. The tester looks at a statement in a requirement or user story and asks, 'What if it isn't? What haven't they thought of here? What could go wrong?' That mindset is quite different from the mindset that a business analyst, system designer, architect, database administrator or developer must bring to creating the work products involved in developing software. While the testers (or reviewers) must assume that the work product under review or test is defective in some way – and it is their job to find those defects – the people developing that work product must have confidence that they understand how to do so properly. Looking at a statement in a requirement or user story, the developer thinks, 'How can I implement this? What technical challenges do I need to solve?'

Having a tester or group of testers who are organizationally separate from development, either as individuals or as an independent test team, can provide significant benefits, such as increased defect-detection percentage. A tester's mindset is a 'different pair of eyes' and independent testers can see things that developers do not see (because of confirmation bias discussed above). This is especially important for large, complex or safety-critical systems.

However, independence from the developers does not mean an adversarial relationship with them. In fact, such a relationship is toxic, often fatally so, to a test team's effectiveness.

The softer side of software testing is often the harder side to master. A tester may have adequate or even excellent technique skills and certifications, but if they do not have adequate interpersonal and communication skills, they will not be an effective tester. Such soft skills can be improved with training and practice. The best testers continuously strive to attain a more professional mindset, and it is a lifelong journey.

CHAPTER REVIEW

Let's review what you have learned in this chapter.

From Section 1.1, you should now know what testing is. You should be able to remember the typical objectives of testing. You should know the difference between testing and debugging. You should know the Glossary keyword terms **debugging**, **test object**, **test objective**, **testing**, **validation** and **verification**.

From Section 1.2, you should now be able to explain why testing is necessary and support that explanation with examples. You should be able to explain the difference between testing and quality assurance and how they work together to improve quality. You should be able to distinguish between an error (made by a person), a defect (in a work product) and a failure (where the component or system does not perform as expected). You should know the difference between the root cause of a defect and the effects of a defect or failure. You should know the Glossary terms **defect**, **error**, **failure**, **quality**, **quality assurance** and **root cause**.

You should be able to explain the seven principles of testing, discussed in Section 1.3.

From Section 1.4, you should now recognize a test process. You should be able to recall the main testing activities of test planning, test monitoring and control, test analysis, test design, test implementation, test execution and test completion. You should be familiar with the work products produced by each test activity. You should know the Glossary terms **coverage**, **test analysis**, **test basis**, **test case**, **test completion**, **test condition**, **test control**, **test data**, **test design**, **test execution**, **test execution schedule**, **test implementation**, **test monitoring**, **test oracle**, **test planning**, **test procedure**, **test suite**, **testware** and **traceability**.

From Section 1.5, you now should be able to explain the psychological factors that influence the success of testing. You should be able to explain and contrast the mindsets of testers and developers, and why these differences can lead to problems.

SAMPLE EXAM QUESTIONS

Question 1 What is NOT a reason for testing?

a. To enable developers to code as quickly as possible.

b. To reduce the risk of failures in operation.

c. To contribute to the quality of the components or systems.

d. To meet any applicable contractual or legal requirements.

Question 2 Consider the following definitions and match the term with the definition.

1. A reason or purpose for designing and executing a test.

2. The component or system to be tested.

3. Confirmation by examination and through provision of objective evidence that the requirements for a specific intended use or application have been fulfilled.

a. 1) test object, 2) test objective, 3) validation.

b. 1) test objective, 2) test object, 3) validation.

c. 1) validation, 2) test basis, 3) verification.

d. 1) test objective, 2) test object, 3) verification.

Question 3 Which statement about quality assurance (QA) is true?

a. QA and testing are the same.

b. QA includes both testing and root cause analysis.

c. Testing is quality control, not QA.

d. QA does not apply to testing.

Question 4 It is important to ensure that test design starts during the requirements definition. Which of the following test objectives supports this?

a. Preventing defects in the system.

b. Finding defects through dynamic testing.

c. Gaining confidence in the system.

d. Finishing the project on time.

Question 5 A test team consistently finds a large number of defects during development, including system testing. Although the test manager understands that this is good defect finding within their budget for her test team and industry, senior management and executives remain disappointed in the test group, saying that the test team misses some bugs that the users find after release. Given that the users are generally happy with the system and that the failures that have occurred have generally been low-impact, which of the following testing principles is most likely to help the test manager explain to these managers and executives why some defects are likely to be missed?

a. Exhaustive testing is impossible.

b. Defect clustering.

c. Pesticide paradox.

d. Absence-of-errors fallacy.

Question 6 What are the benefits of traceability between the test basis and test work products?

a. Traceability means that test basis documents and test work products do not need to be reviewed.

b. Traceability ensures that test work products are limited in number to save time in producing them.

c. Traceability enables test progress and defects to be reported with reference to requirements, which is more understandable to stakeholders.

d. Traceability enables developers to produce code that is easier to test.

Question 7 Which of the following is most important to promote and maintain good relationships between testers and developers?

a. Understanding what managers value about testing.

b. Explaining test results in a neutral fashion.

c. Identifying potential customer work-arounds for bugs.

d. Promoting better quality software whenever possible.

Question 8 Given the following test work products, identify the major activity in a test process that produces it.

1. Test execution schedule.
2. Test cases.
3. Test progress reports.
4. Defect reports.

a. 1) – Test planning, 2) – Test design 3) – Test execution, 4) – Test implementation.

b. 1) – Test execution, 2) – Test analysis 3) – Test completion, 4) – Test execution.

c. 1) – Test control, 2) – Test analysis, 3) – Test monitoring, 4) – Test implementation.

d. 1) – Test implementation, 2) – Test design, 3) – Test monitoring, 4) – Test execution.

CHAPTER TWO

Testing throughout the software development life cycle

Testing is not a stand-alone activity. It has its place within a software development life cycle model and therefore the life cycle applied will largely determine how testing is organized. There are many different forms of testing. Because several disciplines, often with different interests, are involved in the development life cycle, it is important to clearly understand and define the various test levels and types. This chapter discusses the most commonly applied software development models, test levels and test types. Maintenance can be seen as a specific instance of a development process. The way maintenance influences the test process, levels and types and how testing can be organized is described in the last section of this chapter.

2.1 SOFTWARE DEVELOPMENT LIFE CYCLE MODELS

> **SYLLABUS LEARNING OBJECTIVES FOR 2.1 SOFTWARE DEVELOPMENT LIFE CYCLE MODELS (K2)**
>
> **FL-2.1.1** Explain the relationships between software development activities and test activities in the software development life cycle (K2)
>
> **FL-2.1.2** Identify reasons why software development life cycle models must be adapted to the context of project and product characteristics (K1)

In this section, we'll discuss software development models and how testing fits into them. We'll discuss sequential models, focusing on the V-model approach rather than the waterfall. We'll discuss iterative and incremental models such as Rational Unified Process (RUP), Scrum, Kanban and Spiral (or prototyping).

As we go through this section, watch for the Syllabus terms **commercial off-the-shelf (COTS)**, **sequential development model**, and **test level**. You will find these keywords defined in the Glossary (and ISTQB website).

The development process adopted for a project will depend on the project aims and goals. There are numerous development life cycles that have been developed in order to achieve different required objectives. These life cycles range from lightweight and fast methodologies, where time to market is of the essence, through to fully controlled and documented methodologies. Each of these methodologies has its place in modern software development, and the most appropriate development process should be applied to each project. The models specify the various stages of the process and the order in which they are carried out.

The life cycle model that is adopted for a project will have a big impact on the testing that is carried out. Testing does not exist in isolation; test activities are highly related to software development activities. It will define the what, where and when of our planned testing, influence regression testing and largely determine which test techniques to use. The way testing is organized must fit the development life cycle or it will fail to deliver its benefit. If time to market is the key driver, then the testing must be fast and efficient. If a fully documented software development life cycle, with an audit trail of evidence, is required, the testing must be fully documented.

Whichever life cycle model is being used, there are several characteristics of good testing:

- For every development activity there is a corresponding test activity.
- Each test level has test objectives specific to that level.
- The analysis and design of tests for a given test level should begin during the corresponding software development activity.
- Testers should participate in discussions to help define and refine requirements and design. They should also be involved in reviewing work products as soon as drafts are available in the software development cycle.

Recall from Chapter 1, testing Principle 3: 'Early testing saves time and money'. By starting testing activities as early as possible in the software development life cycle, we find defects while they are still small green shoots (in requirements, for example) before they have had a chance to grow into trees (in production). We also prevent defects from occurring at all by being more aware of what should be tested from the earliest point in whatever software development life cycle we are using.

We will look at two categories of software development life cycle models: sequential and iterative/incremental.

Sequential development models

A **sequential development model** is one where the development activities happen in a prescribed sequence – at least that is the idea. The models assume a linear sequential flow of activities; the next phase is only supposed to start when the previous phase is complete. Berard [1993] said that developing software from requirements is like walking on water – it is easier if it is frozen. But practice does not conform to theory: the activities will overlap, and things will be discovered in a later phase that may invalidate assumptions made in previous phases (which were supposed to be finished).

The waterfall model (in Figure 2.1) was one of the earliest models to be designed. It has a natural timeline where tasks are executed in a sequential fashion. We start at the top of the waterfall with a feasibility study and flow down through the various project tasks, finishing with implementation into the live environment. Design flows through into development, which in turn flows into build, and finally on into test. Different models have different levels; the figure shows one possible model. With all waterfall models, however, testing tends to happen towards the end of the life cycle, so defects are detected close to the live implementation date. With this model, it is difficult to get feedback passed backwards up the waterfall and there are difficulties if we need to carry out numerous iterations for a particular phase.

> **Sequential development model** A type of development life cycle model in which a complete system is developed in a linear way of several discrete and successive phases with no overlap between them.

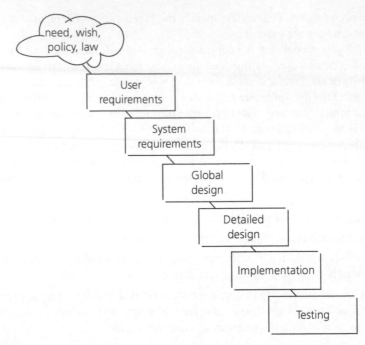

FIGURE 2.1 Waterfall model

The V-model was developed to address some of the problems experienced using the traditional waterfall approach. Defects were being found too late in the life cycle, as testing was not involved until the end of the project. Testing also added lead time due to its late involvement. The V-model provides guidance on how testing begins as early as possible in the life cycle. It also shows that testing is not only an execution-based activity. There are a variety of activities that need to be performed before the end of the coding phase. These activities should be carried out in *parallel* with development activities, and testers need to work with developers and business analysts so they can perform these activities and tasks, producing a set of test deliverables. The work products produced by the developers and business analysts during development are the basis of testing in one or more levels. By starting test design early, defects are often found in the test basis documents. A good practice is to have testers involved even earlier, during the review of the (draft) test basis documents. The V-model is a model that illustrates how testing activities (verification and validation) can be integrated into each phase of the life cycle. Within the V-model, validation testing takes place especially during the early stages, for example reviewing the user requirements, and late in the life cycle, for example during user acceptance testing.

Although variants of the V-model exist, a common type of V-model uses four **test levels**. (See Section 2.2 for more on test levels.) The four test levels used, each with their own objectives, are:

Test level (test stage)
A specific instantiation of a test process.

- Component testing: searches for defects in and verifies the functioning of software components (for example modules, programs, objects, classes, etc.) that are separately testable.
- Integration testing: tests interfaces between components, interactions to different parts of a system such as an operating system, file system and hardware or interfaces between systems.

- System testing: concerned with the behaviour of the whole system/product as defined by the scope of a development project or product. The main focus of system testing is verification against specified requirements.

- Acceptance testing: validation testing with respect to user needs, requirements and business processes conducted to determine whether or not to accept the system.

In practice, a V-model may have more, fewer or different levels of development and testing, depending on the project and the software product. For example, there may be component integration testing after component testing and system integration testing after system testing. Test levels can be combined or reorganized depending on the nature of the project or the system architecture. In the V-model, there may also be overlapping of activities.

Sequential models aim to deliver all of the software at once, that is, the complete set of features required by stakeholders or users, or the software may be delivered in releases containing significant chunks of new functionality. However, typically this may take months or even years of development even for a single release.

Note that the types of work products mentioned in Figure 2.2 on the left side of the V-model are just an illustration. In practice, they come under many different names.

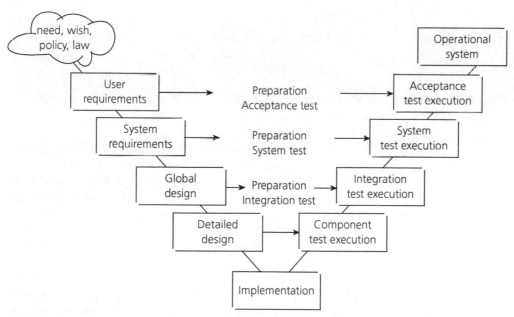

FIGURE 2.2   V-model

Iterative and incremental development models

Not all life cycles are sequential. There are also iterative and incremental life cycles where, instead of one large development timeline from beginning to end, we cycle through a number of smaller self-contained life cycle phases for the same project. As with the V-model, there are many variants of iterative and incremental life cycles.

To better understand the meaning of these two terms, consider the following two sequences of producing a painting.

- **Incremental:** complete one piece at a time (scheduling or staging strategy). Each increment may be delivered to the customer.

Images provided by: Mark Fewster, Grove Software Testing Ltd

- **Iterative:** start with a rough product and refine it, iteratively (rework strategy). Final version only delivered to the customer (although in practice, intermediate versions may be delivered to selected customers to get feedback).

Images provided by: Mark Fewster, Grove Software Testing Ltd

In terms of developing software, a purely iterative model does not produce a working system until the final iteration. The incremental approach produces working versions of parts of the system early on and each of these can be released to the customer. The advantage of this is that the customer can gain early benefit from using the deliveries and, perhaps most importantly, the customers can give valuable feedback. This feedback will influence what is done in future increments. Most iterative approaches also incorporate this feedback loop by delivering some (if not all) of the (intermediate) products created by the iterations.

The painting analogy shown above is not a perfect representation for the iterative approach. If the final product were to comprise 1,000 source code modules, you could be forgiven for thinking that an iterative approach would have people starting the first iteration by writing one line of code in each module and then have the second and subsequent iterations each adding another line of code to each module until they were completed. This is not the case.

In both iterative and incremental models, the features to be implemented are grouped together (for example according to business priority or risk). In this way, the focus is always on the most important of the outstanding features. The various project phases, including their work products and activities, then occur for each group of features. The phases may be done either sequentially or overlapping, and the iterations or increments themselves may be sequential or overlapping.

An iterative development model is shown in Figure 2.3.

FIGURE 2.3 Iterative development model

Testing in incremental and iterative development

During project initiation, high-level test planning and test analysis occurs in parallel with the project planning and business/requirements analysis. Any detailed test
planning, test analysis, test design and test implementation occurs at the beginning
of each iteration.

Test execution often involves overlapping test levels. Each test level begins as
early as possible and may continue after subsequent, higher test levels have started.

In an iterative or incremental life cycle, many of the same tasks will be performed
but their timing and extent may vary. For example, rather than being able to implement the entire test environment at the beginning of the project, it may be more
efficient to implement only the part needed for the current iteration. The testing tasks
may be undertaken in a different order and not necessarily sequentially. There are
likely to be fewer entry and exit criteria between activities compared with sequential
models. Also, much of the test planning and completion reporting are more likely
to occur at the start and end of the project, respectively, rather than at the start and
end of each iteration.

With any of the iterative or incremental life cycle models, the farther ahead the
planning occurs, the farther ahead the scope of the test process can extend.

Common issues with iterative and incremental models include:

- More regression testing.
- Defects outside the scope of the iteration or increment.
- Less thorough testing.

Because the system is being produced a bit at a time, at any given point there will
some part which is completed in some sense, either an increment or the work that was
done iteratively. This part will be tested and may be used by the customer or user to give
feedback. When the next increment or iteration is developed, this will also be tested, but it
is also important to do regression testing of the parts which have already been developed.
The more iterations or increments there are, the more regression testing will be needed
throughout development. (This type of testing is a good candidate for automation.)

Defects that are found in the part that you are currently testing are dealt with in
the usual way, but what about defects found either by regression testing of previously
developed parts, or discovered by accident when testing a new part? These defects do
need to be logged and dealt with, but because they are outside the scope of the current
iteration/increment, they can sometimes fall between the cracks and be forgotten,
neglected or argued about.

There is a danger that the testing may be less thorough in incremental and iterative life cycles, particularly regression testing of previously developed parts, and especially if the regression testing is manual rather than automated. There is also a danger that the testing is less formal, because we are dealing with smaller parts of the system, and formality of the testing may seem like overkill for such a small thing.

Examples of iterative and incremental development models are Rational Unified Process (RUP), Scrum, Kanban and Spiral (or prototyping).

Rational Unified Process (RUP)

RUP is a software development process framework from Rational Software Development, a division of IBM. It consists of four steps:

- Inception: the initial idea, planning (for example what resources would be needed) and go/no-go decision for development, done with stakeholders.
- Elaboration: further detailed investigation into resources, architecture and costs.
- Construction: the software product is developed, including testing.
- Transition: the software product is released to customers, with modifications based on user feedback.

This development process is tailorable for different contexts, and there are tools (and services) to support it. One of the basic principles is that development is iterative, with risk being the primary driver for decisions about the development. Another principle (relevant to us) is that the evaluation of quality (including testing) is continuous throughout development.

In RUP, the increments that are produced, although significantly smaller than what is produced by sequential models, are larger than the increments produced by Agile development (see Scrum below), and would typically take months rather than days or weeks to complete. They might contain groups of related features, for example.

Scrum

Scrum is an iterative and incremental framework for effective team collaboration, which is typically used in Agile development, the most well-known iterative method. It (and Agile) is based on recognizing that change is inevitable and taking a practical empirical approach to changing priorities. Work is broken down into small units that can be completed in a fairly short time (days, a week or two or even a month). The delivery of a unit of work is called a sprint. For software development, a sprint includes all aspects of development for a particular feature or set of small features, everything from requirements (typically user stories) through to testing and (ideally) test automation.

The development teams are small (3 to 9 people) and cross-functional, that is, they include people who perform various roles, and often individuals take on different tasks (such as testing) within the team. The key roles are:

- The Product Owner represents the business, that is, stakeholders and end users.
- The Development team (which includes testers) makes its own decisions about development, that is, they are self-organizing with a high level of autonomy.
- The Scrum Master helps the development team to do their work as efficiently as possible, by interacting with other parts of the organization and dealing with problems. The Scrum Master is not a manager, but a facilitator for the team.

A stand-up meeting of typically around 15 minutes is held each day, for example first thing in the morning, to update everyone with progress from the previous day and plan the work ahead. (This is where the term 'scrum' came from, as in the gathering of a rugby team.)

At the start of a sprint, in the sprint planning meeting, some features are selected to be implemented, with other features being put on a backlog. Acceptance criteria apply to user stories, and are similar to test conditions, saying what needs to work for the user story to be considered working. A definition of done can apply to a user story (which includes but goes beyond satisfaction of the acceptance criteria), but also to unit testing, system testing, iterations and releases. After a sprint completes, a retrospective should be held to assess what went well and what could be improved for the next sprint.

Because development is limited to the sprint duration which is time-boxed, flexibility is in choosing what can be developed in the time. Compare that to sequential models, where all the features are selected first and the time taken to develop all of them is based on that. Thus Scrum (and Agile) enable us to deliver the greatest value soonest, an approach first proposed in the 1980s.

Because the iterations are short, the increments are small, such as a few small features or even a few enhancements or bug fixes.

Kanban

Kanban came from an approach to work in manufacturing at Toyota. It is a way of visualizing work and workflow. A Kanban board has columns for different stages of work, from initial idea through development and testing stages to final delivery to users. The tasks are put on sticky notes which are moved from left to right through the columns (like an assembly line for cars).

A key principle of Kanban is to have a limit for work-in-progress activities. If we concentrate on one task, we are much more efficient at doing it, so this approach is less wasteful than trying to do little bits of lots of different tasks. This focus on eliminating waste makes this a lean approach.

There is also a strong focus on user and customer needs. Iterations can be a fixed length to deliver a single feature or enhancement, or features can be grouped together for delivery. Kanban can span more than one team's work (as opposed to Scrum). If user stories are grouped by feature, work may span more than one column on the Kanban board, sometimes referred to as swim lanes.

Spiral (or prototyping)

The Spiral model, initially proposed by Boehm [1996] is based on risk. There are four steps: determine objectives, identify risks and alternatives, develop and test, and plan the next iteration. Prototypes may be developed as a way of addressing risks; these prototypes may be kept and incorporated into later cycles (an incremental approach), they might be discarded (a throw-away prototype), or they may be re-worked as part of the next cycle.

The diagram of the Spiral model shows development starting small from a centre, and moving in a circular way clockwise through the four stages. Each succeeding cycle builds outwards in a spiral through the phases, developing more functionality each time. The key driver for the Spiral model is that it is risk-driven.

Agile development

In this section, we will describe what Agile development is and then cover the changes that this way of working brings to testing. This is additional to what you need to know for the exam, as the Syllabus does not specifically cover Agile development (the ISTQB Foundation Level Agile Tester Extension Syllabus covers this), but we hope this will give you useful background, especially if you are not familiar with it.

Agile software development is a group of software development methodologies based on iterative and incremental development, where requirements and solutions evolve through collaboration between self-organizing cross-functional teams. Most Agile teams use Scrum, as described above. Typical Agile teams are 5 to 9 people, and the Agile manifesto describes ways of working that are ideal for small teams, and that counteract problems prevalent in the late 1990s, with its emphasis on process and documentation. The Agile manifesto consists of four statements describing what is valued in this way of working:

- individuals and interactions over processes and tools
- working software over comprehensive documentation
- customer collaboration over contract negotiation
- responding to change over following a plan.

While there are several Agile methodologies in practice, the industry seems to have settled on the use of Scrum as an Agile management approach, and Extreme Programming (XP) as the main source of Agile development ideas. Some characteristics of project teams using Scrum and XP are:

- The generation of business stories (a form of lightweight use cases) to define the functionality, rather than highly detailed requirements specifications.
- The incorporation of business representatives into the development process, as part of each iteration (called a sprint and typically lasting 2 to 4 weeks), providing continual feedback and to define and carry out functional acceptance testing.
- The recognition that we cannot know the future, so changes to requirements are welcomed throughout the development process, as this approach can produce a product that better meets the stakeholders' needs as their knowledge grows over time.
- The concept of shared code ownership among the developers, and the close inclusion of testers in the sprint teams.
- The writing of tests as the first step in the development of a component, and the automation of those tests before any code is written. The component is complete when it then passes the automated tests. This is known as test-driven development.
- Simplicity: building only what is necessary, not everything you can think of.
- The continuous integration and testing of the code throughout the sprint, at least once a day.

Proponents of the Scrum and XP approaches emphasize testing throughout the process. Each iteration (sprint) culminates in a short period of testing, often with an independent tester as well as a business representative. Developers are to write and run test cases for their code, and leading practitioners use tools to automate those tests and to measure structural coverage of the tests (see Chapters 4 and 6). Every time a change is made in the code, the component is tested and then integrated with the existing code, which is then tested using the full set of automated component test cases. This gives continuous integration, by which we mean that changes are incorporated continuously into the software build.

Agile development provides both benefits and challenges for testers. Some of the benefits are:

- The focus on working software and good quality code.
- The inclusion of testing as part of and the starting point of software development (test-driven development).
- Accessibility of business stakeholders to help testers resolve questions about expected behaviour of the system.
- Self-organizing teams, where the whole team is responsible for quality and gives testers more autonomy in their work.
- Simplicity of design that should be easier to test.

There are also some significant challenges for testers when moving to an Agile development approach:

- Testers who are used to working with well-documented requirements will be designing tests from a different kind of test basis: less formal and subject to change. The manifesto does not say that documentation is no longer necessary or that it has no value, but it is often interpreted that way.
- Because developers are doing more component testing, there may be a perception that testers are not needed. But component testing and confirmation-based acceptance testing by only business representatives may miss major problems. System testing, with its wider perspective and emphasis on non-functional testing as well as end-to-end functional testing is needed, even if it does not fit comfortably into a sprint.
- The tester's role is different: since there is less documentation and more personal interaction within an Agile team, testers need to adapt to this style of working, and this can be difficult for some testers. Testers may be acting more as coaches in testing to both stakeholders and developers, who may not have a lot of testing knowledge.
- Although there is less to test in one iteration than a whole system, there is also a constant time pressure and less time to think about the testing for the new features.
- Because each increment is adding to an existing working system, regression testing becomes extremely important, and automation becomes more beneficial. However, simply taking existing automated component or component integration tests may not make an adequate regression suite.

Software engineering teams are still learning how to apply Agile approaches. Agile approaches cannot be applied to all projects or products, and some testing challenges remain to be surmounted with respect to Agile development. However, Agile methodologies are showing promising results in terms of both development efficiency and quality of the delivered code.

More information about testing in Agile development and iterative incremental models can be found in books by Black [2017], Crispin and Gregory [2008] and Gregory and Crispin [2015]. There is also an ISTQB certificate for the Foundation Level Agile Tester Extension.

2.1.2 Software development life cycle models in context

As with many aspects of development and testing, there is no one correct or best life cycle model for every situation. Every project and product is different from others, so it is important to choose a development model that is suitable for your own situation or context. The most suitable development model for you may be based on the following:

- the project goal
- the type of product being developed
- business priorities (for example time to market)
- identified product and project risks.

The development of an internal admin system is not the same as a safety-critical system such as flight control software for aircraft or braking systems for cars. These types of development need different life cycle models in order to succeed. The internal admin system may be developed very informally, with different features delivered incrementally. The development (and testing) of safety-critical systems needs to be far more rigorous and may be subject to legal contracts and regulatory requirements, so a sequential life cycle model may be more appropriate.

It is also important to consider organizational and cultural context. If you want to use Scrum for example, good communication between team members is critical.

Commercial off-the-shelf (COTS) (off-the-shelf software) A software product that is developed for the general market, i.e. for a large number of customers, and that is delivered to many customers in identical format.

The context also determines the test levels and/or test activities that are appropriate for a project, and they may be combined or reorganized. For the integration of a **commercial off-the-shelf (COTS)** software product into a system, for example, a purchaser may perform acceptance testing focused on functionality and other attributes (for example integration to the infrastructure and other systems), followed by a system integration test. The acceptance testing can include testing of system functions, but also testing of quality attributes such as performance and other non-functional tests. The testing may be done from the perspective of the end user and may also be done from an operations point of view.

The context within an organization also determines the most suitable life cycle model. For example, the V-model may be used to develop back office systems, so that all new features are integrated and tested before everyone updates to the new system. At the same time, Agile development may be used for the UI (User Interface) to the website, and a Spiral model may be used to develop a new app.

Internet of Things (IoT) systems present special challenges for testing (as well as for development). Many different objects need to be integrated together and tested in realistic conditions, but each object or device may be developed in a different way with a different life cycle model. There is also more emphasis on the later stages of the development life cycle, after objects are actually in use. There may be extensive updates needed to different devices and supporting software systems once users begin using the systems for real. There may also be unforeseen security issues that might require updates. There may even be issues when trying to decommission devices or software for IoT systems. Changing contexts always have an influence on testing, and in our technological world, constant change is definitely the norm, so testing (and development) always needs to adapt to its context.

2.2 TEST LEVELS

SYLLABUS LEARNING OBJECTIVES FOR 2.2 TEST LEVELS (K2)

FL-2.2.1 **Compare the different test levels from the perspective of objectives, test basis, test objects, typical defects and failures, and approaches and responsibilities (K2)**

We have mentioned (and given the definition for) test levels in Section 2.1. The definition of 'test level' is 'an instance of the test process', which is not necessarily the most helpful. The Syllabus here describes test levels as:

groups of test activities that are organized and managed together

The test activities were described in Chapter 1, Section 1.4 (test planning through to test completion). When we talk about test levels, we are looking at those activities performed with reference to development levels (such as those described in the V-model) from components to systems, or even systems of systems.

In this section, we'll look in more detail at the various test levels and show how they are related to other activities within the software development life cycle. The key characteristics for each test level are discussed and defined, to be able to more clearly separate the various test levels. A thorough understanding and definition of the various test levels will identify missing areas and prevent overlap and repetition. Sometimes we may wish to introduce deliberate overlap to address specific risks. Understanding whether we want overlaps and removing the gaps will make the test levels more complementary, leading to more effective and efficient testing. We will look at four test levels in this section.

As we go through this section, watch for the Syllabus terms **acceptance testing**, **alpha testing**, **beta testing**, **component integration testing**, **component testing**, **contractual acceptance testing**, **integration testing**, **operational acceptance testing**, **regulatory acceptance testing**, **system integration testing**, **system testing**, **test basis**, **test case**, **test environment**, **test object**, **test objective** and **user acceptance testing**. These terms are also defined in the Glossary.

While the specific test levels required for – and planned for – a particular project can vary, good practice in testing suggests that each test level has the following clearly identified:

- Specific **test objectives** for the test level.
- The **test basis**, the work product(s) used to derive the test conditions and **test cases**.
- The **test object** (that is, what is being tested such as an item, build, feature or system under test).
- The typical defects and failures that we are looking for at this test level.
- Specific approaches and responsibilities for this test level.

One additional aspect is that each test level needs a **test environment**. Sometimes an environment can be shared by more than one test level: in other situations, a particular environment is needed. For example, acceptance testing should have a test environment that is as similar to production as is possible or feasible.

Test objective A reason or purpose for designing and executing a test.

Test basis The body of knowledge used as the basis for test analysis and design.

Test case A set of preconditions, inputs, actions (where applicable), expected results and postconditions, developed based on test conditions.

Test object The component or system to be tested. See also: test item.

Test environment (test bed, test rig) An environment containing hardware, instrumentation, simulators, software tools and other support elements needed to conduct a test.

In component testing, developers often just use their development environment. In system testing, an environment may be needed with particular external connections, for example.

When these topics are clearly understood and defined for the entire project team, this contributes to the success of the project. In addition, during test planning, the managers responsible for the test levels should consider how they intend to test a system's configuration, if such data is part of a system.

2.2.1 Component testing

> **Component testing** (module testing, unit testing) The testing of individual hardware or software components.

Component testing, also known as unit or module testing, searches for defects in, and verifies the functioning of, software items (for example modules, programs, objects, classes, etc.) that are separately testable.

Component tests are typically based on the requirements and detailed design specifications applicable to the component under test, as well as the code itself (which we'll discuss in Chapter 4 when we talk about white-box testing).

The component under test, the test object, includes the individual components, the data conversion and migration programs used to enable the new release, and database tables, joins, views, modules, procedures, referential integrity and field constraints, and even whole databases.

Component testing: objectives

The different test levels have different objectives. The objectives of component testing include:

- Reducing risk (for example by testing high-risk components more extensively).
- Verifying whether or not functional and non-functional behaviours of the component are as they should be (as designed and specified).
- Building confidence in the quality of the component: this may include measuring structural coverage of the tests, giving confidence that the component has been tested as thoroughly as was planned.
- Finding defects in the component.
- Preventing defects from escaping to later testing.

In incremental and iterative development (for example Agile), automated component regression tests are run frequently, to give confidence that new additions or changes to a component have not caused existing components or links to break.

Component testing may be done in isolation from the rest of the system depending on the context of the development life cycle and the system. Most often, mock objects or stubs and drivers are used to replace the missing software and simulate the interface between the software components in a simple manner. A stub or mock object is called from the software component to be tested; a driver calls a component to be tested (see Figure 2.4). Test harnesses may also be used to provide similar functionality, and service virtualization can give cloud-based functionality to test components in realistic environments.

Component testing may include testing of functionality (for example are the calculations correct) and specific non-functional characteristics such as resource-behaviour (for example memory leaks), performance testing (for example do calculations complete quickly enough), as well as structural testing. Test cases are derived from work products such as the software design or the data model.

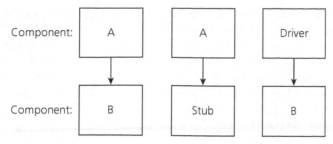

FIGURE 2.4   Stubs and drivers

Component testing: test basis

What is this particular component supposed to do? Examples of work products that can be used as a test basis for component testing include:

- detailed design
- code
- data model
- component specifications (if available).

Component testing: test objects

What are we actually testing at this level? We could say the smallest thing that can be sensibly tested on its own. Typical test objects for component testing include:

- components themselves, units or modules
- code and data structures
- classes
- database models.

Component testing: typical defects and failures

Examples of defects and failures that can typically be revealed by component testing include:

- incorrect functionality (for example not as described in a design specification)
- data flow problems
- incorrect code or logic.

At the end of the description of all the test levels, see Table 2.1 which summarizes the characteristics of each test level.

Component testing: specific approaches and responsibilities

Typically, component testing occurs with access to the code being tested and with the support of the development environment, such as a unit test framework or debugging tool. In practice it usually involves the developer who wrote the code. The developer may change between writing code and testing it. Sometimes, depending on the applicable level of risk, component testing is carried out by a different developer, introducing independence. Defects are typically fixed as soon as they are found, without formally recording them in a defect management tool. Of course, if such defects are recorded, this can provide useful information for root cause analysis.

One approach in component testing, initially developed in Extreme Programming (XP), is to prepare and automate test cases before coding. This is called a test-first approach or test-driven development (TDD). This approach is highly iterative and is based on cycles of developing automated tests, then building and integrating small pieces of code, and executing the component tests until they pass, and is typically done in Agile development. The idea is that the first thing the developer does is to write some automated tests for the component. Of course if these are run now, they will fail because no code is there! Then just enough code is written until those tests pass. This may involve fixing defects now found by the tests and re-factoring the code. (This approach also helps to build only what is needed rather than a lot of functionality that is not really wanted.)

2.2.2 Integration testing

Integration testing
Testing performed to expose defects in the interfaces and in the interactions between integrated components or systems.

Component integration testing
(link testing) Testing performed to expose defects in the interfaces and interactions between integrated components.

System integration testing Testing the combination and interaction of systems.

Integration testing tests interfaces between components and interactions of different parts of a system such as an operating system, file system and hardware or interfaces between systems. Integration tests are typically based on the software and system design (both high-level and low-level), the system architecture (especially the relationships between components or objects) and the workflows or use cases by which the stakeholders will employ the system.

There may be more than one level of integration testing and it may be carried out on test objects of varying size. For example:

- **Component integration testing** tests the interactions between software components and is done after component testing. It is a good candidate for automation. In iterative and incremental development, both component tests and integration tests are usually part of continuous integration, which may involve automated build, test and release to end users or to a next level. At least, this is the theory. In practice, component integration testing may not be done at all, or misunderstood and as a consequence not done well.

- **System integration testing** tests the interactions between different systems, packages and microservices, and may be done after system testing. System integration testing may also test interfaces to and provided by external organizations (such as web services). In this case, the developing organization may control only one side of the interface, resulting in a number of problems: changes may be destabilizing, defects in the external organization's software may block progress in the testing, or special test environments may be needed. Business processes implemented as workflows may involve a series of systems that can even run on different platforms. System integration testing may be done in parallel with other testing activities.

Integration testing: objectives
The objectives of integration testing include:

- Reducing risk, for example by testing high-risk integrations first.
- Verifying whether or not functional and non-functional behaviours of the interfaces are as they should be, as designed and specified.
- Building confidence in the quality of the interfaces.

- Finding defects in the interfaces themselves or in the components or systems being tested together.
- Preventing defects from escaping to later testing.

Automated integration regression tests (such as in continuous integration) provide confidence that changes have not broken existing interfaces, components or systems.

Integration testing: test basis

How are these components or systems supposed to work together and communicate? Examples of work products that can be used as a test basis for integration testing include:

- software and system design
- sequence diagrams
- interface and communication protocol specifications
- use cases
- architecture at component or system level
- workflows
- external interface definitions.

Integration testing: test objects

What are we actually testing at this level? The emphasis here is in testing things with others which have already been tested individually. We are interested in how things work together and how they interact. Typical test objects for integration testing include:

- subsystems
- databases
- infrastructure
- interfaces
- APIs (Application Programming Interfaces)
- microservices.

Integration testing: typical defects and failures

Examples of defects and failures that can typically be revealed by component integration testing include:

- Incorrect data, missing data or incorrect data encoding.
- Incorrect sequencing or timing of interface calls.
- Interface mismatch, for example where one side sends a parameter where the value exceeds 1,000, but the other side only expects values up to 1,000.
- Failures in communication between components.
- Unhandled or improperly handled communication failures between components.
- Incorrect assumptions about the meaning, units or boundaries of the data being passed between components.

Examples of defects and failures that can typically be revealed by system integration testing include:

- inconsistent message structures between systems
- incorrect data, missing data or incorrect data encoding
- interface mismatch
- failures in communication between systems
- unhandled or improperly handled communication failures between systems
- incorrect assumptions about the meaning, units or boundaries of the data being passed between systems
- failure to comply with mandatory security regulations.

At the end of the description of all the test levels, see Table 2.1 which summarizes the characteristics of each test level.

Integration testing: specific approaches and responsibilities

The greater the scope of integration, the more difficult it becomes to isolate failures to a specific interface, which may lead to an increased risk. This leads to varying approaches to integration testing. One extreme is that all components or systems are integrated simultaneously, after which everything is tested as a whole. This is called big-bang integration. Big-bang integration has the advantage that everything is finished before integration testing starts. There is no need to simulate (as yet unfinished) parts. The major disadvantage is that in general it is time-consuming and difficult to trace the cause of failures with this late integration. So big-bang integration may seem like a good idea when planning the project, being optimistic and expecting to find no problems. If one thinks integration testing will find defects, it is a good practice to consider whether time might be saved by breaking down the integration test process.

Another extreme is that all programs are integrated one by one, and tests are carried out after each step (incremental testing). Between these two extremes, there is a range of variants. The incremental approach has the advantage that the defects are found early in a smaller assembly when it is relatively easy to detect the cause. A disadvantage is that it can be time-consuming, since mock objects or stubs and drivers may have to be developed and used in the test. Within incremental integration testing a range of possibilities exist, partly depending on the system architecture:

- Top-down: testing starts from the top and works to the bottom, following the control flow or architectural structure (for example starting from the GUI or main menu). Components or systems are substituted by stubs.
- Bottom-up: testing reverses this approach, starting from the bottom of the control flow upwards. Components or systems are substituted by drivers.
- Functional incremental: integration and testing takes place on the basis of the functions or functionality, as documented in the functional specification.

The preferred integration sequence and the number of integration steps required depend on the location in the architecture of the high-risk interfaces. The best choice is to start integration with those interfaces that are expected to cause the most problems. Doing so prevents major defects at the end of the integration test stage. In order to reduce the risk of late defect discovery, integration should normally be incremental rather than big bang. Ideally, testers should understand the architecture and influence integration planning. If integration tests are planned before components or systems are built, they can be developed in the order required for most efficient testing. A risk analysis of the most complex interfaces can help to focus integration testing. In iterative and incremental development, integration is also incremental. Existing integration tests should be part of the regression tests used in continuous integration. Continuous integration has major benefits because of its iterative nature.

At each stage of integration, testers concentrate solely on the integration itself. For example, if they are integrating component A with component B they are interested in testing the communication between the components, not the functionality of either one. In integrating system X with system Y, again the focus is on the communication between the systems and what can be done by both systems together, rather than defects in the individual systems. Both functional and structural approaches may be used. Testing of specific non-functional characteristics (for example performance) may also be included in integration testing.

Component integration testing is often carried out by developers; system integration testing is generally the responsibility of the testers. Either type of integration testing could be done by a separate team of specialist integration testers, or by a specialist group of developers/integrators, including non-functional specialists. The testers performing the system integration testing need to understand the system architecture. Ideally, they should have had an influence on the development, integration planning and integration testing.

2.2.3 System testing

System testing is concerned with the behaviour of the whole system/product as defined by the scope of a development project or product. It may include tests based on risk analysis reports, system, functional or software requirements specifications, business processes, use cases or other high-level descriptions of system behaviour, interactions with the operating system and system resources. The focus is on end-to-end tasks that the system should perform, including non-functional aspects, such as performance.

In some systems, the quality of the data may be of critical importance, so there would be a focus on data quality. System level tests may be automated to provide a regression suite to ensure that changes have not adversely affected existing system functionality. Stakeholders may use the information from system testing to decide whether the system is ready for user acceptance testing, for example. System testing is also where conformance to legal or regulatory requirements or to external standards is tested.

The test environment is important for system testing; it should correspond to the final production environment as much as possible.

System testing: objectives

The objectives of system testing include:

- reducing risk
- verifying whether or not functional and non-functional behaviours of the system are as they should be (as specified)
- validating that the system is complete and will work as it should and as expected
- building confidence in the quality of the system as a whole
- finding defects
- preventing defects from escaping to later testing or to production.

> **System testing** Testing an integrated system to verify that it meets specified requirements.
> (Note that the ISTQB definition implies that system testing is only about verification of specified requirements. In practice, system testing is often also about validation that the system is suitable for its intended users, as well as verifying against any type of requirement.)

System testing: test basis

What should the system as a whole be able to do? Examples of work products that can be used as a test basis for system testing include:

- software and system requirement specifications (functional and non-functional)
- risk analysis reports
- use cases
- epics and user stories
- models of system behaviour
- state diagrams
- system and user manuals.

System testing: test objects

What are we actually testing at this level? The emphasis here is in testing the whole system, from end to end, encompassing everything that the system needs to do (and how well it should do it, so non-functional aspects are also tested here). Typical test objects for integration testing include:

- applications
- hardware/software systems
- operating systems
- system under test (SUT)
- system configuration and configuration data.

System testing: typical defects and failures

Examples of defects and failures that can typically be revealed by system testing include:

- incorrect calculations
- incorrect or unexpected system functional or non-functional behaviour
- incorrect control and/or data flows within the system
- failure to properly and completely carry out end-to-end functional tasks
- failure of the system to work properly in the production environment(s)
- failure of the system to work as described in system and user manuals.

At the end of the description of all the test levels, see Table 2.1 which summarizes the characteristics of each test level.

System testing: specific approaches and responsibilities

System testing is most often the final test on behalf of development to verify that the system to be delivered meets the specification and to validate that it meets expectations; one of its purposes is to find as many defects as possible. Most often it is carried out by specialist testers that form a dedicated, and sometimes independent, test team within development, reporting to the development manager or project manager. In some organizations system testing is carried out by a third-party team or by business analysts. Again, the required level of independence is based on the applicable risk level and this will have a high influence on the way system testing is organized.

System testing should investigate end-to-end behaviour of both functional and non-functional aspects of the system. An end-to-end test may include all of the steps in a typical transaction, from logging on, accessing data, placing an order, etc. through to logging off and checking order status in a database. Typical non-functional tests include performance, security and reliability. Testers may also need to deal with incomplete or undocumented requirements. System testing of functional requirements starts by using the most appropriate black-box techniques for the aspect of the system to be tested. For example, a decision table may be created for combinations of effects described in business rules. White-box techniques may also be used to assess the thoroughness of testing elements such as menu dialogue structure or web page navigation (see Chapter 4 for more on test techniques).

System testing requires a controlled test environment with regard to, among other things, control of the software versions, testware and the test data (see Chapter 5 for more on configuration management). A system test is executed by the development organization in a (properly controlled) environment. The test environment should correspond to the final target or production environment as much as possible in order to minimize the risk of environment-specific failures not being found by testing.

System testing is often carried out by independent testers, for example an internal test team or external testing specialists. However, if testers are only brought in when system test execution is about to start, you will miss a lot of opportunities to save time and money, as well as aggravation. If there are defects in specifications, such as missing functions or incorrect descriptions of business processes, these may not be picked up before the system is built. Because many defects result from misunderstandings, the discussions (indeed arguments) about them tend to be worse the later they are discovered. The developers will defend their understanding because that is what they have built. The independent testers or end-users may realize that what was built was not what was wanted. This situation can lead to defects being missed in testing (if they are based on wrong specifications) or things being reported as defects that actually are not (due to misunderstandings). These are known as false negative and false positive results respectively. Referring back to testing Principle 3, early test involvement saves time and money, so have testers involved in user story refinement and static testing such as reviews.

2.2.4 Acceptance testing

When the development organization has performed its system test (and possibly also system integration tests) and has corrected all or most defects, the system may be delivered for **acceptance testing**. Acceptance tests typically produce information to assess the system's readiness for release or deployment to end-users or customers. Although defects are found at this level, that is not the main aim of acceptance testing. (If lots of defects are found at this late stage, there are serious problems with the whole system, and major project risks.) The focus is on validation, the use of the system for real, how suitable the system is to be put into production or actual use by its intended users. Regulatory and legal requirements, and conformance to standards may also be checked in acceptance testing, although they should also have been addressed in an earlier level of testing, so that the acceptance test is confirming compliance to the standards.

Acceptance testing
Formal testing with respect to user needs, requirements, and business processes conducted to determine whether or not a system satisfies the acceptance criteria and to enable the user, customers or other authorized entity to determine whether or not to accept the system.

Acceptance testing: objectives

The objectives of acceptance testing include:

● establishing confidence in the quality of the system as a whole

● validating that the system is complete and will work as expected

● verifying that functional and non-functional behaviours of the system are as specified.

Different forms of acceptance testing

Acceptance testing is quite a broad category, and it comes in several different flavours or forms. We will look at four of these.

User acceptance testing (UAT)

User acceptance testing is exactly what it says. It is acceptance testing done by (or on behalf of) users, that is, end-users. The focus is on making sure that the system is really fit for purpose and ready to be used by real intended users of the system. The UAT can be done in the real environment or in a simulated operational environment (but as realistic as possible). The aim of testing here is to build confidence that the system will indeed enable the users to do what they need to do in an efficient way. The system needs to fulfil the requirements and meet their needs. The users focus on their business processes, which they should be able to perform with a minimum of difficulty, cost and risk.

Operational acceptance testing (OAT)

Operational acceptance testing focuses on operations and may be performed by system administrators. The main purpose is to give confidence to the system administrators or operators that they will be able to keep the system running, and recover from adverse events quickly and without additional risk. It is normally performed in a simulated production environment and is looking at operational aspects, such as:

● testing of backups and restoration of backups

● installing, uninstalling and upgrading

● disaster recovery

● user management

● maintenance tasks

● data loading and migration tasks

● checking for security vulnerabilities (for example ethical hacking)

● performance and load testing.

Contractual and regulatory acceptance testing

If a system has been custom-developed for another company, there is normally a legal contract describing the responsibilities, schedule and costs of the project. The contract should also include or refer to acceptance criteria for the system, which should have been defined and agreed when the contract was first taken out. Having agreed the acceptance criteria in advance, **contractual acceptance testing** is focused on whether or not the system meets those criteria. This form of testing is often performed by users or independent testers.

Regulatory acceptance testing is focused on ensuring that the system conforms to government, legal or safety regulations. This type of testing is also often performed by

---

User acceptance testing Acceptance testing conducted in a real or simulated operational environment by intended users focusing on their needs, requirements and business processes.

Operational acceptance testing (production acceptance testing) Operational testing in the acceptance test phase, typically performed in a (simulated) operational environment by operations and/or systems administration staff focusing on operational aspects, for example recoverability, resource-behaviour, installability and technical compliance.

Contractual acceptance testing Acceptance testing conducted to verify whether a system satisfies its contractual requirements.

Regulatory acceptance testing Acceptance testing conducted to verify whether a system conforms to relevant laws, policies and regulations.

independent testers. It may be a requirement to have a representative of the regulatory body present to witness or to audit the tests.

For both of these forms of acceptance testing, the aim is to build confidence that the system is in conformance with the contract or regulations.

Alpha and beta testing

Alpha and beta testing are typically used for COTS software, such as software packages that can be bought or downloaded by consumers. Feedback is needed from potential or existing users in their market before the software product is put out for sale commercially. The testing here is looking for feedback (and defects) from real users and customers or potential customers. Sometimes free software is offered to those who volunteer to do beta testing.

The difference between alpha and beta testing is only in where the testing takes place. **Alpha testing** is at the company that developed the software, and beta testing is done in the users' own offices or homes. In alpha testing, a cross-section of potential users are invited to use the system. Developers observe the users and note problems. Alpha testing may also be carried out by an independent test team. Alpha testing is normally mentioned first, but these two forms can be done in any order, or only one could be done (or none).

Beta testing sends the system or software package out to a cross-section of users who install it and use it under real-world working conditions. The users send records of defects with the system to the development organization, where the defects are repaired. Beta testing is more visible, and is increasingly popular to be done remotely. For example, crowd testing, where people or potential users from all over the world remotely test an application, can be a form of beta testing. One of the advantages of beta testing is that different users will have a great variety of different environments (browsers, other software, hardware configurations, etc.), so the testing can cover many more combinations of factors.

Acceptance testing: test basis

How do we know that the system is ready to be used for real? Examples of work products that can be used as a test basis for the various forms of acceptance testing include:

- business processes
- user or business requirements
- regulations, legal contracts and standards
- use cases
- system requirements
- system or user documentation
- installation procedures
- risk analysis reports.

For operational acceptance testing (OAT), there are some additional aspects with specific work products that can be a test basis:

- backup and restore/recovery procedures
- disaster recovery procedures
- non-functional requirements
- operations documentation

Alpha testing
Simulated or actual operational testing conducted in the developer's test environment, by roles outside the development organization.

Beta testing (field testing) Simulated or actual operational testing conducted at an external site, by roles outside the development organization.

- deployment and installation instructions
- performance targets
- database packages
- security standards or regulations.

Note that it is particularly important to have very clear, well-tested and frequently rehearsed procedures for disaster recovery and restoring backups. If you are in the situation of having to perform these procedures, then you may be in a state of panic, since something serious will have already gone wrong. In that psychological state, it is very easy to make mistakes, and here mistakes could be disastrous. There are stories of organizations who compounded one disaster by accidentally deleting their backups, or who find that their backups are unusable or incomplete! This is why restoring from backups is an important test to do regularly.

Acceptance testing: test objects

What are we actually testing at this level? The emphasis here is in gaining confidence, based on the particular form of acceptance testing: user confidence, confidence in operations, confidence that we have met legal or regulatory requirements, and confidence that real users will like and be happy with the software we are selling. Some of the things we are testing are similar to the test objects of system testing. Typical test objects for acceptance testing include:

- system under test (SUT)
- system configuration and configuration data
- business processes for a fully integrated system
- recovery systems and hot sites (for business continuity and disaster recovery testing)
- operational and maintenance processes
- forms
- reports
- existing and converted production data.

Acceptance testing: typical defects and failures

Examples of defects and failures that can typically be revealed by acceptance testing include:

- system workflows do not meet business or user requirements
- business rules are not implemented correctly
- system does not satisfy contractual or regulatory requirements
- non-functional failures such as security vulnerabilities, inadequate performance efficiency under high load, or improper operation on a supported platform.

At the end of the description of all the test levels, see Table 2.1 which summarizes the characteristics of each test level.

Acceptance testing: specific approaches and responsibilities

The acceptance test should answer questions such as: 'Can the system be released?', 'What, if any, are the outstanding (business) risks?' and 'Has development met their obligations?' Acceptance testing is most often the responsibility of the user or customer, although other stakeholders may be involved as well. The execution of the acceptance test requires a test environment that is, for most aspects, representative of the production environment ('as-if production').

The goal of acceptance testing is to establish confidence in the system, part of the system or specific non-functional characteristics, for example usability of the system. Acceptance testing is most often focused on a validation type of testing, where we are trying to determine whether the system is fit for purpose. Finding defects should not be the main focus in acceptance testing. Although it assesses the system's readiness for deployment and use, it is not necessarily the final level of testing. For example, a large-scale system integration test may come after the acceptance of a system.

Acceptance testing may occur at more than just a single level, for example:

- A COTS software product may be acceptance tested when it is installed or integrated.
- Acceptance testing of the usability of a component may be done during component testing.
- Acceptance testing of a new functional enhancement may come before system testing.

User acceptance testing focuses mainly on the functionality, thereby validating the fitness for use of the system by the business user, while the operational acceptance test (also called production acceptance test) validates whether the system meets the requirements for operation. The user acceptance test is performed by the users and application managers. In terms of planning, the user acceptance test usually links tightly to the system test, and will, in many cases, be organized partly overlapping in time. If the system to be tested consists of a number of more or less independent subsystems, the acceptance test for a subsystem that meets its exit criteria from the system test can start while another subsystem may still be in the system test phase. In most organizations, system administration will perform the operational acceptance test shortly before the system is released. The operational acceptance test may include testing of backup/restore, data load and migration tasks, disaster recovery, user management, maintenance tasks and periodic check of security vulnerabilities.

Note that organizations may use other terms, such as factory acceptance testing and site acceptance testing for systems that are tested before and after being moved to a customer's site.

In iterative development, different forms of acceptance testing may be done at various times, and often in parallel. At the end of an iteration, a new feature may be tested to validate that it meets stakeholder and user needs. This is user acceptance testing. If software for general release (COTS) is being developed, alpha and beta testing may be used at or near the end of an iteration or set of iterations. Operational and regulatory acceptance testing may also occur at the end of an iteration or set of iterations.

Test level characteristics: summary

Table 2.1 summarizes the characteristics of the different test levels: the test basis, test objects and typical defects and failures. We have covered these in the various sections, but it is useful to contrast them in order to distinguish them from each other. We have omitted some of the detail to make the table easier to take in at a glance. Note that some of the typical defects for integration testing are only for system integration testing (SIT).

TABLE 2.1 Test level characteristics

	Component testing	Integration testing	System testing	Acceptance testing
Objectives	reduce risk verify functional and non-functional behaviour build confidence in components find defects prevent defects to higher levels	reduce risk verify functional and non-functional behaviour build confidence in interfaces find defects prevent defects to higher levels	reduce risk verify functional and non-functional behaviour validate completeness, works as expected build confidence in whole system find defects prevent defects to higher levels	establish confidence in whole system and its use validate completeness, works as expected verify functional and non-functional behaviour
Test basis	detailed design code data models component specifications	software/system design sequence diagrams interface and communication protocol specs use cases architecture (component or system) workflows external interface definitions	requirement specs (functional and non-functional) risk analysis reports use cases epics and user stories models of system behaviour state diagrams system and user manuals	business processes user, business, system requirements regulations, legal contracts and standards use cases documentation installation procedures risk analysis

	Component testing	Integration testing	System testing	Acceptance testing
Test objects	components, units, modules code data structures classes database models	subsystems databases infrastructure interfaces APIs microservices	applications hardware/software operating systems system under test system configuration and data	system under test (SUT) system configuration and data business processes recovery systems operation and maintenance processes forms reports existing and converted production data
Typical defects and failures	wrong functionality data flow problems incorrect code/logic	data problems inconsistent message structure (SIT) timing problems interface mismatch communication failures incorrect assumptions not complying with regulations (ST)	incorrect calculations incorrect or unexpected behaviour incorrect data/control flows cannot complete end-to-end tasks does not work in production environment(s) not as described in manuals/documentation	system workflows do not meet business or user needs business rules not correct contractual or regulatory problems non-functional failures (performance, security)

2.3 TEST TYPES

In this section, we'll look at different test types. We'll discuss tests that focus on the functionality of a system, which informally is *testing what the system does*. We'll also discuss tests that focus on non-functional attributes of a system, which informally is *testing how well the system does what it does*. We'll introduce testing based on the system's structure. Finally, we'll look at testing of changes to the system, both confirmation testing (testing that the changes succeeded) and regression testing (testing that the changes did not affect anything unintentionally).

The test types discussed here can involve the development and use of a model of the software or its behaviours. Such models can occur in structural testing when we use control flow models or menu structure models. Such models in non-functional testing can involve performance models, usability models and security threat models. They can also arise in functional testing, such as the use of process flow models, state transition models or plain language specifications. Examples of such models will be found in Chapter 4.

As we go through this section, watch for the Syllabus terms **functional testing**, **non-functional testing**, **test type** and **white-box testing**. You will find these terms defined in the Glossary as well.

Test types are introduced as a means of clearly defining the objective of a certain test level for a program or project. We need to think about different types of testing because testing the functionality of the component or system may not be sufficient at each level to meet the overall test objectives. Focusing the testing on a specific test objective and, therefore, selecting the appropriate type of test, helps make it easier to make and communicate decisions about test objectives. Typical objectives may include:

- Evaluating functional quality, for example whether a function or feature is complete, correct and appropriate.

- Evaluating non-functional quality characteristics, for example reliability, performance efficiency, security, compatibility and usability.

- Evaluating whether the structure or architecture of the component or system is correct, complete and as specified.

- Evaluating the effects of changes, looking at both the changes themselves (for example defect fixes) and also the remaining system to check for any unintended side-effects of the change. These are confirmation testing and regression testing, respectively, and are discussed in Section 2.3.4.

A **test type** is focused on a particular test objective, which could be the testing of a function to be performed by the component or system; a non-functional quality characteristic, such as reliability or usability; the structure or architecture of the component or system; or related to changes, that is, confirming that defects have been fixed (confirmation testing, or re-testing) and looking for unintended changes (regression testing). Depending on its objectives, testing will be organized differently. For example, component testing aimed at performance would be quite different from component testing aimed at achieving decision coverage.

Test type A group of test activities based on specific test objectives aimed at specific characteristics of a component or system.

2.3.1 Functional testing

The function of a system (or component) is what it does. This is typically described in work products such as business requirements specifications, functional specifications, use cases, epics or user stories. There may be some functions that are assumed to be provided that are not documented. They are also part of the requirements for a system, though it is difficult to test against undocumented and implicit requirements. Functional tests are based on these functions, described in documents or understood by the testers, and may be performed at all test levels (for example tests for components may be based on a component specification).

Functional testing considers the specified behaviour and is often also referred to as black-box testing (specification-based testing). This is not entirely true, since black-box testing also includes non-functional testing (see Section 2.3.2).

Functional testing Testing conducted to evaluate the compliance of a component or system with functional requirements.

Functional testing can also be done focusing on suitability, interoperability testing, security, accuracy and compliance. Security testing, for example, investigates the functions (for example a firewall) relating to detection of threats, such as viruses, from malicious outsiders.

Testing of functionality could be done from different perspectives, the two main ones being requirements-based or business-process-based.

Requirements-based testing uses a specification of the functional requirements for the system as the basis for designing tests. A good way to start is to use the table of contents of the requirements specification as an initial test inventory or list of items to test (or not to test). We should also prioritize the requirements based on risk criteria (if this is not already done in the specification) and use this to prioritize the tests. This will ensure that the most important and most critical tests are included in the testing effort.

Business-process-based testing uses knowledge of the business processes. Business processes describe the scenarios involved in the day-to-day business use of the system. For example, a personnel and payroll system may have a business process along the lines of: someone joins the company, he or she is paid on a regular basis, and he or she finally leaves the company. User scenarios originate from object-oriented development but are nowadays popular in many development life cycles. They also take the business processes as a starting point, although they start from tasks to be performed by users. Use cases are a very useful basis for test cases from a business perspective.

The techniques used for functional testing are often specification-based, but experience-based techniques can also be used (see Chapter 4 for more on test techniques). Test conditions and test cases are derived from the functionality of the component or system. As part of test design, a model may be developed, such as a process model, state transition model or a plain-language specification.

The thoroughness of functional testing can be measured by a coverage measure based on elements of the function that we can list. For example, we can list all of the options available from every pull-down menu. If our set of tests has at least one test for each option, then we have 100% coverage of these menu options. Of course, that does not mean that the system or component is 100% tested, but it does mean that we have at least touched every one of the things we identified. When we have traceability between our tests and functional requirements, we can identify which requirements we have not yet covered, that is, have not yet tested (coverage gaps). For example, if we covered only 90% of the menu options, we could add tests so that the untested 10% are then covered.

Special skills or knowledge may be needed for functional testing, particularly for specialized application domains. For example, medical device software may need medical knowledge both for the design and testing of such systems. The worst thing that a heart pacemaker can do is not to stop giving the electrical stimulant to the heart (the heart may still limp along less efficiently). The worst thing is to speed up, giving the signal much too frequently; this can be fatal. Other specialized application areas include gaming or interactive entertainment systems, geological modelling for oil and gas exploration, or automotive systems.

2.3.2 Non-functional testing

This test type is the testing of the quality characteristics, or non-functional attributes of the system (or component or integration group). Here we are interested in how well or how fast something is done. We are testing something that we need to measure on a scale of measurement, for example time to respond.

Non-functional testing, as functional testing, is performed at all test levels. Non-functional testing includes, but is not limited to, performance testing, load testing, stress testing, usability testing, maintainability testing, reliability testing, portability testing and security testing. It is the testing of how well the system works.

Many have tried to capture software quality in a collection of characteristics and related sub-characteristics. In these models, some elementary characteristics keep on reappearing, although their place in the hierarchy can differ. The International Organization for Standardization (ISO) has defined a set of quality characteristics in ISE/IEC 25010 [2011].

A common misconception is that non-functional testing occurs only during higher levels of testing such as system test, system integration test and acceptance test. In fact, non-functional testing may be performed at all test levels; the higher the level of risk associated with each type of non-functional testing, the earlier in the life cycle it should occur. Ideally, non-functional testing involves tests that quantifiably measure characteristics of the systems and software. For example, in performance testing we can measure transaction throughput, resource utilization and response times. Generally, non-functional testing defines expected results in terms of the external behaviour of the software. This means that we typically use black-box test techniques. For example, we could use boundary value analysis to

Non-functional testing Testing conducted to evaluate the compliance of a component or system with non-functional requirements.

define the stress conditions for performance tests, and equivalence partitioning to identify types of devices for compatibility testing, or to identify user groups for usability testing (novice, experienced, age range, geographical location, educational background).

The thoroughness of non-functional testing can be measured by the coverage of non-functional elements. If we had at least one test for each major group of users, then we would have 100% coverage of those user groups that we had identified. Of course, we may have forgotten an important user group, such as those with disabilities, so we have only covered the groups we have identified.

If we have traceability between non-functional tests and non-functional requirements, we may be able to identify coverage gaps. For example, an implicit requirement is for accessibility for disabled users.

Special skills or knowledge may be needed for non-functional testing, such as for performance testing, usability testing or security testing (for example for specific development languages).

More about non-functional testing is found in other ISTQB qualification Syllabuses, including the Advanced Test Analyst, the Advanced Technical Test Analyst, and the Advanced Security Tester, the Foundation Performance Testing, and the Foundation Usability Testing Syllabus.

2.3.3 White-box testing

The third test type looks at the internal structure or implementation of the system or component. If we are talking about the structure of a system, we may call it the system architecture. Structural elements also include the code itself, control flows, business processes and data flows. **White-box testing** is also referred to as structural testing or glass-box because we are interested in what is happening inside the box.

White-box testing is most often used as a way of measuring the thoroughness of testing through the coverage of a set of structural elements or coverage items. It can occur at any test level, although it is true to say that it tends to be mostly applied at component testing and component integration testing, and generally is less likely at higher test levels, except for business process testing. At component integration level it may be based on the architecture of the system, such as a calling hierarchy or the interfaces between components (the interfaces themselves can be listed as coverage items). The test basis for system, system integration or acceptance testing could be a business model, for example business rules.

At component level, and to a lesser extent at component integration testing, there is good tool support to measure code coverage. Coverage measurement tools assess the percentage of executable elements (for example statements or decision outcomes) that have been exercised (that is, they have been covered) by a test suite. If coverage is not 100%, then additional tests may need to be written and run to cover those parts that have not yet been exercised. This of course depends on the exit criteria. (Coverage and white-box test techniques are covered in Chapter 4.)

Special skills or knowledge may be needed for white-box testing, such as knowledge of the code (to interpret coverage tool results) or how data is stored (for database queries).

White-box testing (clear-box testing, code-based testing, glass-box testing, logic-coverage testing, logic-driven testing, structural testing, structure-based testing) Testing based on an analysis of the internal structure-based of the component or system.

2.3.4 Change-related testing

The final test type is the testing of changes. This category is slightly different to the others because if you have made a change to the software, you will have changed the way it functions, how well it functions (or both) and its structure. However, we are looking here at the specific types of tests relating to changes, even though they may include all of the other test types. There are two things to be particularly aware of when changes are made: the change itself and any other effects of the change.

Confirmation testing (re-testing)

Confirmation testing
(re-testing) Dynamic testing conducted after fixing defects with the objective to confirm that failures caused by those defects do not occur anymore.

When a test fails and we determine that the cause of the failure is a software defect, the defect is reported and we can expect a new version of the software that has had the defect fixed. In this case we will need to execute the test again to confirm that the defect has indeed been fixed. This is known as **confirmation testing** (also known as re-testing).

When doing confirmation testing, it is important to ensure that steps leading up to the failure are carried out in exactly the same way as described in the defect report, using the same inputs, data and environment, and possibly extending beyond the test to ensure that the change has indeed fixed all of the problems due to the defect. If the test now passes, does this mean that the software is now correct? Well, we now know that at least one part of the software is correct – where the defect was. But this is not enough. The fix may have introduced or uncovered a different defect elsewhere in the software. The way to detect these unexpected side-effects of fixes is to do regression testing.

Regression testing

Regression testing
Testing of a previously tested component or system following modification to ensure that defects have not been introduced or have been uncovered in unchanged areas of the software as a result of the changes made.

Like confirmation testing, **regression testing** involves executing test cases that have been executed before. The difference is that, for regression testing, the test cases probably passed the last time they were executed (compare this with the test cases executed in confirmation testing – they failed the last time).

The term regression testing is something of a misnomer. It would be better if it were called anti-regression testing because we are executing tests with the intent of checking that the system has *not* regressed (that is, it does not now have more defects in it as a result of some change). More specifically, the purpose of regression testing is to make sure (as far as is practical) that modifications in the software or the environment have not caused unintended adverse side effects and that the system still meets its requirements.

It is common for organizations to have what is usually called a regression test suite or regression test pack. This is a set of test cases that is specifically used for regression testing. They are designed to collectively exercise most functions (certainly the most important ones) in a system, but not test any one in detail. It is appropriate to have a regression test suite at every level of testing (component testing, integration testing, system testing, etc.). In some cases, all of the test cases in a regression test suite would be executed every time a new version of software is produced; this makes them ideal candidates for automation. However, it is much better to be able to select subsets for execution, especially if the regression test suite is very large. In Agile development, a selection of regression tests would be run to meet the objectives of a particular iteration. Automation of regression tests should start as early as possible in the project. See Chapter 6 for more on test automation.

Regression tests are executed whenever the software changes, either as a result of fixes or new or changed functionality. It is also a good idea to execute them when some aspect of the environment changes, for example when a new version of the host operating system is introduced or the production environment has a new version of the Java Virtual Machine or anti-malware software.

Maintenance of a regression test suite should be carried out so it evolves over time in line with the software. As new functionality is added to a system, new regression tests should be added. As old functionality is changed or removed, so too should regression tests be changed or removed. As new tests are added, a regression test suite may become very large. If all the tests have to be executed manually it may not be possible to execute them all every time the regression suite is used. In this case, a subset of the test cases has to be chosen. This selection should be made considering the latest changes that have been made to the software. Sometimes a regression test suite of automated tests can become so large that it is not always possible to execute them all. It may be possible and desirable to eliminate some test cases from a large regression test suite, for example if they are repetitive (tests which exercise the same conditions) or can be combined (if they are always run together). Another approach is to eliminate test cases when the risk associated with that test is so low that it is not worth running it anymore.

Both confirmation testing and regression testing are done at all test levels.

In iterative and incremental development, changes are more frequent, even continuous and the software is refactored frequently. This makes confirmation testing and regression testing even more important. But iterative development such as Agile should also include continuous testing, and this testing is mainly regression testing. For IoT systems, change-related testing covers not only software systems but the changes made to individual objects or devices, which may be frequently updated or replaced.

2.3.5 Test types and test levels

We mentioned as we went through the test types that each test type is applicable at every test level. The testing is different, depending on the test level and test type, of course, but the Syllabus gives examples of each test type at each test level to illustrate the point.

Functional tests at each test level

Let's use a banking example to look at the different levels of testing. There are many features in a financial application. Some of them are visible to users and others are behind the scenes but equally important for the whole application to work well. The more technical and more detailed aspects should be tested at the lower levels, and the customer-facing aspects at higher levels. We will also look at examples of the different test types showing the different testing for functional, non-functional, white-box and change-related testing.

- Component testing: how the component should calculate compound interest.
- Component integration testing: how account information from the user interface is passed to the business logic.
- System testing: how account holders can apply for a line of credit.

- System integration testing: how the system uses an external microservice to check an account holder's credit score.
- Acceptance testing: how the banker handles approving or declining a credit application.

Non-functional tests at each test level

- Component testing: the time or number of CPU cycles to perform a complex interest calculation.
- Component integration testing: checking for buffer overflow (a security flaw) from data passed from the user interface to the business logic.
- System testing: portability tests on whether the presentation layer works on supported browsers and mobile devices.
- System integration testing: reliability tests to evaluate robustness if the credit score microservice does not respond.
- Acceptance testing: usability tests for accessibility of the banker's credit processing interface for people with disabilities.

White-box tests at each test level

- Component testing: achieve 100% statement and decision coverage for all components performing financial calculations.
- Component integration testing: coverage of how each screen in the browser interface passes data to the next screen and to the business logic.
- System testing: coverage of sequences of web pages that can occur during a credit line application.
- System integration testing: coverage of all possible inquiry types sent to the credit score microservice.
- Acceptance testing: coverage of all supported financial data file structures and value ranges for bank-to-bank transfers.

Change-related tests at each test level

- Component testing: automated regression tests for each component are included in the continuous integration framework and pipeline.
- Component integration testing: confirmation tests for interface-related defects are activated as the fixes are checked into the code repository.
- System testing: all tests for a given workflow are re-executed if any screen changes.
- System integration testing: as part of continuous deployment of the credit scoring microservice, automated tests of the interactions of the application with the microservice are re-executed.
- Acceptance testing: all previously failed tests are re-executed after defects found in acceptance testing are fixed.

Note that not every test type will occur at every test level in every system! However, it is a good idea to think about how every test type might apply at each test level, and try to implement those tests at the earliest opportunity within the development life cycle.

2.4 MAINTENANCE TESTING

FL-2.4.1   Summarize triggers for maintenance testing (K2)

FL-2.4.2   Describe the role of impact analysis in maintenance testing (K2)

Once deployed, a system is often in service for years or even decades. During this time, the system and its operational environment are often corrected, changed or extended. As we go through this section, watch for the Syllabus terms **impact analysis** and **maintenance testing**. You will find these terms also defined in the Glossary.

Testing that is executed during this life cycle phase is called **maintenance testing**. Maintenance testing, along with the entire process of maintenance releases, should be carefully planned. Not only must planned maintenance releases be considered, but the process for developing and testing hot fixes must be as well. Maintenance testing includes any type of testing of changes to an existing, operational system, whether the changes result from modifications, migration or retirement of the software or system.

> **Maintenance testing**
> Testing the changes to an operational system or the impact of a changed environment to an operational system.

Modifications can result from planned enhancement changes such as those referred to as minor releases, that include new features and accumulated (non-emergency) bug fixes. Modifications can also result from corrective and more urgent emergency changes. Modifications can also involve changes of environment, such as planned operating system or database upgrades, planned upgrade of COTS software, or patches to correct newly exposed or discovered vulnerabilities of the operating system.

Migration involves moving from one platform to another. This can involve abandoning a platform no longer supported or adding a new supported platform. Either way, testing must include operational tests of the new environment as well as of the changed software. Migration testing can also include conversion testing, where data from another application will be migrated into the system being maintained.

Note that maintenance testing is different from testing for maintainability (which is the degree to which a component or system can be modified by the intended maintainers). In this section, we'll discuss maintenance testing.

The same test process steps will apply as for testing during development and, depending on the size and risk of the changes made, several levels of testing are carried out: a component test, an integration test, a system test and an acceptance test. If testing is done more formally, an application for a change may be used to produce a test plan for testing the change, with test cases changed or created as needed. In less formal testing, thought needs to be given to how the change should be tested, even if this planning, updating of test cases and execution of the tests is part of a continuous process.

The scope of maintenance testing depends on several factors, which influence the test types and test levels. The factors are:

- Degree of risk of the change, for example a self-contained change is a lower risk than a change to a part of the system that communicates with other systems.

- The size of the existing system, for example a small system would need less regression testing than a larger system.
- The size of the change, which affects the amount of testing of the changes that would be needed. The amount of regression testing is more related to the size of the system than the size of the change.

2.4.1 Triggers for maintenance

As stated, maintenance testing is done on an existing operational system. There are three possible triggers for maintenance testing:

- modifications
- migration
- retirement.

Modifications include planned enhancement changes (for example release-based), corrective and emergency changes and changes of environment, such as planned operating system or database upgrades, or patches to newly exposed or discovered vulnerabilities of the operating system and upgrades of COTS software.

Modifications may also be of hardware or devices, not just software components or systems. For example, in IoT systems, new or significantly modified hardware devices may be introduced to a working system. The emphasis in maintenance testing would likely focus on different types of integration testing and security testing at all test levels.

Maintenance testing for migration (for example from one platform to another) should also include operational testing of the new environment, as well as the changed software. It is important to know that the platform you will be transferring to is sound before you start migrating your own files and applications.

Maintenance testing for the retirement of a system may include the testing of data migration or archiving, if long data-retention periods are required. Testing of restore or retrieve procedures after archiving may also be needed. There is no point in trying to save and preserve something that you can no longer access. These procedures should be regularly tested and action taken to migrate away from technology that is reaching the end of its life. You may remember seeing magnetic tape on old movies, which was thought to be a good long-term archiving solution at the time.

2.4.2 Impact analysis and regression testing

As mentioned earlier, maintenance testing usually consists of two parts:

- testing the changes
- regression tests to show that the rest of the system has not been affected by the maintenance work.

Impact analysis The identification of all work products affected by a change, including an estimate of the resources needed to accomplish the change.

In addition to testing what has been changed, maintenance testing includes extensive regression testing to parts of the system that have not been changed. Some systems will have extensive regression suites (automated or not) where the costs of executing all of the tests would be significant. A major and important activity within maintenance testing is **impact analysis**. During impact analysis, together with stakeholders, a decision is made on what parts of the system may be unintentionally affected and therefore need more extensive regression testing. Risk analysis will help to decide where to focus regression testing. It is unlikely that the team will have time to repeat all the existing tests, so this gives us the best value for the time and effort we can spend in regression testing.

If the test specifications from the original development of the system are kept, one may be able to reuse them for regression testing and to adapt them for changes to the system. This may be as simple as changing the expected results for your existing tests. Sometimes additional tests may need to be built. Extension or enhancement to the system may mean new areas have been specified and tests would be drawn up just as for the development. Do not forget that automated regression tests will also need to be updated in line with the changes; this can take significant effort, depending on the architecture of your automation (see Chapter 6).

Impact analysis can also be used to help make a decision about whether or not a particular change should be made. If the change has the potential to cause high-risk vulnerabilities throughout the system, it may be a better decision not to make that change.

There are a number of factors that make impact analysis more difficult:

- Specifications are out of date or missing (for example business requirements, user stories, architecture diagrams).
- Test cases are not documented or are out of date.
- Bi-directional traceability between tests and the test basis has not been maintained.
- Tool support is weak or non-existent.
- The people involved do not have domain and/or system knowledge.
- The maintainability of the software has not been taken into enough consideration during development.

Impact analysis can be very useful in making maintenance testing more efficient, but if it is not, or cannot be, done well, then the risks of making the change are greatly increased.

CHAPTER REVIEW

Let's review what you have learned in this chapter.

From Section 2.1, you should now understand the relationship between development activities and test activities within a development life cycle and be familiar with sequential life cycle models (waterfall and V-model) and iterative/incremental life cycle models (RUP, Scrum, Kanban and Spiral). You should be able to recall the reasons for different levels of testing and characteristics of good testing in any life cycle model. You should be able to give reasons why software development life cycle models need to be adapted to the context of the project and product being developed. You should know the Glossary terms **commercial off-the-shelf (COTS), sequential development model** and **test level**.

From Section 2.2, you should know the typical levels of testing (component, integration, system and acceptance testing). You should be able to compare the different levels of testing with respect to their major objectives, the test basis, typical objects of testing, typical defects and failures, and approaches and responsibilities for each test level. You should know the Glossary terms **acceptance testing**, **alpha testing**, **beta testing**, **component integration testing**, **component testing**, **contractual acceptance testing**, **integration testing**, **operational acceptance testing**, **regulatory acceptance testing**, **system integration testing**, **system testing**, **test basis**, **test case**, **test environment**, **test object**, **test objective** and **user acceptance testing**.

From Section 2.3, you should know the four major types of test (functional, non-functional, structural and change-related) and should be able to provide some concrete examples for each of these. You should understand that functional and structural tests occur at any test level and be able to explain how they are applied in the various test levels. You should be able to identify and describe non-functional test types based on non-functional requirements and product quality characteristics. Finally, you should be able to explain the purpose of confirmation testing (re-testing) and regression testing in the context of change-related testing. You should know the Glossary terms **functional testing**, **non-functional testing**, **test type** and **white-box testing**.

From Section 2.4, you should be able to compare maintenance testing to testing of new applications. You should be able to identify triggers and reasons for maintenance testing, such as modifications, migration and retirement. Finally, you should be able to describe the role of regression testing and impact analysis within maintenance testing. You should know the Glossary terms **impact analysis** and **maintenance testing**.

SAMPLE EXAM QUESTIONS

Question 1 Which of the following statements is true?

a. Overlapping test levels and test activities are more common in sequential life cycle models than in iterative incremental models.

b. The V-model is an iterative incremental life cycle model because each development activity has a corresponding test activity.

c. When completed, iterative incremental life cycle models are more likely to deliver the full set of features originally envisioned by stakeholders than sequential models.

d. In iterative and incremental life cycle models, delivery of usable software to end-users is much more frequent than in sequential models.

Question 2 What level of testing is typically performed by system administration staff?

a. Regulatory acceptance testing.

b. System testing.

c. System integration testing.

d. Operational acceptance testing.

Question 3 Which of the following is a test type?

a. Component testing.

b. Functional testing.

c. System testing.

d. Acceptance testing.

Question 4 Consider the three triggers for maintenance, and match the event with the correct trigger:

1. Data conversion from one system to another.

2. Upgrade of COTS software.

3. Test of data archiving.

4. System now runs on a different platform and operating system.

5. Testing restore or retrieve procedures.

6. Patches for security vulnerabilities.

a. Modification: 2 and 3, Migration: 1 and 5, Retirement: 4 and 6.

b. Modification: 2 and 6, Migration: 1 and 4, Retirement: 3 and 5.

c. Modification: 2 and 4, Migration: 1 and 3, Retirement: 5 and 6.

d. Modification: 1 and 5, Migration: 2 and 3, Retirement: 4 and 6.

Question 5 Which of these is a functional test?

a. Measuring response time on an online booking system.

b. Checking the effect of high volumes of traffic in a call centre system.

c. Checking the online bookings screen information and the database contents against the information on the letter to the customers.

d. Checking how easy the system is to use, particularly for users with disabilities such as impaired vision.

Question 6 Which of the following is true, regarding the process of testing emergency fixes?

a. There is no time to test the change before it goes live, so only the best developers should do this work and should not involve testers as they slow down the process.

b. Just run the retest of the defect actually fixed.

c. Always run a full regression test of the whole system in case other parts of the system have been adversely affected.

d. Retest the changed area and then use risk assessment to decide on a reasonable subset of the whole regression test to run in case other parts of the system have been adversely affected.

Question 7 A regression test:

a. Is only run once.

b. Will always be automated.

c. Will check unchanged areas of the software to see if they have been affected.

d. Will check changed areas of the software to see if they have been affected.

Question 8 Non-functional testing includes:

a. Testing to see where the system does not function correctly.

b. Testing the quality attributes of the system including reliability and usability.

c. Gaining user approval for the system.

d. Testing a system feature using only the software required for that function.

Question 9 Beta testing is:

a. Performed by customers at their own site.

b. Performed by customers at the software developer's site.

c. Performed by an independent test team.

d. Useful to test software developed for a specific customer or user.

CHAPTER THREE
Static techniques

Static test techniques provide a powerful way to improve the quality and productivity of software development. This chapter describes static test techniques, including reviews, and provides an overview of how they are conducted. The fundamental objective of static testing is to improve the quality of software work products by assisting engineers to recognize and fix their own defects early in the software development process. While static testing techniques will not solve all the problems, they are enormously effective. Static techniques can improve both quality and productivity by impressive factors. Static testing is not magic and it should not be considered a replacement for dynamic testing, but all software organizations should consider using reviews in all major aspects of their work, including requirements, design, implementation, testing and maintenance. Static analysis tools implement automated checks, for example on code.

3.1 STATIC TECHNIQUES AND THE TEST PROCESS

SYLLABUS LEARNING OBJECTIVES FOR 3.1 STATIC TECHNIQUES AND THE TEST PROCESS (K2)

FL-3.1.1   **Recognize types of software work product that can be examined by the different static testing techniques (K1)**

FL-3.1.2   **Use examples to describe the value of static testing (K2)**

FL-3.1.3   **Explain the difference between static and dynamic techniques, considering objectives, types of defects to be identified, and the role of these techniques within the software life cycle (K2)**

In this section, we consider how static testing techniques fit into the overall test process. Dynamic testing requires that we run the item or system under test, but static testing techniques allow us to find defects directly in work products, without the execution of the code and without the need to isolate the failure to locate the underlying defect. Static techniques include both reviews and static analysis, each of which we'll discuss in this chapter. Static techniques are efficient ways to find and remove defects, and can find certain defects that are hard to find with dynamic testing. As we go through this section, watch for the Syllabus terms **dynamic testing**, static analysis and **static testing**. You will find these terms also defined in the Glossary.

In Chapter 1, we saw that testing is defined as all life cycle activities, both static and dynamic, to do with planning, preparing and evaluating software and related work products. As indicated in that definition, two approaches can be used to achieve these objectives, static testing and dynamic testing. Static analysis is a form of automated static testing.

The definitions of **static analysis** and **static testing** are very similar, and to be honest, are somewhat confusing! The definition of static analysis would apply equally well to reviews, which are a form of static testing but are not part of static analysis. Generally, static analysis involves the use of tools to do the analysis; in fact, the Syllabus describes them as 'tool-driven evaluation' of code or work products. The key difference is: considering the code we want to evaluate, **dynamic testing** actually executes that code; static testing (including static analysis) does NOT execute the code we are evaluating.

One area where static analysis is often used (and is critical for) is in safety-critical systems such as flight control software, medical devices or nuclear power control software. However static analysis is also very important in security testing, as it can identify malicious code (which does not make itself visible in execution). In continuous delivery and continuous deployment, the automated build systems also frequently make use of static analysis as part of the build process.

Static analysis The process of evaluating a component or system without executing it, based on its form, structure, content or documentation.

Static testing Testing a work product without code being executed.

Dynamic testing Testing that involves the execution of the software of a component or system.

3.1.1 Work products that can be examined by static testing

Static analysis is most often used to evaluate code against various criteria, such as adherence to coding standards, thresholds for complexity, spelling and grammar correctness and reading difficulty (the last few for work products other than code). However, static testing is broader than automated evaluations; reviews can be applied to any type of work product, including:

- Any type of specification: business requirements, functional requirements, security requirements.
- Epics, user stories and acceptance criteria.
- Code.
- Testware, that is, any type of work product to do with testing, for example test plans, test conditions, test cases, test procedures and automated test scripts.
- User guides, help text, wizards and other things designed to help the user to more effectively use the system.
- Web pages (there are also static analysis tools to analyze whether any links are broken for example).
- Contracts (a particularly important work product to review, as a lot of money may be riding on the specific wording), project plans, schedules and budgets.
- Models such as activity diagrams or other models used in model-based testing (MBT).

(Note that there is an ISTQB Foundation Level Model-Based Tester Extension Syllabus.)

Reviews apply to any work product; the reviewers need to be able to read and understand it, but can then provide feedback about it. See Section 3.2 for more on reviews.

Static analysis of software code is done using a tool to analyze the code with respect to the criteria of interest. For example, static analysis tools can identify dead code, a section of code that can never be reached from anywhere else in the code. This dead code can never be executed, so should be removed, as it could be confusing to leave it in. Static analysis can also identify a variable whose value is used before it has been defined. This type of defect can cause failures which are difficult to find by dynamic testing.

There are also tools that can analyze natural language text, for example in requirements, to catch some typos, assess readability level (ease of understandability), etc., so these are also a form of static analysis.

3.1.2 Benefits of static testing

Studies have shown that as a result of reviews, a significant increase in productivity and product quality can be achieved Gilb and Graham [1993] and van Veenendaal [1999]. Reducing the number of defects early in the product life cycle also means that less time would be spent on testing and maintenance. The use of static testing, such as reviews on software work products, has two major advantages:

- Since static testing can start early in the life cycle, early feedback on quality issues can be established, for example an early validation of user requirements rather than late in the life cycle during acceptance testing. Feedback during design review or backlog refinement is more useful than after a feature has been built.
- By detecting defects at an early stage, rework costs are most often relatively low, and thus relatively cheap improvements to the quality of software products can be achieved, as many of the follow-on costs of late updates are avoided, for example additional regression tests, confirmation tests, etc.

Additional benefits of static testing may include:

- Defects are more efficiently detected and corrected, particularly since this is done before dynamic test execution.
- Defects that are not easily found by dynamic testing, such as security vulnerabilities, are identified.
- Defects in future design and code are prevented by uncovering inconsistencies, ambiguities, contradictions, omissions, inaccuracies and redundancies in requirements.
- Since rework effort is substantially reduced, development productivity figures are likely to increase.
- Reduced development cost and time.
- Reduced testing cost and time. If defects are found and fixed before test execution starts, there are fewer to find in testing, so more tests pass, and there are fewer defect reports to write and fewer confirmation tests to run after fixes. This saves both time and money.
- Reduced total cost of quality over the software's lifetime. If defects are found and fixed early, then there should be fewer that get through to later testing or operation. The defects that are not there do not need to be investigated or fixed, saving time and money.

- Improved communication within the team, since there is an exchange of information between the participants during reviews, which can lead to an increased awareness of quality issues.

In conclusion, static testing is a very suitable method for improving the quality of software work products. This applies primarily to the assessed work products themselves. It is also important that the quality improvement is not achieved just once, but has a more permanent nature. The feedback from the static testing process to the development process allows for process improvement, which supports the avoidance of similar errors being made in the future. This is particularly useful for sprint or project retrospectives.

3.1.3 Differences between static and dynamic testing

Static and dynamic testing have the same objectives: to assess the quality of work products and identify defects as early as possible. But static and dynamic testing are not the same. They find different types of defect, so they are complementary and are best used together. It does not make sense to ask if one is better than the other; both are useful and needed.

With dynamic testing methods, software is executed using a set of input values and its output is then examined and compared to what is expected. During static testing, software work products are examined manually, or with a set of tools, but not executed. Dynamic testing can be started early by identifying test conditions and test cases as early as possible in the life cycle (as we discussed in Chapter 1 Section 1.4), but dynamic test execution can only be applied to software code. Dynamic execution is applied as a technique to detect defects and to determine quality attributes of the code. This dynamic testing option is not applicable for the majority of the software work products. Among the questions that arise are:

- How can we evaluate or analyze a work product, such as a requirement specification, a user story, a design document, a test plan or a user manual?
- How can we effectively examine the source code before execution?

As discussed above, one powerful technique that can be used is static testing, for example reviews. In principle, all human-readable software work products can be tested using review techniques.

Types of defects that are easier to find during static testing include:

- Requirements defects, such as inconsistencies, ambiguities, contradictions, omissions, inaccuracies, redundancies.
- Design defects, such as inefficient algorithms or database structures, high coupling or low cohesion.
- Coding defects, such as variables with undefined values, variables that are declared but never used, unreachable code, duplicate code. All of these can be found by static analysis tools.
- Deviations from standards, for example lack of adherence to coding standards.
- Incorrect interface specifications, such as different units of measurement used by the calling system than by the called system. In 1999, a Mars Orbiter burned up in the atmosphere due to one team using metric units of measurement and the other using imperial units of measurement, as described in Nasa [1999].

- Security vulnerabilities, for example buffer overflow susceptibility.

- Traceability problems, such as gaps or inaccuracies or lack of coverage (for example missing tests for an acceptance criterion).

- Maintainability defects, such as improper modularization, poor reusability, code that is difficult to analyze and modify (often referred to as code smells). These defects do not show up in dynamic testing but can be critical for long-term costs of the system.

Compared to dynamic testing, static testing finds defects rather than failures. You may recall that in Chapter 1 Section 1.2.3 we made a distinction between errors, defects and failures. An error is a mistake made by a human being (for example in writing code), a defect is something that is wrong (for example in the code itself) and a failure is when the system or component does not perform as it should (for example returns the wrong balance). Static testing does not cause the system or component to do anything, so it cannot find failures; only dynamic testing can do that. However, static testing does find defects directly. Dynamic testing has to investigate the failure to find a defect.

In addition to finding defects, the objectives of reviews are often also informational, communicational and educational. Participants learn about the content of software work products to help them understand the role of their own work and to plan for future stages of development. Reviews often represent project milestones and support the establishment of a baseline for a software product. The type and quantity of defects found during reviews can also help testers focus their testing and select effective classes of tests. In some cases, customers/users or product owners attend the review meeting and provide feedback to the development team, so reviews are also a means of customer/user communication.

3.2 REVIEW PROCESS

SYLLABUS LEARNING OBJECTIVES FOR 3.2 REVIEW PROCESS (K3)

FL-3.2.1   **Summarize the activities of the work product review process (K2)**

FL-3.2.2   **Recognize the different roles and responsibilities in a formal review (K1)**

FL-3.2.3   **Explain the differences between different review types: informal review, walkthrough, technical review and inspection (K2)**

FL-3.2.4   **Apply a review technique to a work product to find defects (K3)**

FL-3.2.5   **Explain the factors that contribute to a successful review (K2)**

In this section, we will focus on reviews as a distinct – and distinctly useful – form of static testing. We'll discuss the process for carrying out reviews. We'll talk about who does what in a review meeting and as part of the review process. We'll cover types of reviews that you can use. We'll look at different variations for reviews based on different ways to prepare for and perform reviews, and finally we will look at success factors to enable the most effective and efficient reviews possible. As we go through this section, watch for the Syllabus terms **ad hoc reviewing**, **checklist-based reviewing**, **formal review**, **informal review**, **inspection**, **perspective-based reading**, **review**, **role-based reviewing**, **scenario-based reviewing**, **technical review** and **walkthrough**. You will find these terms also defined in the Glossary.

One reason why reviews are so useful is that having a different person look at a work product is a way to overcome cognitive bias, the tendency to see what we intended rather than what we actually wrote.

Review A type of static testing during which a work product or process is evaluated by one or more individuals to detect issues and to provide improvements.

Informal review A type of review without a formal (documented) procedure.

Formal review A form of review that follows a defined process with a formally documented output.

Reviews vary from very informal to formal (that is, well-structured and regulated). Although inspection is perhaps the most documented and formal review technique, it is certainly not the only one. The formality of a review process is related by factors such as the maturity of the development process, any legal or regulatory requirements or the need for an audit trail. In practice, the **informal review** is perhaps the most common type of review. Informal reviews are applied at various times during the early stages in the life cycle of a work product. A two-person team can conduct an informal review, as the author can ask a colleague to review a work product or code. Pair working (pair programming, pair testing or a tester and developer pairing) is also an informal way to review the work products that both are working on. In later stages, reviews often involve more people and a meeting. This normally involves peers of the author, who try to find defects in the work product under review and discuss these defects in a review meeting. The goal is to help the author and to improve the quality of the work product. Informal reviews come in various shapes and forms, but all have one characteristic in common: they are not documented.

Formal reviews generally have team participation, documented results of the review and specified procedures to follow in carrying out the review.

Different reviews may have a different focus or objective for the review. For example, one objective may be to find defects. This is often at least one of the objectives of most types of review, formal or informal. Sometimes the objective is for all participants to gain knowledge and understanding; although a walkthrough is normally used for this purpose, an informal review could also meet this goal, and it is often a by-product (if not an explicit objective) for technical reviews or inspections. Another objective may be to hold discussions and come to a consensus about technical issues; this is normally the focus of a technical review.

The standard that covers review processes is ISO/IEC 20246 [2017].

3.2.1 Work product review process

In contrast to informal reviews, formal reviews follow a formal process. Informal reviews may perform at least some of the same activities to some extent. The review process consists of the following main activities:

Planning

The Foundation Syllabus specifies the following elements of the planning activity:

● Defining the scope of the review: the purpose of the review, what work products (for example documents) or parts of work products to review and the quality characteristics to be evaluated in the review.

- Estimating effort and the timeframe for the review.
- Identifying review characteristics such as the type of review with roles, activities and checklists.
- Selecting the people to participate in the review and allocating roles to each reviewer.
- Defining the entry and exit criteria for more formal review types (for example inspections).
- Checking that entry criteria are met before the review starts (for more formal review types).

Let's examine these in more detail.

The review process for a particular review may begin with a request for review by the author to the review leader, who takes overall responsibility for the review, for example scheduling (dates, time, place and invitation) of the review. On a project level, the project planning needs to allow time for review and rework activities, thus providing engineers with time to thoroughly participate in reviews.

For more formal reviews, for example inspections, the facilitator performs an entry check and defines at this stage formal exit criteria. The entry check is carried out to ensure that the reviewers' time is not wasted on a work product that is not ready for review. A work product containing too many obvious mistakes is clearly not ready to enter a formal review process, and it could even be very harmful to the review process. It would possibly de-motivate both reviewers and the author. Also, the review is likely to be less effective because the numerous obvious and minor defects will conceal the major defects.

The following are possible entry criteria for a formal review:

- A short check of a work product sample by the review leader (or expert) does not reveal many major defects.
- The work product to be reviewed is available with line numbers (if relevant).
- The work product has been cleaned up by running any applicable automated checks, such as static analysis or spelling and grammar assessments.
- References needed for the review are stable and available.
- The work product author is prepared to join the review team and feels confident with the quality of the product.

If the work product passes the entry check, the review leader and author decide which part(s) of it to review. Because the human mind can comprehend a limited set of pages at one time, the number should not be too high. The maximum number of pages depends, among other things, on the objective, review type and work product type. It should be derived from practical experiences within the organization. For a review, the maximum size is usually between 10 and 20 pages. In formal inspection, only a page or two may be looked at in depth in order to find the most serious defects that are not obvious.

After the work product size has been set and the pages to be checked have been selected, the review leader determines, in co-operation with the author, the composition of the review team. The team normally consists of four to six participants, including facilitator (moderator) and author. To improve the effectiveness of the review, different roles may be assigned to each of the participants. These roles help the reviewers focus on particular types of defects during individual review.

This reduces the chance of different reviewers finding the same defects. The review leader or facilitator assigns the roles to the reviewers. (See below on role-based reviewing.)

Quality characteristics may also be evaluated and documented in a review, for example, the testability of a design or the readability or understandability of user help or installation instructions. These may also be assigned roles.

Initiate review

The Foundation Syllabus specifies the following activities for initiating a review:

- Distributing the work products (physically or electronically) and any other relevant material such as logging forms, checklists or related work products.
- Explaining the scope, objectives, process, roles and work products to the participants.
- Answering any questions that participants may have about the review.

Let's examine these in more detail.

The goal of this set of activities is to get everybody on the same wavelength regarding the work product under review and to commit to the time that will be spent on checking (that is, individual reviewing). The result of the entry check and defined exit criteria are discussed in case of a more formal review. This stage of the review process is important to increase the motivation of reviewers and thus the effectiveness of the review process. At customer sites, we have measured results of up to 70% more major defects found per page as a result of performing a kick-off meeting, a form of review initiation, as described in van Veenendaal and van der Zwan [2001].

The review initiation may be done remotely, or it may involve a meeting (in person or using video conferencing). If a meeting is held, the reviewers receive a short introduction to the objectives of the review and the work products. The relationships between the work product under review and the other work products (for example sources or predecessor work products) are explained, especially if the number of related work products is high.

Role assignments, checking rate, the pages to be reviewed, the roles to be taken by each person, process changes and possible other questions are also discussed during this meeting.

Whether or not a meeting is held, the facilitator (moderator) ensures that each reviewer is clear about their responsibilities, and answers any questions that they may have, either about the work products, or the review process itself.

Individual review (that is, individual preparation)

The Foundation Syllabus specifies the following activities for the individual review:

- Reviewing all or part of the work documents(s).
- Noting potential defects, recommendations and questions.

Let us examine these in more detail.

In the individual review, the participants work alone on the work product under review using the related work products, procedures, rules and checklists provided. The individual participants identify defects, recommendations, questions and comments, according to their understanding of the work product and the particular role they have been given. All issues are recorded, preferably using a logging form. Spelling mistakes are recorded on the work product under review, but not mentioned during the meeting. The annotated work product may be given to the author at the end of the logging meeting. Using checklists during individual reviewing can make reviews more effective and efficient, for example a specific checklist based on perspectives such as user, maintainer, tester or operations, or a checklist for typical coding problems. This may also be an assigned role.

A critical success factor for a thorough preparation is the number of pages individually reviewed per hour. This is called the checking rate. The optimum checking rate is the result of a mix of factors, including the type of work product, its complexity, the number of related work products and the experience of the reviewer. Usually the checking rate is in the range of five to ten pages per hour, but may be much less for formal inspection, for example one page per hour. During preparation, participants should not exceed the checking rate they have been asked to use. By collecting data and measuring the review process, company-specific criteria for checking rate and work product size (see Planning) can be set, preferably specific to a work product type.

Issue communication and analysis

The Foundation Syllabus specifies the following activities for issue communication and analysis:

- Communicating identified potential defects, for example in a review meeting.
- Analyzing potential defects, assigning ownership and status to them.
- Evaluating and documenting quality characteristics.
- Evaluating the review findings against the exit criteria to make a review decision (reject; major changes needed; accept, possibly with minor changes).

Let's examine these in more detail.

In a formal review, the things found by the individual reviewers are communicated to the author of the work product (or the person who will fix defects), and may also be communicated to the other reviewers. We may refer to these as issues at this point because we do not yet know if they are defects or not. The issues may be communicated electronically, or in a review meeting, which may consist of the following activities (partly depending on the review type): logging, discussion and decision making.

Logging in a review meeting

During logging, the issues, that is, potential defects, that have been identified during the individual review are mentioned page by page, reviewer by reviewer, and are logged either by the author or by a scribe. A separate person to do the logging (a scribe) is especially useful for formal review types such as an inspection. To ensure progress and efficiency, no real discussion is allowed during logging. If an issue needs discussion, the item is noted as a discussion item and then handled in the discussion part of the meeting. A detailed discussion on whether or not an issue is a defect is not very meaningful, as it is much more efficient to simply log it and proceed to the next one. Furthermore, in spite of the opinion of the team, a discussed and discarded defect may well turn out to be a real one during rework.

Every defect and its severity should be logged. The participant who identifies the defect may propose the severity, or the facilitator may assign a severity. If reviewers assign severity, it is important that the meaning of each category is understood by all reviewers in the same way. Otherwise, one reviewer may regard everything as critical, for example, skewing the review results. Severity classes could be:

- *Critical:* defects will cause downstream damage; the scope and impact of the defect is beyond the work product under inspection.

- *Major:* defects could cause a downstream effect (for example a fault in a design can result in an error in the implementation).
- *Minor:* defects are not likely to cause downstream damage (for example non-compliance with the standards and templates).

In order to keep the added value of reviews, spelling errors are not part of the defect classification. Spelling defects are noted by the participants in the work product under review and given to the author at the end of the meeting, or could be dealt with in a separate proofreading exercise.

During logging, the focus is on logging as many defects as possible within a certain timeframe. To ensure this, the facilitator tries to keep a good logging rate (number of defects logged per minute). In a well-led and disciplined formal review meeting, the logging rate should be between one and two defects logged per minute.

Discussion part of a review meeting

For a more formal review, the issues classified as discussion items will be handled during a discussion part of the review meeting, which occurs after the logging has been completed. Less formal reviews will often not have separate logging and discussion parts and will start immediately with logging mixed with discussion (which may lead to fewer defects being found). Participants can take part in the discussion by bringing forward their comments and reasoning. In the discussion part of the meeting, the facilitator or moderator takes care of people issues. For example, they prevent discussions from getting too personal, rephrase remarks if necessary and call for a break to cool down heated discussions and/or participants.

Reviewers who do not need to be in the discussion may leave, or stay as a learning exercise. The facilitator also paces this part of the meeting and ensures that all discussed items either have an outcome by the end of the meeting or are noted as an action point if the issue cannot be solved during the meeting. The outcome of discussions is documented for future reference.

Quality characteristics may also be evaluated and documented at this point, for example, the testability of a design or the readability or understandability of user help or installation instructions.

Decision-making part of a review meeting

At the end of the meeting, a decision on the work product under review has to be made by the participants, sometimes based on formal exit criteria. The most important exit criterion may be the average number of critical and/or major defects found per page (for example no more than three critical/major defects per page). If the number of defects found per page exceeds a certain level, the work product may need to be reviewed again, after it has been reworked. If the work product complies with the exit criteria, it will be checked later by the review leader, facilitator or one or more participants. Subsequently, the work product can leave the review process.

In addition to the number of defects per page, other exit criteria are used that measure the thoroughness of the review process, such as ensuring that all pages have been checked at the right rate. The average number of defects per page is only a valid quality indicator if these process criteria are met.

If a project is under pressure, the review leader or facilitator will sometimes be forced to skip re-reviews and exit with a defect-prone work product. Setting (and agreeing to) quantified exit criteria helps the review leader or facilitator to make firm decisions at all times. Even if a limited sample of a work product has been (formally) reviewed, an estimate of remaining defects per page can give an indication of likely problems later on.

For informal reviews, some of these activities may be performed, but informally. For example, potential defects may be emailed to the author of the work product with a suggested severity classification. The author may then evaluate exit criteria, possibly checking back with the reviewer(s).

Fixing and reporting

The Foundation Syllabus specifies the following activities for fixing and reporting:

- Creating defect reports for those findings that require changes.
- Fixing defects found (typically done by the author) in the work product reviewed.
- Communicating defects to the appropriate person or team (when found in a work product related to the work product reviewed).
- Recording updated status of defects (in formal reviews), potentially including the agreement of the comment originator.
- Gathering metrics (for more formal review types), for example of defects fixed, deferred, etc.
- Checking that exit criteria are met (for more formal review types).
- Accepting the work product when the exit criteria are reached.

Let's examine these in more detail.

Defect reports may have been recorded in a general defect logging tool (for example also used by testers) or may have been recorded in a review log.

During fixing, the author will improve the work product under review step by step, based on the issues or defects detected by the individual reviewers and/or those found in the review meeting. Not every issue that is reported is a defect that leads to a fix. It is often the author's responsibility to judge if an issue really is a defect which has to be fixed, though in some cases the review meeting participants may make those decisions. If nothing is done about an issue for a certain reason, it should still be reported to show that the author has considered it.

Changes that are made to the work product should be easy to identify by anyone who will be confirming that the fixes are correct. For example, the author may turn on 'track changes' in a document.

Sometimes an issue raised affects a work product that is not under the direct control of the author of the reviewed work product. For example, reviewing a feature to be implemented may reveal an inconsistency or omission in the user story or requirements specification that it is based on. If the author cannot update the user story or requirement specification directly, they need to communicate this to whoever can update the related work product.

As defects are fixed, the status of those defects should be updated wherever they are managed. In some reviews, the originator of the comment or defect would then confirm that the defect has been fixed adequately, that the author has correctly understood their comment and fixed the right problem in the right way.

In order to control and optimize the review process, a number of measurements are collected by the facilitator at each step of the process. Examples of such measurements include number of defects found, number of defects found per page, time spent checking per page, total review effort, etc. It is the responsibility of the facilitator or moderator to ensure that the information is correct and stored for future analysis.

The facilitator or moderator is responsible for ensuring that satisfactory actions have been taken on all logged defects, process improvement suggestions and change requests. Although the facilitator or moderator checks to make sure that the author has taken action on all known defects, it is not necessary for them to check all the corrections in detail. If it is decided that all participants will check the updated work product, the facilitator or moderator takes care of the distribution and collects the feedback. For more formal review types the review leader or facilitator checks for compliance to the exit criteria.

When all of the exit criteria have been met, including fixing, checking of fixes and confirming that the review process was properly carried out, then the work product can be formally accepted. This may be particularly important in safety-critical systems.

3.2.2 Roles and responsibilities in a formal review

The participants in any type of formal review should have adequate knowledge of the review process. The best, and most efficient, review situation occurs when the participants gain some kind of advantage for their own work during reviewing. In the case of an inspection or technical review, participants should have been properly trained, as both types of review have proven to be far less successful without trained participants. This indeed is a critical success factor.

The best formal reviews come from well-organized teams, guided by trained facilitators (moderators). Within a review team, six types of roles can be distinguished: author, management, facilitator (or moderator), review leader, reviewers and scribe (or recorder).

The author

The author has two main responsibilities:

● Creating the work product under review.
● Fixing defects in the work product (if necessary).

The author's basic goal should be to learn as much as possible with regard to improving the quality of the work product, but also to improve his or her ability to write future work products. The author's task is to illuminate unclear areas and to understand the defects found.

Management

Management has a number of very important responsibilities in successful reviews, including:

● Ensuring that reviews are planned.
● Deciding on the execution of reviews.
● Assigning staff, budget and time.
● Monitoring ongoing cost effectiveness.
● Executing control decisions in the event of inadequate outcomes.

The role of management in reviews is often underestimated, but without adequate support from managers, reviews are seldom successful. The manager needs to believe in reviews, and to ensure that they will be carried out as part of development. This includes allowing time in schedules for reviews to be done (and also any resulting rework!). Managers should also keep an eye on the effectiveness of reviews and encourage increasing effectiveness and efficiency, so that the greatest benefits are gained from reviews. The manager should have clear objectives for the review process(es) and should determine whether those objectives have been met. The manager will ensure that any review training requested by the participants takes place. Of course, a manager can also be involved in the review itself, depending on his or her background, playing the role of a review leader or reviewer if this would be helpful. In some review types, the manager should not be the moderator or facilitator of the review meeting (for example inspection).

Facilitator (often called moderator)

The responsibilities of the facilitator or moderator are:

- Ensuring the effective running of review meetings (when held).
- Mediating, if necessary, between the various points of view.
- Being the person upon whom the success of the review often depends.

The facilitator or moderator leads each individual review process. The facilitator performs the entry check and checks on the fixes, in order to control the quality of the input and output of the review process. The moderator also schedules the meeting, disseminates work products and other relevant materials, organizes the meeting, coaches other team members, paces the meeting, leads possible discussions and stores the data that is collected.

Review leader

The responsibilities of the review leader are:

- Taking overall responsibility for the review.
- Deciding who will be involved.

Depending on the size of the organization, the role of the review leader may be taken by a manager, or by the facilitator (moderator). If review leader is a separate role, they will be working closely with both of these roles.

In some organizations, there is no distinction made between the review leader and the facilitator in practice. The main difference is that the review leader is responsible for the review happening, and organizes the people involved, but may not be involved in the review meeting (if this is how issues are communicated). The facilitator's main role is in dealing with the people while the review is happening, ensuring that the review meetings are run well, and making sure that interpersonal issues do not disrupt the review process.

Reviewers

The responsibilities of the reviewers are:

- Being subject matter experts, persons working on the project, stakeholders with an interest in the work product, and/or individuals with specific technical or business backgrounds.
- Identifying potential defects in the work product under review.
- Representing different perspectives as requested, for example tester, developer, user, operator, business analyst, usability expert, etc.

The role of the reviewers (also called checkers or inspectors) is to be another set of eyes to look at the work products from a fresh point of view. The reviewers check any material for defects, mostly prior to the meeting. The level of thoroughness required depends on the type of review. The level of domain knowledge or technical expertise needed by the reviewers also depends on the type of review. Reviewers should be chosen to represent different perspectives in the review process. In addition to the work product under review, reviewers also receive other material, including source work products, standards, checklists, etc. In general, the fewer source and reference work products provided, the more domain expertise is neeeded regarding the content of the work product under review.

Scribe (or recorder)

The responsibilities of the scribe or recorder are:

- Collating potential defects found during the individual review activity.
- Recording new potential defects, open points and decisions from the review meeting (when held).

During the logging meeting, the scribe (or recorder) has to record each defect mentioned and any suggestions for process improvement. In practice, it is often the author who plays the role of scribe, ensuring that the log is readable and understandable. If authors record their own defects, or at least make their own notes in their own words, it helps them to understand the log better when they look through it afterwards to fix the defects found. However, having someone other than the author take the role of the scribe (for example the facilitator) can have significant advantages, since the author is freed up to think about the work product rather than being tied down with lots of writing.

The role of the scribe or recorder may be less relevant, or even irrelevant, if the defects, discussion points, decisions and other issues raised in the review are recorded electronically, although the scribe may be the person doing that recording during a meeting.

Although we have described the roles and responsibilities as though they are all separate and distinct, this does not mean that they are done by different people. One person may take on more than one role and perform the responsibilities for multiple roles. The determination of who does what role also depends on the type of review.

3.2.3 Types of review

The different review types have different objectives and can be used for different purposes, but the most common objective of all review types is to uncover defects in the work product being reviewed. The type of review should be chosen, based on a number of factors, including the needs of the project, available resources, product type and risks, business domain and company culture.

The main review types, their main characteristics and attributes are described below.

Informal review (for example buddy check, pairing, pair review)

An informal review is characterized by the following attributes:

- Main purpose/objective: detecting potential defects.
- Possible additional purposes: generating new ideas or solutions, quickly solving minor problems.

- Not based on a formal (documented) review process.
- May not involve a review meeting.
- May be performed by a colleague of the author (buddy check) or by more people.
- Results may be documented (but often are not).
- Varies in usefulness depending on the reviewer(s).
- Use of checklists is optional.
- Very commonly used in Agile development.

An informal review may simply be one person saying to a colleague, 'Could you have a quick look at what I've just done?' The colleague may spend less than an hour looking through and giving any comments back to the author, such as typos, something missing, or a 'But have you thought of this?' comment. With the right person reviewing, this buddy check can be very effective (and at little cost in time). Other forms of informal review include pair working, when one person works with another to produce a work product, the second person continually evaluating (that is, reviewing) what the first person is typing.

Walkthrough

A **walkthrough** is characterized by the following attributes:

- Main purposes: find defects, improve the software product, consider alternative implementations, evaluate conformance to standards and specifications.
- Possible additional purposes: exchanging ideas about techniques or style variations, training of participants, achieving consensus.
- Individual preparation before the review meeting is optional.
- Review meeting is typically led by the author of the work product.
- Use of a scribe is mandatory.
- Use of checklists is optional.
- May take the form of scenarios, dry runs or simulations.
- Potential defect logs and review reports may be produced.
- May vary in practice from quite informal to very formal.

> **Walkthrough** (Structured walkthrough) A type of review in which an author leads members of the review through a work product and the members ask questions and make comments about possible issues.

Within a walkthrough, the author does most of the preparation. The participants, who are selected from different departments and backgrounds, are not generally required to do a detailed study of the work products in advance (but it is an option). Because of the way the meeting is structured, a large number of people can participate and this larger audience can bring a great number of diverse viewpoints regarding the contents of the work product being reviewed. If the audience represents a broad cross-section of skills and disciplines, it can give assurance that no major defects are missed in the walkthrough. A walkthrough is especially useful for higher-level work products, such as requirement specifications and architectural documents.

A walkthrough is often used to transfer knowledge and educate a wider audience about a particular work product. In some cases, the educational value of a walkthrough is more important than finding defects (although defects should be welcomed).

If a large number of people are present, a scribe (someone other than the author) may be used to record the discussion, the questions raised and any decisions taken at the meeting.

Technical review

Technical review
A formal review type by a team of technically-qualified personnel that examines the suitability of a work product for its intended use and identifies discrepancies from specifications and standards.

A **technical review** is characterized by the following attributes:

- Main purposes: gaining consensus, detecting potential defects.
- Possible further purposes: evaluating quality and building confidence in the work product, generating new ideas, motivating and enabling authors to improve future work products, considering alternative implementations.
- Reviewers should be technical peers of the author, and technical experts in relevant disciplines.
- Individual preparation before the review meeting is required.
- Review meeting is optional, ideally led by a trained facilitator (typically not the author).
- Scribe is mandatory, ideally not the author.
- Use of checklists is optional.
- Potential defect logs and review reports are typically produced.

A technical review is often a discussion meeting that focuses on achieving consensus about the technical content of a work product that all the participants have studied before the meeting. During technical reviews, defects are found by experts, who focus on the content of the work product. The experts who participate in a technical review may include, for example, architects, chief designers and key users. It is useful to have an independent facilitator, especially if there are a number of strong opinions about technical issues. Technical reviews are typically less formal than inspections, but generally more formal than walkthroughs. In practice, technical reviews may vary from quite informal to very formal.

Inspection

Inspection A type of formal review to identify issues in a work product, which provides measurement to improve the review process and the software development process.

An **inspection** is characterized by the following attributes:

- Main purposes: detecting potential defects, evaluating quality and building confidence in the work product, preventing future similar defects through author learning and root cause analysis.
- Possible further purposes: motivating and enabling authors to improve future work products and the software development process, achieving consensus.
- A defined process is followed, with formal documented outputs, based on rules and checklists.
- There are clearly defined roles, such as those specified in Section 3.2.2 which are mandatory and may include a dedicated reader who reads/paraphrases the work product aloud during the review meeting.
- Individual preparation before the review meeting is required.

- Reviewers are either peers of the author or experts in other disciplines that are relevant to the work product.
- Specified entry and exit criteria are used.
- A scribe is mandatory.
- The review meeting is led by a trained facilitator/moderator (not the author).
- The author cannot act as the review leader, facilitator, reader or scribe.
- Potential defect logs and review reports are produced.
- Metrics are collected and used to improve the entire software development process, including the inspection process.

Inspection is the most formal review type. The work product under inspection is prepared and checked thoroughly by the reviewers before the meeting, comparing the work product with its sources and other referenced work products, and using rules and checklists. In the inspection meeting, the defects found are logged and any discussion is postponed until the discussion part of the meeting. This makes the inspection meeting a very efficient meeting.

Depending on the organization and the objectives of a project, inspections can be balanced to serve a number of goals. For example, if the time to market is extremely important, the emphasis in inspections will be on efficiency. In a safety-critical market, the focus will be on effectiveness.

When inspections are done well, they not only help to identify defects in the work products being reviewed, but the emphasis on process improvement and learning leads to better ways of producing work products, both for the author and for other reviewers.

All review types
A single work product may be the subject of more than one review. If more than one type of review is used, the order may vary. For example, an informal review may be carried out before a technical review to make sure the work product is ready for the technical review, or an inspection may be carried out on a requirements specification or epic before a walkthrough with customers. No one of the types of review is the winner, but the different types serve different purposes at different stages in the life cycle of a work product.

A peer review is where all of the reviewers are at the same or similar organizational level as the author, that is, the author's equals are reviewing the work. A peer review is not another type of review, as all of the types of review could be carried out by peers, from informal review to inspection.

All review types have as at least one of their purposes to find defects. Section 3.1.3 gave some examples of defects that can be found by static testing, including reviews. The most important thing is to find the most severe defects, those that represent the highest risk to the organization. Reviewing the most important work products is one way to get greater value from reviews. For example, a decimal point error may not be very important in a report about sales of low-volume items, but a decimal point error in a multi-million dollar or euro contract could be very significant. The types of defect found depend on the work product, as well as on the reviewers, and the way in which the reviews are carried out.

3.2.4 Applying review techniques

Suppose you have agreed to participate in a review of some type. You have been given the work product to review, with instructions about which parts to concentrate on, and perhaps some related documentation. How do you actually do the individual reviewing, the 'individual preparation' of the review process?

There are a number of techniques that can be used, whatever type of review is being performed. The main aim is to find defects, but some of these techniques will be more effective than others in some situations.

The Syllabus lists five different techniques (although you could argue that the first one is more the absence of any technique).

Ad hoc reviewing

If you have been given no instructions or guidance for how to review, then you will probably be doing an **ad hoc review**. You will likely read the work product from the beginning, and you may notice a few things that you note as possible defects. If you are a very good reviewer, this may be quite effective, but if you really are not sure what you are supposed to be looking out for, you may not find much that is useful. If everyone uses only ad hoc reviewing, the reviewers are likely to all find the same things, which is wasteful.

Ad hoc reviewing
A review technique carried out by independent reviewers informally, without a structured process.

Checklist-based reviewing

Checklist-based reviewing is often far more effective, because there is helpful guidance given about what to look for in the supplied checklist. The checklist would be one of the things distributed when the review is initiated. Different reviewers may have different checklists. This helps to cut down the number of duplicate defects found by reviewers. A checklist may contain items to check or questions.

Checklist-based reviewing A review technique guided by a list of questions or required attributes.

The checklist may contain questions relating to the work product, such as 'Have references been given for claims shown?', 'Are all pointers valid?' or 'Has the customer's viewpoint been considered?' It is a good idea to organize a checklist so that if the answer to a question is 'No', then there is a potential defect. The best checklist questions are often derived from something that went wrong or was missed in a previous review. If a major defect was missed, adding a specific question to a checklist to look for that type of defect is very effective.

However, checklists should not just be allowed to grow and grow. It is important to review the checklists regularly, and to remove questions that are no longer useful, so that the checklist is focused on the most important things. The longer a checklist is, the less likely it is to be fully used, so it is also a good idea to limit the size of the checklist to one page, and to put the most important checklist questions at the beginning.

Checklists are useful when reviewing any type of work product, from unit or component code to user stories or Help text. The questions would, of course, be different for each work product, as they are targeted at potential defects for that type of work product. For example, code-specific questions (about pointers) would be appropriate for a unit code checklist, and customer-related questions would be appropriate for a user story or requirements specification checklist.

When checklists are used well, this is a very effective review technique; if all of the checklist questions are evaluated, this is a systematic search for previous or typical defect types.

One last word of warning about checklist-based reviews: do not be constrained to check only what is on the checklist. The checklist can help to guide you to look for specific things, but also be aware of other things, and take inspiration from the checklist to look for related potential defects outside of the checklist.

Scenario-based reviewing and dry runs

A **scenario-based review** is one where the reviewers are given a structured perspective on how to work through a work product from a particular point of view. For example, if use cases are used, a use case can be a scenario to work through how the system will work from each actor's point of view (people and other systems).

> **Scenario-based reviewing** A review technique where the review is guided by determining the ability of the work product to address specific scenarios.

When you are stepping through the scenario, this is also called a 'dry run', a term used for a rehearsal before a big event or speech. In this sense, going through the scenario is a rehearsal for the system. We are looking at the way the system is expected to be used, which is an important aspect of validation.

A scenario is a different way of reviewing from using a checklist. You are looking at how the system will be used from a specific perspective, and this can be more focused than just a list of questions or points to check. When using a scenario, we are acting out realistic ways of using the system and validating whether or not it will meet user needs and expectations. A checklist is more likely to be focused on verifying individual aspects, such as types of defect, that have occurred previously.

As with checklists, do not be constrained by the scenario, but use it as inspiration for finding other defects outside of the scenario. With user-focused scenarios, be particularly aware of missing features.

Role-based reviewing

Role-based reviewing is similar to scenario-based reviewing, but the viewpoints are different stakeholders rather than just users. Roles can include specific end-user types, such as experienced versus inexperienced, age-related (children, teenagers, adults, seniors), or accessibility roles such as vision impaired, hearing impaired, etc.

> **Role-based reviewing** A review technique where reviewers evaluate a work product from the perspective of different stakeholder roles.

Personas may also be used, which are typically based on a profile of a specific set of characteristics. A persona is the characterization of a user who represents the target audience for your system. A number of different personas are used to represent a range of user profiles, needs or desires. For example, one persona may be a young adult who is single and likes skiing; another may be a married elderly person with significant health problems. Each persona is described in detail (job, where they live, income level, etc.). Each persona would represent a role in role-based reviewing.

Figure 3.1 shows some different roles with respect to documents or work products used within a review. The roles represent views of the work product under review:

- Focus on higher-level work products, for example does the design comply to the requirements (Type 1 in Figure 3.1).
- Focus on standards, for example internal consistency, clarity, naming conventions, templates (Type 2).
- Focus on related work products at the same level, for example interfaces between software functions (Type 3).
- Focus on usage of the work product, for example for testability or maintainability (Type 4).

FIGURE 3.1   Basic review roles for a work product under review

The author may raise additional specific roles and questions to be addressed. The moderator has the option to also fulfil a role, alongside the task of being the facilitator. Checking the work product improves the facilitator's ability to lead the meeting, because it ensures better understanding. Furthermore, it improves the review efficiency because the facilitator replaces an engineer who would otherwise have to check the work product and attend the meeting. It is recommended that the facilitator take the role of checking compliance to standards, since this tends to be a highly objective role, with less discussion about the defects found.

Roles can also be organizational, such as from the perspective of a system administrator or user administrator. They can also be from testing perspectives such as performance testing or security testing.

In inspection, viewpoint roles can also include reviewing from the perspective of contractual issues, manufacturing (if relevant), legal issues, design or testing, operations or delivery or a third-party supplier. In addition to these viewpoint roles, there can be procedural roles, such as checking all financial calculations, starting from the back, looking for the most important things or cross-checking within or between work products. There may also be document or work product roles where each reviewer is given special responsibility for using one particular related work product. For example, if there are three user stories that are related to the work product being reviewed, and there are three reviewers, each would pay special attention to one of the three user stories.

Perspective-based reading

| Perspective-based reading (Perspective-based reviewing) A review technique whereby reviewers evaluate the work product from different viewpoints. |

Perspective-based reading is similar to role-based reviewing, but rather than playing a specific role, the reviewer typically tries to perform the tasks on a high level that they would be doing with the work product under review (taking that perspective), for example, as a tester making some test designs. Stakeholder perspectives include end-users, marketing, designer, tester or operations. These are similar to some of the inspection roles, and in fact this technique was devised for inspections. This technique goes beyond role-based and is therefore typically more expensive, but it also finds more defects.

The benefits of this technique (and also role-based and scenario-based reviewing) are that each individual reviewer has their own specialty within the review, and will be looking in more depth within their own assigned area. This makes the review more effective (since there is deeper checking) but also more efficient, since there is less duplication of issues found by different reviewers. Checklists can also be used for the different perspectives.

Another approach to perspective-based reading is for the reviewers to use the work product to generate other work products from it. When doing perspective-based reading on a requirements specification, a tester-perspective reviewer would be generating acceptance tests. This can help to identify missing information needed for the tests.

Perspective-based reading combines aspects of all of the review techniques (except ad hoc) and so can be the most effective. There is no one right way to do reviews, but when reviewers look at the work product in different ways, using checklists, scenarios, roles or perspectives, then the best results are gained. More information is available in Shull, Rus and Basili [2000].

3.2.5 Success factors for reviews

Implementing (formal) reviews is not easy. There is no one way to success and there are numerous ways to fail. The most common reasons for failure in reviews are due to either organizational factors or people-related factors. We will look at aspects of both of these.

One aspect (which is not emphasized in the Syllabus) is the importance of having a champion, the person who will lead the process on a project or organizational level. They need expertise, enthusiasm and a practical mindset in order to guide moderators and participants. The authority of this champion should be clear to the entire organization.

Organizational success factors for reviews

To be successful, a review culture should be part of the mindset of the organization, and there are a number of aspects which can make or break the effectiveness and efficiency of reviews within an organization.

Have clear objectives

Each review should have clear objectives. These are defined during the planning stage, communicated to all participants and may be used to measure the exit criteria or definition of done for the review.

Pick the right review type and technique

In the previous subsections, we discussed a number of review types and techniques, each of which has its strengths and weaknesses, and advantages and disadvantages in use. You should be careful to select and use review types and techniques that will best enable the achievement of the objectives of the project and the review itself. Be sure to consider the type, importance and risk level of the work product to be reviewed, and the reviewers who will participate. For example, do not try to review everything by inspection; fit the review to the risk associated with specific parts of the work product. Some work products may only warrant an informal review and others will repay using inspection. Of course, it is also of utmost importance that the right people are involved. Consider the work product to be reviewed. Would a checklist-based review technique or a role-based technique be the most suitable for identifying defects?

Review materials need to be kept up to date

We use work products that support the review process to perform a review. These work products need to be up to date and of good quality in order to support the reviews. Review materials, such as checklists, need reviewing too! When significant defects are found in work products (either in reviews or in testing), add an item to the relevant checklist so that this type of work product defect can be identified earlier next time. At regular intervals, check to make sure that all of the items or questions on a checklist are still relevant, and remove any that are not useful any more.

Limit the scope of the review

Large documents or work products should be reviewed in small chunks, so that feedback can be given to the authors while they are still working on the work product. Early and frequent feedback is more effective and more efficient, partly because if a particular type of defect is detected early, the author can be aware of this in the rest of the work product; this prevents that type of defect from appearing in the parts of the work product written later.

It takes time

Reviews take time, and this time needs to be scheduled. But it is not just the time for review meetings. It is more important to allow adequate time for reviewers to do the preparation and individual studying of the work product before any meeting, as this is when most defects are identified. Skimping on preparation time is a false economy. The review meetings must be scheduled with adequate notice, so that reviewers can plan the review time into their own work schedules. It is not realistic to expect reviewers to be able to drop everything for a review, they need to balance their own work with the review work.

Management support is critical

Management support is essential for success. Managers should, among other things, incorporate adequate time for review activities in project schedules. They should visibly support the review process and help to foster a culture where reviews are seen as valuable both to the organization and to the individual. Managers especially must commit not to use metrics or other information from reviews for the evaluation of the author or the participants. If people are blamed for making mistakes, they do not make fewer mistakes, they hide them better!

One of the authors was called in to give training for reviews in an organization where the manager claimed to be very much in favour of using them. This sounded good, but during the training, it became clear that something was not right; there was great resistance to the idea of reviews. When raised with the manager, he said, 'But I am really supporting reviews here – that way I can find out who puts in the most defects and fire them.' Needless to say, reviews did not work in this organization!

To ensure that reviews become part of the day-to-day activities, the hours to be spent should be made visible within each project plan. The engineers involved should be prompted to schedule time for preparation and, very importantly, rework. Tracking these hours will improve planning of the next review. As stated earlier, management plays an important part in planning of review activities.

Report quantified and aggregated results and benefits at a high (not individual) level to all those involved as soon as possible, including discussion of the consequences of defects if they had not been found this early. Costs should of course be tracked, but benefits, especially when problems do not occur in the future, should be made visible by quantifying the benefits as well as the costs.

People-related success factors for reviews

Reviews are about evaluating someone's work product. Some reviewers tend to get too personal when they are not well managed by the facilitator (moderator). People issues and psychological aspects should be dealt with by the facilitator and should be part of the review training, thus making the review a positive experience for the author. During the review, defects should be welcomed. This is much more likely when they are expressed objectively. It is important that all participants create and operate in an atmosphere of trust.

Pick the right reviewers

The people chosen to participate in a review have a significant impact on the success and outcome of the review. Different review types or techniques may require different skills from the reviewers, and different types of work product may require different skills. For example, if code is being reviewed, the reviewers must at least be able to read and understand the code, so developer skills are needed. If role-based review techniques are used, people who have or can adopt those particular perspectives are needed as reviewers. If someone will be using a particular work product in their own work (for example a developer who will be working to implement a feature in a user story), that person would be a good candidate to include on the review team, as they have a vested interest in understanding their source (the user story), clarifying any ambiguities and removing any defects before they use it in their own development work.

Use testers

As discussed in Chapter 1, testers are professional pessimists. This focus on what could go wrong makes them good contributors to reviews, provided they observe the earlier points about keeping the review experience a positive one. In addition to providing valuable input to the review itself, testers who participate in reviews often learn about the product. This supports earlier testing, one of the principles discussed in Chapter 1. Using testers as reviewers is also beneficial to the testers, as the review can help them identify relevant test conditions and test cases, and to begin preparing the tests earlier.

Each participant does their review work well

Each reviewer has responsibilities and possibly roles to play in the review. It is important that each of them takes the reviewing work seriously and does it to the best of their ability. This includes spending adequate time on the review activities, and paying attention to detail as needed, for example by using a checklist.

Limit the scope of the review and pick things that really count

As mentioned under the organizational factors, do not try to review too much at one time. Even if a limited scope has not been formally defined, reviewers should be selective about what they spend their time on. Select the work products for review that are most important in a project. Reviewing highly critical, upstream work products like requirements and architecture will most certainly show the benefits of the review process to the project. This investment in review hours will have a clear and high return on investment.

Another advantage of limiting the scope of a review is that it is easier to concentrate on a small piece of work rather than trying to take in a large amount. Reviewers need to keep up their concentration on the important things, both in individual preparation and in any review meeting.

Defects found should be welcomed

The attitude towards defects found in reviews is critical to success. Any defect found is an opportunity to improve not only the quality of the work product that it was found in but also to become aware of other similar defects in the same or in different work products. When reviews are working well, many more defects are prevented than are found.

But the attitude towards defects by the author of the work product is also critical. Defects should be acknowledged and appreciated (even if you are not sure at the time whether it really is a defect or not, acknowledge the point made by the person reporting it). Defects should be reported and handled objectively; defect reporting should never become personal, as this creates ill will and damages the review process and culture.

Review meetings are well managed

The role of the facilitator or moderator in the review meeting is one of the major factors in making the whole review experience useful and pleasant. The meeting should be focused on the review objectives, and any discussion should be tightly controlled. It is all too easy for discussions in meetings to go on and on, but if the purpose of the review is to identify defects as efficiently as possible, then most discussion is probably unnecessary. All review participants should feel that their time in the review (including the meeting) has been a valuable use of their time.

Trust is critical

As mentioned in the earlier section, it is very important that the defect information is considered sensitive data and handled accordingly. Even the rumour of a manager wanting to use review data to evaluate people is enough to destroy the effectiveness of a review process. There needs to be an atmosphere of trust among the reviewers; they all know that they are helping each other get better, and they need to be confident that the data will be used in the right way.

How you communicate is important

Particularly in review meetings, subliminal factors such as body language and tone of voice may damage the openness of a good review atmosphere. In addition, if defects raised are criticized, for example by the author, then reviewers are much less likely to raise other defects, so something very important may be missed. Language is important as well. Contrast 'There may be a problem here' (objective wording), with 'You did it wrong here' (personal attack).

Follow the rules but keep it simple

Follow all the formal rules until you know why and how to modify them, but make the process only as formal as the project culture or maturity level allows. Do not become too theoretical or too detailed. Checklists and roles are recommended to increase the effectiveness of defect identification.

Train participants

It is important that training is provided in review techniques, especially the more formal techniques, such as inspection. Otherwise the process is likely to be impeded by those who do not understand the process and the reasoning behind it. Special training should be provided to the facilitators (moderators) to prepare them for their critical role in the review process.

Continuously improve process and tools

Continuous improvement of process guidelines and supporting tools (for example checklists), based upon the ideas of participants, ensures the motivation of the engineers involved. Motivation is the key to a successful change process. There should also be an emphasis, in addition to defect finding, on learning and process improvement which becomes part of the culture of the organization.

Just do it!

Finally, the review process is simple but not easy. Every step of the process is clear, but experience is needed to execute them correctly. Try to get experienced people to observe and help where possible. But most importantly, start doing reviews and start learning from every review.

More information about successful reviews can be found in Weigers [2002], van Veenendaal [2004], Sauer [2000] and Kramer and Legeard [2016].

CHAPTER REVIEW

Let's review what you have learned in this chapter.

From Section 3.1, you should be able to recognize the software work products that can be examined by static testing techniques. You should be able to explain the value of static testing by using examples. You should be able to explain the difference between static testing and dynamic testing in terms of their objectives, types of defects to be found, and the role of these techniques within the software life cycle. You should know the Glossary terms **dynamic testing**, **static analysis** and **static testing**.

From Section 3.2, you should be able to summarize the activities of the work product review process. You should recognize the different roles and responsibilities in a formal review. You should be able to explain the differences between the various types of review: informal review, walkthrough, technical review and inspection. You should be able to apply a review technique to a work product to find defects. Finally, you should be able to explain the factors for successful performance of reviews, both organizational and people-related. You should know the Glossary terms **ad hoc reviewing**, **checklist-based reviewing**, **formal review**, **informal review**, **inspection**, **perspective-based reading**, **review**, **role-based reviewing**, **scenario-based reviewing**, **technical review** and **walkthrough**. Finally, you should be able to carry out a review, particularly the individual reviewing of a work product, as this is K3 level in the Syllabus.

SAMPLE EXAM QUESTIONS

Question 1 Which of the following artefacts can NOT be examined using review techniques?

a. Software code.

b. User story.

c. Test designs.

d. User's intentions.

Question 2 Which of the following are the main activities of the work product review process?

1. Planning.

2. Initiate review.

3. Select reviewers.

4. Individual review.

5. Review meeting.

6. Evaluating review findings against exit criteria.

7. Issue communication and analysis.

8. Fixing and reporting.

a. 1, 2, 4, 7, 8.

b. 2, 3, 4, 5, 8.

c. 1, 2, 3, 5, 7.

d. 1, 4, 5, 6, 7.

Question 3 Which statement about static and dynamic testing is True?

a. Static testing and dynamic testing have different objectives.

b. Static testing and dynamic testing find the same types of defect.

c. Static testing identifies defects through failures; dynamic testing finds defects directly.

d. Static testing can find some types of defect with less effort than dynamic testing.

Question 4 What statement about reviews is True?

a. Inspections are led by a trained moderator, but this is not necessary for technical reviews.

b. Technical reviews are led by a trained leader, inspections are not.

c. In a walkthrough, the author does not attend.

d. Participants for a walkthrough always need to be thoroughly trained.

Question 5 Which statement below is True?

a. Management ensures effective running of review meetings; the review leader decides who will be involved.

b. Management is responsible for review planning; the facilitator monitors ongoing cost effectiveness.

c. Management organizes when and where reviews will take place; the review leader assigns staff, budget and time.

d. Management decides on the execution of reviews; the facilitator is often the person on whom the success of the review depends.

Question 6 Match the following characteristics with the type of review.

1. Led by the author.

2. Undocumented.

3. Reviewers are technical peers of the author.

4. Led by a trained moderator or leader.

5. Uses entry and exit criteria.

INSP: Inspection

TR: Technical review

IR: Informal review

W: Walkthrough

a. INSP: 4, TR: 3, IR: 2 and 5, W: 1

b. INSP: 4 and 5, TR: 3, IR: 2, W: 1

c. INSP: 1 and 5, TR: 3, IR: 2, W: 4

d. INSP: 5, TR: 4, IR: 3, W: 1 and 2

Question 7 Which of the following statements about success factors in reviews are True?

1. Reviewers should try to review as much of the work product as they can.

2. The author acknowledges and appreciates defects found in their work.

3. Each review has clear objectives, which are communicated to the reviewers.

4. Testers are not normally involved in reviews, as their work focuses on test design.

5. Checklists should be standardized and used for all types of work product.

a. 2 and 3.

b. 1, 2 and 3.

c. 1, 2 and 4.

d. 2, 3 and 5.

Question 8 Which review technique is this: reviewing a requirements specification or user story from the point of view of an end-user of the system, using a checklist?

a. Checklist-based.

b. Role-based.

c. Perspective-based.

d. Scenario-based.

Question 9 Consider the following specification for review:

When you sign up, you must give your first and last name, postal address, phone number, email address and password. When you log in, you must give your last name, phone number and password. You are logged in until you select Log Out followed by answering 'Yes' to 'Are you sure?' When you are logged in, you can update your details, but you need to confirm the change by entering a secure code sent to your phone. You then need to log in again.

The following are potential defects in the specification:

1. Incorrect timeout for the secure code sent to the phone.

2. Buffer overflow for lengthy postal address.

3. Cannot change your phone number, as the code is sent to the old number.

4. Details are stored as an additional entry in the database for every change.

Which of the potential defects above would be most likely to be found by a review performed by developers?

a. 2 and 3.

b. 2, 3 and 4.

c. 1, 2 and 4.

d. 1 and 4.

EXERCISE

Perform an individual review of the functional specification shown in Document 3.1, using a checklist-based review. The checklist is as follows:

1. Do all requirements give sufficient detail needed for determining the expected results for tests?

2. Are all dependencies and restrictions specified?

3. Are alternatives specified for all options?

Make a list of potential defects in the specification, noting the severity level of each (High, Medium or Low). Note which checklist question has found the defect. Solution ideas are given in the next section.

DOCUMENT 3.1 Functional requirements specification

Functional requirements

This specification describes the required functionality of the booking system for a sports centre.

Browsing the facilities

Customers will be able to view all the available facilities using the following options to filter the selection:

- None – shows all facilities
- Outdoor/indoor
- Sport – selected from a pull-down list
- Date – using a standard calendar
- Time – selected from a pull-down list

Each facility shown will include colour-coded information on availability (not available, already booked, and available for booking) and the time slots.

Selecting a facility

Any facility available for booking can be selected by clicking on the required time period. A confirmation message will be displayed. The user may either cancel the message and return to the list of facilities or continue to the booking details page.

Booking details

If the customer is not already logged in, the customer login dialogue will be displayed.

Details of the facility together with any relevant regulations (such as age restrictions, footwear and no-show conditions, etc.) will be displayed. The customer name, member ID and mobile phone number fields will be pre-filled. The customer can either cancel or confirm the details. Confirming the details takes the customer to the payment details page; cancelling returns the customer to the list of facilities page.

Payment details

Payment can be made by credit card. The following details are required:

- Card type – Visa or Mastercard
- Name on card – as printed on card
- Card number – 16 digits, no spaces
- Expiry date – mm/yy
- CVC code – last 3 digits on the signature strip

Having entered these details, the system will seek authorization for the payment. When this is received a final confirmation message is displayed. The customer can choose to cancel or confirm. If confirmed, the booking is made and a confirmation email is sent to the customer's email address (as specified in their customer profile). If the payment authorization fails, an error message is displayed.

EXERCISE SOLUTION

The following are some potential defects in the functional requirement shown in Document 3.1. This is not an exhaustive list; you may have found others. We have noted the checklist question number used to discover each issue, and a severity level of High, Medium or Low.

TABLE 3.1   Potential defects in the functional requirements specification

Defect	Description	Checklist	Severity
1	Need to know the specific colours in the colour coding to be able to see if the test passes or fails.	1	M
2	Need to know what all the facilities are, in order to check if they are displayed correctly.	1	M
3	What facilities are in the 'Sport' pull-down list?	2	M
4	What are the rules for selection of options? Does Date have to be selected before Time, for example? Can you select only one option?	2	H
5	If login fails, what is supposed to happen: can you continue to book anyway?	3	H
6	If login is successful, what screen is displayed, already selected, or back to list?	3	L
7	Can filters be combined? For example can you select Indoor and Tennis?	2	L
8	Is it possible to choose more than one time slot at once, for example 3 consecutive half-hour times?	2	M
9	If credit card authorization fails, what happens after the error message is shown?	3	L
10	The customer can cancel after authorization has gone through? Has payment already been taken? If so, will it be refunded? Automatically?	3	H
11	When booking is cancelled after authorization, what screen is shown after the error message?	3	L
12	Missing from specification: Is cancellation possible after a booking has been made, either by customer or by the sports centre? Is a refund given? Automatically?	none	H

As mentioned above, these are some suggested potential defects. Note that we have phrased many of them as questions, which may be less threatening to the author of the requirements document. Note also that we have noted an additional high severity defect which was not specifically triggered by an item in the checklist.

CHAPTER FOUR

Test techniques

C hapter 3 covered static testing, looking at work products and code, but not running the code we are interested in. This chapter looks at dynamic testing, where the software we are interested in is run by executing tests on the running code.

4.1 CATEGORIES OF TEST TECHNIQUES

SYLLABUS LEARNING OBJECTIVES FOR 4.1 CATEGORIES OF TEST TECHNIQUES (K2)

FL-4.1.1   **Explain the characteristics, commonalities and differences between black-box test techniques, white-box test techniques and experience-based test techniques (K2)**

In this section we will look at the different types of test techniques, how they are used, how they differ and the factors to consider when choosing a test technique. The three types or categories are distinguished by their primary source: a description of what the system should do (for example requirements, user stories, etc.), the structure of the system or component, or a person's experience. All categories are useful and the three are complementary.

The purpose of a test technique is to identify test conditions, test cases and test data. Test conditions are identified during analysis, and then used to define test cases and test data during test design, which are then used in test implementation. For example, in risk-based testing strategies, we identify risk items (which are the test conditions) when performing an analysis of the risks to product quality. Those risk items, along with their corresponding levels of risk, are subsequently used to design the test cases and implement the test data. Risk-based testing will be discussed in Chapter 5.

In this section, look for the definitions of the Glossary terms **black-box test technique**, **coverage**, **experience-based test technique**, **test technique** and **white-box test technique**.

4.1.1 Choosing test techniques

In this section we will look at the factors that go into the decision about which techniques to use when.

Which technique is best? This is the wrong question! Each technique is good for certain things, and not as good for other things. For example, one of the benefits of white-box techniques is that they can find things in the code that are not supposed to be there, such as Trojan Horses or other malicious code. However, if there are parts of the specification that are missing from the code, black-box techniques can find that. White-box techniques can only test what is there. If there are things missing both from the specification and from the code, then only experience-based techniques would find them. Each individual technique is aimed at particular types of defect as well. For example, state transition testing is unlikely to find boundary defects.

The choice of which **test technique** to use depends on a number of factors, which we discuss below.

Some techniques are more applicable to certain situations and test levels; others are applicable to all test levels. The best testing uses a combination of test techniques.

This chapter covers the most popular and commonly used software test techniques. There are many others that fall outside the scope of the Syllabus that this book is based on. With so many testing techniques to choose from, how are testers to decide which ones to use?

The use of techniques can vary in formality, from very informal (with little or no documentation) to very formal, where information about test conditions and why particular techniques are used is recorded. The level of formality also depends on other factors as discussed below. For example, safety or regulatory industries require a higher level of formality. The maturity of the organization, the life cycle model being used, and the knowledge and skills of the testers also influence the level of formality.

Perhaps the single most important thing to understand is that the best test technique is no single test technique. Because each test technique is good at finding one specific class of defect, using just one technique will help ensure that many (perhaps most but not all) defects of that particular class are found. Unfortunately, it may also help to ensure that many defects of other classes are missed! Using a variety of techniques will therefore help ensure that a variety of defects are found, resulting in more effective testing.

So how can we choose the most appropriate test techniques to use? The decision will be based on a number of factors, both internal and external.

The factors that influence the decision about which technique to use are:

- *Type of component or system.* The type of component (for example embedded, graphical, financial, etc.) will influence the choice of techniques. For example, a financial application involving many calculations would benefit from boundary value analysis.

- *Component or system complexity.* More complex components or systems are likely to have more defects, and defects may be harder to find. Using a different technique to address aspects of that complexity will give better defect detection from the testing. For example, a simple field with numerical input would be a good candidate for equivalence partitioning and boundary value analysis, but a screen with many fields, with complex dependencies, calculations and validation rules depending on aspects that change over time, would benefit from additional techniques such as decision table testing, state transition testing and white-box test techniques.

- *Regulatory standards.* Some industries have regulatory standards or guidelines that govern the test techniques used. For example, the aircraft industry requires the use of equivalence partitioning, boundary value analysis and state transition testing for high integrity systems, together with statement, decision or modified condition decision coverage depending on the level of software integrity required.

Test technique (test case design technique, test specification technique, test design technique) A procedure used to derive and/or select test cases.

- *Customer or contractual requirements.* Sometimes contracts specify particular test techniques to use (most commonly statement or branch coverage).

- *Risk levels and risk types.* The greater the risk level (for example safety-critical systems), the greater the need for more thorough, formal testing. Commercial risk may be influenced by quality issues (so more thorough testing would be appropriate) or by time to market issues (so exploratory testing would be a more appropriate choice). Risk type might, for example, tell us that a risk is related to usability, performance, security or functionality. Of course, the correct test technique needs to be chosen that is able to address the risk type that is being mitigated.

- *Test objectives.* If the test objective is simply to gain confidence that the software will cope with typical operational tasks, then use cases would be a sensible approach. If the objective is for very thorough testing, then more rigorous and detailed techniques (including white-box test techniques) should be chosen.

- *Available documentation.* Whether or not documentation (for example a work product such as a requirements specification) exists, and how up-to-date it is, will affect the choice of test techniques. The content and style of the work products will also influence the choice of techniques (for example, if decision tables or state graphs have been used, then the associated test techniques should be used).

- *Tester knowledge and skills.* How much testers know about the system and about test techniques will clearly influence their choice of techniques. Experience-based techniques are particularly based on tester knowledge and skills.

- *Available tools.* If tools are available for a particular technique, then that technique may be a good choice. Since test techniques are based on models, the models available (that is, developed and used during the specification, design and implementation of the system) will to some extent govern which test techniques can be used. For example, if the specification contains a state transition diagram, state transition testing would be a good technique to use.

- *Time and budget.* Ultimately how much time there is available will always affect the choice of test techniques. When more time is available, we can afford to select more techniques. When time is severely limited, we will be limited to those that we know have a good chance of helping us find just the most important defects.

- *Software development life cycle model.* A sequential life cycle model will lend itself to the use of more formal techniques, whereas an iterative life cycle model may be better suited to using an exploratory test approach.

- *Expected use of the software.* If the software is to be used in safety-critical situations, for example medical monitoring devices or car-driving technology, then the testing should be more thorough, and more techniques should be chosen.

- *Previous experience with using the test techniques on the component or system to be tested.* Testers tend to use techniques that they are familiar with and more skilled at, rather than less familiar techniques. With this familiarity, you can become very effective at finding similar defects to those that have occurred before. But be aware that you may get better results from using a technique that is less familiar, and when you do use it, you will increase your skill and familiarity with it.

● *The types of defects expected in the component or system.* Knowledge of the likely defects will be very helpful in choosing test techniques (since each technique is good at finding a particular type of defect). This knowledge could be gained through experience of testing a previous version of the system and previous levels of testing on the current version.

It is important to remember that intelligent, experienced testers see test techniques (and indeed test strategies, which we'll discuss in Chapter 5) as tools to be employed wherever needed and useful. You should use whatever techniques and strategies, in whatever combinations, make sense to ensure adequate coverage of the system under test, and achievement of the objectives of testing. Feel free to combine the test techniques discussed in this chapter with whatever inspiration you have, along with process-related, rule-based and data-driven techniques. Use your brain and do what makes sense.

4.1.2 Categories of test techniques and their characteristics

There are many different types of software test techniques, each with its own strengths and weaknesses. Each individual technique is good at finding particular types of defect and relatively poor at finding other types. For example, a technique that explores the upper and lower limits of a single input range is more likely to find boundary value defects than those associated with combinations of inputs. Similarly, testing performed at different stages in the software development life cycle will find different types of defects; component testing is more likely to find coding logic defects than system design defects or user experience problems.

Each test technique falls into one of a number of different categories. Broadly speaking there are two main categories, static and dynamic. Static test techniques, as discussed in Chapter 3, do not execute the code being examined and are generally used before any tests are executed on the software. They could be called non-execution techniques. Most static test techniques can be used to test any form of work product including source code, design documents and models, user stories, functional specifications and requirement specifications. Static analysis is a tool-supported type of static testing that concentrates on testing formal languages and so is most often used to statically test source code.

In this chapter we look at dynamic test techniques, which are subdivided into three more categories: black-box (also known as specification-based, behavioural or behaviour-based techniques), white-box (structure-based or structural techniques) and experience-based. Black-box test techniques include both functional and non-functional techniques (that is, testing of quality characteristics). The techniques covered in the Syllabus are summarized in Figure 4.1.

Black-box test techniques

The first of the dynamic test techniques we will look at are the **black-box test techniques**. They are called black-box because they view the software as a black box with inputs and outputs, but they have no knowledge of how the system or component is structured inside the box. In essence, the tester is concentrating on what the software does, not how it does it.

Black-box test technique (black-box technique, specification-based technique, specification-based test technique) A procedure to derive and/or select test cases based on an analysis of the specification, either functional or non-functional, of a component or system, without reference to its internal structure.

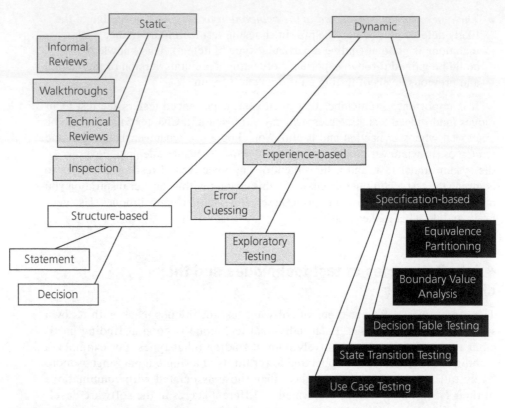

FIGURE 4.1 Test techniques

All black-box test techniques have the common characteristic that they are based on a model (formal or informal) of some aspect of the system, which enables test conditions and test cases to be derived from them in a systematic way.

Common characteristics of black-box test techniques include the following:

● Test conditions, test cases and test data are derived from a test basis that may include software requirements, specifications, use cases and user stories. The source of information for black-box tests is some description of what the system or software is supposed to do.

● Test cases may be used to detect gaps between the requirements and the implementation of the requirements, as well as deviations from the requirements. One of the strengths of test cases is that they make things specific, and this often highlights different understandings about the test basis, showing what is missing or interpreted differently.

● Coverage is measured based on the items tested in the test basis and the technique applied to the test basis. As we will see later, whenever you can make a list of some things that could be tested and can tell whether or not they have been tested, then you can measure coverage. Coverage at black-box level is based on items from the test basis. For example, does every requirement described have at least one test that exercises it?

Black-box test techniques are appropriate at all levels of testing (component testing through to acceptance testing) where a specification or other test basis exists. When performing system or acceptance testing, the requirements specification or functional specification may form the basis of the tests. When performing component or integration testing, a design document or low-level specification may form the basis of the tests.

Notice that the definition mentions both functional and non-functional testing. Functional testing is concerned with what the system does, its features or functions. Non-functional testing is concerned with examining how well the system does something, rather than what it does. Non-functional aspects (also known as quality characteristics or quality attributes) include performance, usability, portability, maintainability, etc. Techniques to test these non-functional aspects are less procedural and less formalized than those of other categories, as the actual tests are more dependent on the type of system, what it does and the resources available for the tests.

Non-functional testing is part of the Syllabus and is also covered in Chapter 2. There are techniques for deriving non-functional tests [Gilb 1988], but they are not covered at the Foundation level.

Categorizing test techniques into black-box and white-box is mentioned in a number of testing books, including Beizer [1990], Black [2007] and Copeland [2004].

White-box test techniques

White-box test techniques (which are also dynamic rather than static) use the internal structure of the software to derive test cases. They are commonly called white-box or glass-box techniques (implying you can see into the system/box) since they require knowledge of how the software is implemented, that is, how it works. For example, a structural technique may be concerned with exercising loops in the software. Different test cases may be derived to exercise the loop once, twice and many times. This may be done regardless of the functionality of the software. All structure-based techniques have the common characteristic that they are based on how the software under test is constructed or designed. This structural information is used to assess which parts of the software have been exercised by a set of tests (often derived by other techniques). Additional test cases can then be derived in a systematic way to cover the parts of the structure that have not been touched by any test before.

Common characteristics of white-box test techniques include the following:

> **White-box test technique** (structural test technique, structure-based test technique, structure-based technique, white-box technique) A procedure to derive and/or select test cases based on an analysis of the internal structure of a component or system.

- Test conditions, test cases and test data are derived from a test basis that may include code, software architecture, detailed design or any other source of information regarding the structure of the software. White-box test techniques are most commonly used for code structure, but these techniques are also useful for other structures. For example, the menu structure of an app could be tested using white-box techniques.

- **Coverage** is measured based on the items tested within a selected structure, for example the code statements, the decisions, the interfaces, the menu structure or any other identified structural element. See Section 4.3 for more on coverage.

> **Coverage** (test coverage) The degree to which specified coverage items have been determined to have been exercised by a test suite, expressed as a percentage.

- White-box test techniques determine the path through the software that either was taken or that you want to be taken, and this is determined by specific inputs to the software. However, in order to be a test, we also need to know what the expected outcome of the test case should be, even though this does not affect the path taken. A test oracle of some kind, for example a specification, is used to determine the expected outcome.

White-box test techniques can also be used at all levels of testing. Developers use white-box techniques in component testing and component integration testing, especially where there is good tool support for code coverage. White-box techniques are also used in system and acceptance testing, but the structures are different. For example, the coverage of major business transactions could be the structural element in system or acceptance testing.

Experience-based test techniques

Experience-based test technique (experience-based technique) A procedure to derive and/or select test cases based on the tester's experience, knowledge and intuition.

In **experience-based test techniques**, people's knowledge, skills and background are a prime contributor to the test conditions, test cases and test data. The experience of both technical and business people is important, as they bring different perspectives to the test analysis and design process. Due to previous experience with similar systems, they may have insights into what could go wrong, which is very useful for testing. Both structural and behavioural insights are used to design experience-based tests.

All experience-based test techniques have the common characteristic that they are based on human knowledge and experience, both of the system itself (including the knowledge of users and stakeholders) and of likely defects. Test cases are therefore derived in a less systematic way, but may be more effective.

Experience-based test techniques are used to complement black-box and white-box techniques, and are also used when there is no specification, or if the specification is inadequate or out-of-date. This may be the only type of technique used for low-risk systems, but this approach may be particularly useful under extreme time pressure. In fact this is one of the factors leading to exploratory testing.

4.2 BLACK-BOX TEST TECHNIQUES

> **SYLLABUS LEARNING OBJECTIVES FOR 4.2 BLACK-BOX TEST TECHNIQUES (K3)**
>
> **FL-4.2.1** Apply equivalence partitioning to derive test cases from given requirements (K3)
>
> **FL-4.2.2** Apply boundary value analysis to derive test cases from given requirements (K3)
>
> **FL-4.2.3** Apply decision table testing to derive test cases from given requirements (K3)
>
> **FL-4.2.4** Apply state transition testing to derive test cases from given requirements (K3)
>
> **FL-4.2.5** Explain how to derive test cases from a use case (K2)

In this section we will look in detail at four black-box test techniques. These four techniques are K3 in the Syllabus. This means that you need to be able to use these techniques to design test cases. We will also cover briefly (not at K3 level) the technique of use case testing. In Section 4.3, we will look at the K2 white-box test techniques.

In this section, look for the definitions of the Glossary terms **boundary value analysis**, **decision table testing**, **equivalence partitioning**, **state transition testing** and **use case testing**.

The four black-box test techniques we will cover in detail are:

- Equivalence partitioning.
- Boundary value analysis.
- Decision table testing.
- State transition testing.

4.2.1 Equivalence partitioning

Equivalence partitioning (EP) is a good all round black-box test technique. It can be applied at any level of testing and is often a good technique to use first. It is a common sense approach to testing, so much so that most testers practice it informally even though they may not realize it. However, while it is better to use the technique informally than not at all, it is much better to use the technique in a formal way to attain the full benefits that it can deliver. This technique will be found in most testing books, including Myers [2011], Copeland [2004], Jorgensen [2014] and Kaner *et al.* [2013].

The idea behind the technique is to divide (that is, to partition) a set of test conditions into groups or sets where all elements of the set can be considered the same, so the system should handle them equivalently, hence 'equivalence partitioning'. **Equivalence partitions** are also known as equivalence classes: the two terms mean exactly the same thing.

The EP technique then requires that we need test only one condition from each partition. This is because we are assuming that all the conditions in one partition will be treated in the same way by the software. If one condition in a partition works, we assume all of the conditions in that partition will work, and so there is little point in testing any of these others. Conversely, if one of the conditions in a partition does not work, then we assume that none of the conditions in that partition will work so again there is little point in testing any more in that partition. Of course these are simplifying assumptions that may not always be right, but if we write them down, at least it gives other people the chance to challenge the assumptions we have made and hopefully help to identify better partitions. If you have time, you may want to try more than one value from a partition, especially if you want to confirm a selection of typical user inputs.

For example, a savings account in a bank earns a different rate of interest depending on the balance in the account. In order to test the software that calculates the interest due, we can identify the ranges of balance values that earn the different rates of interest. For example, if a balance in the range $0 up to $100 has a 3% interest rate, a balance over $100 and up to $1,000 has a 5% interest rate, and balances of $1,000 and over have a 7% interest rate, we would initially identify three valid equivalence partitions and one invalid partition as shown below.

Invalid partition	Valid (for 3% interest)		Valid (for 5%)		Valid (for 7%)
−$0.01	$0.00	$100.00	$100.01	$999.99	$1,000.00

Equivalence partitioning (partition testing) A black-box test technique in which test cases are designed to exercise equivalence partitions by using one representative member of each partition.

Equivalence partition (equivalence class) A portion of the value domain of a data element related to the test object for which all values are expected to be treated the same based on the specification.

Notice that we have identified four partitions here, even though the specification only mentions three. This illustrates a very important task of the tester: not only do we test what is in our specification, but we also think about things that have not been specified. In this case we have thought of the situation where the balance is less than zero. We have not (yet) identified an invalid partition on the right, but this would also be a good thing to consider. In order to identify where the 7% partition ends, we would need to know what the maximum balance is for this account (which may not be easy to find out). In our example we have left this open for the time being. Note that non-numeric input is also an invalid partition (for example the letter 'a') but we discuss only the numeric partitions for now.

We have made an assumption here about what the smallest difference is between two values. We have assumed two decimal places, that is $100.00, but we could have assumed zero decimal places (that is $100) or more than two decimal places (for example $100.0000). In any case it is a good idea to state your assumptions: then other people can see them and let you know if they are correct or not.

We have also made an assumption about exactly which amount starts the new interest rate: a cent over to go into the 5% interest rate, but exactly on the $1,000.00 to go into the 7% rate. By making our assumptions explicit, and documenting them in this technique, we may highlight any differences in understanding exactly what the specification means.

When designing the test cases for this software we would ensure that the three valid equivalence partitions are each covered once, and we would also test the invalid partition at least once. So for example, we might choose to calculate the interest on balances of −$10.00, $50.00, $260.00 and $1,348.00. If we had not specifically identified these partitions, it is possible that at least one of them could have been missed at the expense of testing another one several times over. Note that we could also apply EP to outputs as well. In this case we have three interest rates: 3%, 5% and 7%, plus the error message for the invalid partition (or partitions). In this example, the output partitions line up exactly with the input partitions.

How would someone test this without thinking about the partitions? A naïve tester (let's call him Robbie) might have thought that a good set of tests would be to test every $50. That would give the following tests: $50.00, $100.00, $150.00, $200.00, $250.00, ... say up to $800.00 (then Robbie would have got tired of it and thought that enough tests had been carried out). But look at what Robbie has tested: only two out of four partitions! So if the system does not correctly handle a negative balance or a balance of $1,000 or more, he would not have found these defects, so the naïve approach is less effective than EP. At the same time, Robbie has four times more tests (16 tests versus our four tests using equivalence partitions), so he is also much less efficient! This is why we say that using techniques such as this makes testing both more effective and more efficient.

Note that when we say a partition is invalid, it does not mean that it represents a value that cannot be entered by a user or a value that the user is not supposed to enter. It just means that it is not one of the expected inputs for this particular field. The software should correctly handle values from the invalid partition, by replying with an error message such as 'Balance must be at least $0.00'.

Note also that the invalid partition may be invalid only in the context of crediting interest payments. An account that is overdrawn will require some different action.

Here is a summary of EP characteristics:

● Valid values should be accepted by the component or system. An equivalence partition containing valid values is called a valid equivalence partition.

- Invalid values should be rejected by the component or system. An equivalence partition containing invalid values is called an invalid equivalence partition.

- Partitions can be identified for any data element related to the test object, including inputs, outputs, internal values, time-related values (for example before or after an event) and for interface parameters (for example integrated components being tested during integration testing).

- Any partition may be divided into sub-partitions if required, where smaller differences of behaviour are defined or possible. For example, if a valid input range goes from –100 to 100, then we could have three sub-partitions: valid and negative, valid and zero, and valid and positive.

- Each value belongs to one and only one equivalence partition from a set of partitions. However, it is possible to apply EP more than once and end up with different sets of partitions, as we will see later under 'Applying more than once' in the section on 'Extending equivalence partitioning and boundary value analysis').

- When values from valid partitions are used in test cases, they can be combined with other valid values in the same test, as the whole set should pass. We can therefore test many valid values at the same time.

- When values from invalid partitions are used in test cases, they should be tested individually, that is, not combined with other invalid equivalence partitions, to ensure that failures are not masked. Failures can be masked when several failures occur at the same time but only one is visible, causing the other failures to be undetected.

- EP is applicable at all test levels.

We have more things to say about EP (including how to measure coverage), but we will return to that after we cover boundary value analysis, since the two techniques are closely related.

4.2.2 Boundary value analysis

Boundary value analysis (BVA) is based on testing at the boundaries between partitions that are ordered, such as a field with numerical input or an alphabetical list of values in a menu. It is essentially an enhancement or extension of EP and can also be used to extend other black-box (and white-box) test techniques. If you have ever done 'range checking', you were probably using the BVA technique, even if you were not aware of it. Note that we have both valid boundaries (in the valid partitions) and invalid boundaries (in the invalid partitions).

As an example, consider a printer that has an input option of the number of copies to be made, from 1 to 99.

Invalid	Valid		Invalid
0	1	99	100

To apply BVA, we will take the minimum and maximum (boundary) values from the valid partition (1 and 99 in this case) together with the first or last value respectively in each of the invalid partitions adjacent to the valid partition (0 and 100 in this case). In this example we would have three EP tests (one from each of the three partitions) and four boundary value tests.

> **Boundary value analysis** A black-box test technique in which test cases are designed based on boundary values.

Let's return to the savings account system described in the previous section:

Invalid partition	Valid (for 3% interest)		Valid (for 5%)		Valid (for 7%)
−$0.01	$0.00	$100.00	$100.01	$999.99	$1,000.00

Because the boundary values are defined as those values on the edge of a partition, we have identified the following boundary values: −$0.01 (an invalid boundary value because it is at the edge of an invalid partition), $0.00, $100.00, $100.01, $999.99 and $1,000.00, all valid boundary values.

So by applying BVA we will have six tests for boundary values. Compare what our naïve tester Robbie had done: he did actually hit one of the boundary values ($100) though it was more by accident than design. So in addition to testing only half of the partitions, Robbie has only tested one-sixth of the boundaries (so he will be less effective at finding any boundary defects). If we consider all of our tests for both EP and BVA, the techniques give us a total of ten tests, compared to the 16 that Robbie had, so we are still considerably more efficient as well as being over three times more effective (testing four partitions and six boundaries, so ten conditions in total compared to three).

Note that in this savings account interest example, we have valid partitions next to other valid partitions. If we were to consider an invalid boundary for the 3% interest rate, we have −$0.01, but what about the value just above $100.00? The value of $100.01 is not an *invalid* boundary; it is actually a *valid* boundary because it falls into a valid partition. So the partition for 5%, for example, has no invalid boundary values associated with partitions next to it.

A good way to represent the valid and invalid partitions and boundaries is in a table such as Table 4.1:

TABLE 4.1 Equivalence partitions and boundaries

Test conditions	Valid partitions	Invalid partitions	Valid boundaries	Invalid boundaries
Balance in account	$0.00 − $100.00	< $0.00	$0.00	− $0.01
	$100.01 − $999.99	> $Max	$100.00	$Max + 0.01
	$1,000.00 − $Max	non-integer (if balance is an input field)	$100.01	
			$999.99	
			$1,000.00	
			$Max	
Interest rates	3%	Any other value	Not applicable	Not applicable
	5%	Non-integer		
	7%	No interest calculated		

By showing the values in the table, we can see that no maximum has been specified for the 7% interest rate. We would now want to know what the maximum value is for an account balance, so that we can test that boundary. This is called an open boundary, because one of the sides of the partition is left open, that is, not defined. But that doesn't mean we can ignore it. We should still try to test it, but how? We have called it $Max to remind ourselves to investigate this.

Open boundaries are more difficult to test, but there are ways to approach them. Actually the best solution to the problem is to find out what the boundary should be specified as! One approach is to go back to the specification to see if a maximum has been stated somewhere else for a balance amount. If so, then we know what our boundary value is. Another approach might be to investigate other related areas of the system. For example, the field that holds the account balance figure may be only six figures plus two decimal figures. This would give a maximum account balance of $999,999.99 so we could use that as our maximum boundary value. If we really cannot find anything about what this boundary should be, then we probably need to use an intuitive or experience-based approach to probe various large values trying to make it fail.

We could also try to find out about the lower open boundary. What is the lowest negative balance? Although we have omitted this from our example, setting it out in the table shows that we have omitted it, so helps us be more thorough if we wanted to be.

Representing the partitions and boundaries in a table such as this also makes it easier to see whether or not you have tested each one (if that is your objective). To achieve 100% coverage for EP, we need to ensure that there is at least one test for each identified equivalence partition. To achieve 100% coverage of boundary values, we need to ensure that there is at least one test for each boundary value identified. Of course, just one test for either a partition or a boundary may not be sufficient testing, but it does show some degree of thoroughness, since we have not left any partition or boundary untested.

BVA can be applied at all test levels.

Extending equivalence partitioning and boundary value analysis

So far, by using EP and BVA we have identified conditions that could be tested, that is, partitions and boundary values. The techniques are used to identify test conditions, which could be at a fairly high level (for example low interest account) or at a detailed level (for example value of $100.00). We have been looking at applying these techniques to ranges of numbers. However, we can also apply the techniques to other things.

Applying to more than numbers

For example, if you are booking a flight, you have a choice of Economy/Coach, Premium Economy, Business or First Class tickets. Each of these is an equivalence partition in its own right and should be tested, but it does not make sense to talk about boundaries for this type of partition, which is a collection of valid things. The invalid partition would be an attempt to type in any other type of flight class (for example Staff). If this field is implemented using a drop-down list, then it should not be possible to type anything else in, but it is still a good test to try at least once in some drop-down field. When you are analyzing the test basis (for example a requirements specification or user story), EP can help to identify where a drop-down list would be appropriate.

When trying to identify a defect, you might try several values in a partition. If this results in different behaviour where you expected it to be the same, then there may be two (or more) partitions where you initially thought there was only one.

We can apply EP and BVA to all levels of testing. The examples here were at a fairly detailed level, probably most appropriate in component testing or in the detailed testing of a single screen.

At a system level, for example, we may have three basic configurations which our users can choose from when setting up their systems, with a number of options for each configuration. The basic configurations could be system administrator, manager and customer liaison. These represent three equivalence partitions that could be tested. We could have serious problems if we forget to test the configuration for the system administrator, for example.

Applying more than once

We can also apply EP and BVA more than once to the same specification item. For example, if an internal telephone system for a company with 200 telephones has three-digit extension numbers from 100 to 699, we can identify the following partitions and boundaries:

- Digits (characters 0 to 9) with the invalid partition containing non-digits.
- Number of digits, 3 (so invalid boundary values of two digits and four digits).
- Range of extension numbers, 100 to 699 (so invalid boundary values of 099 and 700).
- Extensions that are in use and those that are not (two valid partitions, no boundaries).
- The lowest and highest extension numbers that are in use could also be used as boundary values.

One test case could test more than one of these partitions/boundaries. For example, Extension 409 which is in use would test four valid partitions: digits, the number of digits, the valid range and the in use partition. It also tests the boundary values for digits 0 and 9.

How many test cases would we need to test all of these partitions and boundaries, both valid and invalid? We would need a non-digit, a two-digit and a four-digit number, the values of 99, 100, 699 and 700, one extension that is not in use, and possibly the lowest and highest extensions in use. This is 10 or 11 test cases: the exact number would depend on what we could combine in one test case.

Using EP and BVA helps us to identify tests that are most likely to find defects, and to use fewer test cases to find them. This is because the contents of a partition are representative of all of the possible values. Rather than test all ten individual digits, we test one in the middle (for example 4) and the two edges (0 and 9). Instead of testing every possible non-digit character, one can represent all of them.

Applying to output

As we mentioned earlier, we can also apply these techniques to output partitions. Consider the following extension to our bank interest rate example. Suppose that a customer with more than one account can have an extra 1% interest on this account if they have at least $1,000 in it. Now we have two possible output values (7% interest and 8% interest) for the same account balance, so we have identified another test condition (8% interest rate). (We may also have identified that same output condition by looking at customers with more than one account, which is a partition of types of customer.)

Applying to more than human inputs

EP can be applied to different types of input as well. Our examples have concentrated on inputs that would be typed in (by a human) when using the system. However, systems receive input data from other sources as well, such as from other systems via some interface. This is also a good place to look for partitions (and boundaries). For example, the value of an interface parameter may fall into valid and invalid equivalence partitions. This type of defect is often difficult to find in testing once the interfaces have been joined together, so is particularly useful to apply in integra tion testing, either component integration, for example between APIs (Application Programming Interfaces) or system integration. If you are receiving data from a third-party supplier, a value sent by the supplier may be larger than the maximum value your system is expecting. If you do not check the value when it arrives, this could cause problems.

Boundary value analysis can be applied to a whole string of characters (for example a name or address). The number of characters in the string is a partition, for example between 1 and 30 characters is the valid partition with valid boundaries of 1 and 30. The invalid boundaries would be zero characters (null, just hit the Return key) and 31 characters. Both of these should produce an error message.

Partitions can also be identified when setting up test data. If there are different types of record, your testing will be more representative if you include a data record of each type. The size of a record is also a partition with boundaries, so we could include maximum and minimum size records in the test database.

If you have some inside knowledge about how the data is physically organized, you may be able to identify some hidden boundaries. For example, if an overflow storage block is used when more than 255 characters are entered into a field, the boundary value tests would include 255 and 256 characters in that field. This may be verging on white-box testing, since we have some knowledge of how the data is structured, but it does not matter how we classify things as long as our testing is effective at finding defects. Don't get hung up on a fine distinction: just do whatever testing makes sense, based on what you know. An old Chinese proverb says, 'It doesn't matter whether the cat is white or black; all that matters is that the cat catches mice'.

Two- and three-value boundary analysis

With BVA, we think of the boundary as a dividing line between two things. Hence we have a value on each side of the boundary, but the boundary itself is not a value.

Invalid	Valid	Invalid
0	1 99	100

Looking at the values for our printer example, 0 is in an invalid partition, 1 and 99 are in the valid partition and 100 is in the other invalid partition. So the boundary is between the values of 0 and 1, and between the values of 99 and 100. There is a school of thought that regards an actual value as a boundary value. By tradition, these are the values in the valid partition (that is, the values specified). This approach then requires three values for every boundary, so you would have 0, 1 and 2 for the left boundary, and 98, 99 and 100 for the right boundary in this example. The boundary values are said to be on and either side of the boundary and the value that is 'on' the boundary is generally taken to be in the valid partition.

Note that Beizer [1990] and Kaner, Padmanabhan and Hoffman [2013] talk about domain testing, a generalization of EP, with three-value boundaries. Beizer makes a distinction between open and closed boundaries, where a closed boundary is one where the point is included in the domain. So the convention is for the valid partition to have closed boundaries. You may be pleased to know that you do not have to know this for the exam! Three-value boundary testing is covered in ISO/IEC/IEEE 29119-4 [2015].

So which approach is best? If you use the two-value approach together with EP, you are equally effective and slightly more efficient than the three-value approach. (We will not go into the details here, but this can be demonstrated.) In this book we will use the two-value approach. In the exam, you may have a question based on either the two-value or the three-value approach, but it should be clear what the correct choice is in either case.

Designing test cases using EP and BVA

Having identified the test conditions that you wish to test, in this instance by using EP and BVA, the next step is to design the test cases. The more test conditions that can be covered in a single test case, the fewer test cases will be needed in order to cover all the conditions. This is usually the best approach to take for positive tests and for tests that you are reasonably confident will pass. However if a test fails, then we need to find out why it failed. Which test condition was handled incorrectly? We need to get a good balance between covering too many and too few test conditions in our tests.

Let's look at how one test case can cover one or more test conditions. Using the bank balance example, our first test could be of a new customer with a balance of $500. This would cover a balance in the partition from $100.01 to $999.99 and an output partition of a 5% interest rate. We would also be covering other partitions that we have not discussed yet, for example a valid customer, a new customer, a customer with only one account, etc. All of the partitions covered in this test are valid partitions.

When we come to test invalid partitions, the safest option is probably to try to cover only one invalid test condition per test case. This is because programs may stop processing input as soon as they encounter the first problem. So if you have an invalid customer name, invalid address and invalid balance, you may get an error message saying 'Invalid input' and you do not know whether the test has detected only one invalid input or all of them. This is also why specific error messages are much better than general ones!

However, if it is known that the software under test is required to process all input regardless of its validity, then it is sensible to continue as before and design test cases that cover as many invalid conditions in one go as possible. For example, if every invalid field in a form has some red text above or below the field saying that this field is invalid and why, then you know that each field has been checked, so you have tested all of the error processing in one test case. In either case, there should be separate test cases covering valid and invalid conditions.

To cover the boundary test cases, it may be possible to combine all of the minimum valid boundaries for a group of fields into one test case and also the maximum valid boundary values. The invalid boundaries could be tested together if the validation is done on every field; otherwise they should be tested separately, as with the invalid partitions.

Why do both equivalence partitioning and boundary value analysis?

Technically, because every boundary is in some partition, if you did only BVA you would also have tested every equivalence partition. However, this approach may cause problems if that value fails – was it only the boundary value that failed or did the whole partition fail? Also by testing only boundaries we would probably not give the users much confidence as we are using extreme values rather than normal values. The boundaries may be more difficult (and therefore more costly) to set up as well.

For example, in the printer copies example described earlier we identified the following boundary values:

Invalid	Valid		Invalid
0	1	99	100

Suppose we test only the valid boundary values 1 and 99 and nothing in between. If both tests pass, this seems to indicate that all the values in between should also work. However, suppose that one page prints correctly, but 99 pages do not. Now we do not know whether any set of more than one page works, so the first thing we would do would be to test for say ten pages, which is a value from the equivalence partition.

We recommend that you test the partitions separately from boundaries. This means choosing partition values that are NOT boundary values.

However, if you use the three-value boundary value approach, then you would have valid boundary values of 1, 2, 98 and 99, so having a separate equivalence value in addition to the extra two boundary values would not give much additional benefit. But notice that one equivalence value, for example 10, replaces both of the extra two boundary values (2 and 98). This is why EP with two value BVA is more efficient than three-value BVA.

Which partitions and boundaries you decide to exercise (you do not need to test them all), and which ones you decide to test first, depends on your test objectives. If your goal is the most thorough approach, then follow the procedure of testing valid partitions first, then invalid partitions, then valid boundaries and finally invalid boundaries. However, if you are under time pressure (and who isn't?), then you can't test as much as you would like. Now your test objectives will help you decide what to test. If you are after user confidence of typical transactions with a minimum number of tests, you might do valid partitions only. If you want to find as many defects as possible as quickly as possible, you may start with boundary values, both valid and invalid. If you want confidence that the system will handle bad inputs correctly, you may do mainly invalid partitions and boundaries. Your previous experience of types of defects can help you find similar defects; for example, if there are typically a lot of boundary defects, then you would start by testing boundaries.

EP and BVA are described in most testing books, including Myers [2011], Copeland [2004], Kaner, Padmanabhan and Hoffman [2013] and Jorgensen [2014]. EP and BVA are described in ISO/IEC/IEEE 29119-4 [2015], including designing tests and measuring coverage.

4.2.3 Decision table testing

The techniques of EP and BVA are often applied to specific situations or inputs. However, if different combinations of inputs result in different actions being taken, this can be more difficult to show using EP and BVA, which tend to be more focused on the user interface. The other two specification-based techniques, **decision table testing** and state transition testing, are more focused on business logic or business rules.

A decision table is a good way to deal with combinations of things (for example inputs). This technique is sometimes also referred to as a 'cause-effect' table. The reason for this is that there is an associated logic diagramming technique called 'cause-effect graphing' which was sometimes used to help derive the decision table. (Myers describes this as a combinatorial logic network [Myers 2011]). However, most people find it more useful just to use the table described in Copeland [2004].

Decision table testing A black-box test technique in which test cases are designed to execute the combinations of inputs and/or stimuli (causes) shown in a decision table.

If you begin using decision tables to explore what the business rules are that should be tested, you may find that the analysts and developers find the tables very helpful and want to begin using them too. Do encourage this, as it will make your job easier in the future. Decision tables provide a systematic way of stating complex business rules, which is useful for developers as well as for testers. Decision tables can be used in test design whether or not they are used in development, as they help testers explore the effects of combinations of different inputs and other software states that must correctly implement business rules. Helping the developers do a better job can also lead to better relationships with them.

Testing combinations can be a challenge, as the number of combinations can often be huge. Testing all combinations may be impractical, if not impossible. We have to be satisfied with testing just a small subset of combinations, but it's not easy to choose which combinations to test and which not to test. If you don't have a systematic way of selecting combinations, an arbitrary subset will be used and this may well result in an ineffective test effort.

Decision tables aid the systematic selection of effective test cases and can have the beneficial side-effect of finding problems and ambiguities in the specification. It is a technique that works well in conjunction with EP. The combination of conditions explored may be combinations of equivalence partitions.

In addition to decision tables, there are other techniques that deal with testing combinations of things: pairwise testing and orthogonal arrays. These are described in Copeland [2004]. Other sources of techniques are Pol, Teunissen and van Veenendaal [2001] and Black [2007]. Decision tables and cause–effect graphing are described in ISO/IEC/IEEE 29119-4 [2015], including designing tests and measuring coverage.

Using decision tables for test design

The first task is to identify a suitable function or subsystem that has a behaviour which reacts according to a combination of inputs or events. The behaviour of interest must not be too extensive (that is, should not contain too many inputs) otherwise the number of combinations will become cumbersome and difficult to manage. It is better to deal with large numbers of conditions by dividing them into subsets and dealing with the subsets one at a time.

Once you have identified the aspects that need to be combined, then you put them into a table, listing all the combinations of True and False for each of the aspects. Take an example of a loan application, where you can enter the amount of the monthly repayment or the number of years you want to take to pay it back (the term of the loan). If you enter both, we assume that the system will make a compromise between the two if they conflict. The two conditions are the repayment amount and the term, so we put them in a table (see Table 4.2).

TABLE 4.2 Empty decision table

Conditions	Rule 1	Rule 2	Rule 3	Rule 4
Repayment amount has been entered				
Term of loan has been entered				

Next, we will identify all of the combinations of True and False (see Table 4.3). With two conditions, each of which can be True or False, we will have four combinations (two to the power of the number of things to be combined). Note that if we have three things to combine, we will have eight combinations, with four things, there are 16, etc. This is why it is good to tackle small sets of combinations at a time. In order to keep track of which combinations we have, we will alternate True and False on the bottom row, put two Trues and then two Falses on the row above the bottom row, etc., so the top row will have all Trues and then all Falses (and this principle applies to all such tables).

TABLE 4.3 Decision table with input combinations

Conditions	Rule 1	Rule 2	Rule 3	Rule 4
Repayment amount has been entered	T	T	F	F
Term of loan has been entered	T	F	T	F

We are using T and F for the inputs in our example; we could also have used Y and N or 1 (the number one) and 0 (zero) respectively. The conditions can also be numbers, numeric ranges or enumerated types (for example red, green or blue).

The next step (at least for this example) is to identify the correct outcome for each combination (see Table 4.4). In this example, we can enter one or both of the two fields. Each combination is sometimes referred to as a rule. In this example, we are using Y for the actions which should occur and leaving it blank if that action should not occur. Other options are to use X or 1 if an action should occur, and N, F, '–' or 0 for actions that should not occur. We could use a number or range of numbers if an outcome occurs for those numbers and does not occur for others. You could also use discrete values, for example an action should occur if an input is red, which does not occur if it is green or yellow.

TABLE 4.4 Decision table with combinations and outcomes

Conditions	Rule 1	Rule 2	Rule 3	Rule 4
Repayment amount has been entered	T	T	F	F
Term of loan has been entered	T	F	T	F
Actions/Outcomes				
Process loan amount	Y	Y		
Process term	Y		Y	

At this point, we may now realize that we had not thought about what happens if the customer doesn't enter anything in either of the two fields. The table has highlighted a combination that was not mentioned in the specification for this example. We could assume that this combination should result in an error message, so we need to add another action (see Table 4.5). This highlights the strength of this technique to discover omissions and ambiguities in specifications. It is not unusual for some combinations to be omitted from specifications; therefore this is also a valuable technique to use when reviewing the test basis.

TABLE 4.5 Decision table with additional outcome

Conditions	Rule 1	Rule 2	Rule 3	Rule 4
Repayment amount has been entered	T	T	F	F
Term of loan has been entered	T	F	T	F
Actions/Outcomes				
Process loan amount	Y	Y		
Process term	Y		Y	
Error message				Y

Suppose we change our example slightly, so that the customer is not allowed to enter both repayment and term. Now our table will change, because there should also be an error message if both are entered, so it will look like Table 4.6.

TABLE 4.6 Decision table with changed outcomes

Conditions	Rule 1	Rule 2	Rule 3	Rule 4
Repayment amount has been entered	T	T	F	F
Term of loan has been entered	T	F	T	F
Actions/Outcomes				
Process loan amount		Y		
Process term			Y	
Error message	Y			Y

You might notice now that there is only one Yes in each column, that is, our actions are mutually exclusive: only one action occurs for each combination of conditions. We could represent this in a different way by listing the actions in the cell of one row, as shown in Table 4.7. Note that if more than one action results from any of the combinations, then it would be better to show them as separate rows rather than combining them into one row.

TABLE 4.7 Decision table with outcomes in one row

Conditions	Rule 1	Rule 2	Rule 3	Rule 4
Repayment amount has been entered	T	T	F	F
Term of loan has been entered	T	F	T	F
Actions/Outcomes				
Result	Error message	Process loan amount	Process term	Error message

The final step of this technique is to write test cases to exercise each of the four rules in our table.

In this example we started by identifying the input conditions and then identifying the outcomes. However, in practice it might work the other way around – we can see that there are a number of different outcomes and have to work back to understand what combination of input conditions actually drive those outcomes. The technique works just as well doing it in this way and may well be an iterative approach as you discover more about the rules that drive the system.

Credit card worked example

Let's look at another example. If you are a new customer opening a credit card account, you will get a 15% discount on all your purchases today. If you are an existing customer and you hold a loyalty card, you get a 10% discount. If you have a coupon, you can get 20% off today (but it cannot be used with the new customer discount). Discount amounts are added, if applicable. This is shown in Table 4.8.

In Table 4.8, the conditions and actions are listed in the left-hand column. All the other columns in the decision table each represent a separate rule, one for each combination of conditions. We may choose to test each rule/combination and if there are only a few, this will usually be the case. However, if the number of rules/combinations is large we are more likely to sample them by selecting a rich subset for testing.

Note that we have put X for the discount for two of the columns (Rules 1 and 2). This means that this combination should not occur. You cannot be both a new customer and already hold a loyalty card! There should be an error message stating this, but even if we don't know what that message should be, it will still make a good test.

TABLE 4.8 Decision table for credit card example

Conditions	Rule 1	Rule 2	Rule 3	Rule 4	Rule 5	Rule 6	Rule 7	Rule 8
New customer (15%)	T	T	T	T	F	F	F	F
Loyalty card (10%)	T	T	F	F	T	T	F	F
Coupon (20%)	T	F	T	F	T	F	T	F
Actions								
Discount (%)	X	X	20	15	30	10	20	0

Because we have exactly the same action (and presumably the same error message) for both columns 1 and 2, we can see that having a coupon makes no difference to the outcome, that is, we do not care whether you have a coupon or not, as it makes no difference to the actions or outcome. This means that we can slightly collapse or shorten the table as shown in Table 4.9. We have put a dash (–) to show that it does not matter whether coupon is True or False. This is not very significant for such a small example. We could also put 'N/A' (Not Applicable) to show that this value does not affect the outcome. We can combine two or more columns in this way, as long as they all have the same resulting actions or outcomes. See Copeland [2004] for more information.

With more complex decision tables, being able to collapse the table by combining columns (or deleting a column) can make the table much easier to read and understand. For clarity, we have just removed 'Rule 2' and kept the other rule numbers as they were. This could be changed to make the rule numbers sequential in the final table. More information about collapsing decision tables is covered in the ISTQB Advanced Level Test Analyst Syllabus.

TABLE 4.9 Collapsed decision table for credit card example

Conditions	Rule 1	Rule 3	Rule 4	Rule 5	Rule 6	Rule 7	Rule 8
New customer (15%)	T	T	T	F	F	F	F
Loyalty card (10%)	T	F	F	T	T	F	F
Coupon (20%)	–	T	F	T	F	T	F
Actions							
Discount (%)	X	20	15	30	10	20	0

We have made an assumption in Rule 3. Since the coupon has a greater discount than the new customer discount, we assume that the customer will choose 20% rather than 15%. We cannot add them, since the coupon cannot be used with the new customer discount. The 20% action is an assumption on our part, and we should check that this assumption (and any other assumptions that we make) is correct, by asking the person who wrote the specification or the users.

For Rule 5, however, we can add the discounts, since both the coupon and the loyalty card discount should apply (at least that is our assumption).

Rules 4, 6 and 7 have only one type of discount and Rule 8 has no discount, so is 0%.

If we are applying this technique thoroughly, we would have one test for each column or rule of our decision table. The advantage of doing this is that we may test a combination of things that otherwise we might not have tested and that could find a defect. Coverage of decision table testing is measured by the number of columns that have at least one test case, divided by the total number of columns.

However, if we have a lot of combinations, it may not be possible or sensible to test every combination. Or if we are time-constrained, we may not have time to test all combinations. Do not just assume that all combinations need to be tested; it is better to prioritize and test the most important combinations. Having the full table enables us to see which combinations we decided to test and which not to test this time.

There may also be many different actions as a result of the combinations of conditions. In the example above we just had one: the discount to be applied. The decision table shows which actions apply to each combination of conditions.

In the example above all the conditions are binary, that is, they have only two possible values: True or False (or, if you prefer Yes or No). Often it is the case that conditions are more complex, having potentially many possible values. Where this is the case the number of combinations is likely to be very large, so the combinations may only be sampled rather than exercising all of them.

4.2.4 State transition testing

State transition testing is used where some aspect of the system can be described in what is called a 'finite state machine'. This simply means that the system can be in a limited (finite) number of different states, and the transitions from one state to another are determined by the rules of the 'machine'. This is the model on which the system and the tests are based. Any system where you get a different output for the same input, depending on what has happened before, is a finite state system. A finite state system is often shown as a state diagram (see Figure 4.2).

For example, if you request to withdraw $100 from a bank ATM, you may be given cash. Later you may make exactly the same request but be refused the money (because your balance is insufficient). This later refusal is because the state of your bank account has changed from having sufficient funds to cover the withdrawal to having insufficient funds. When the same event can result in two different transitions, depending on some True/False condition (in this case sufficient funds), this is referred to as a 'guard condition' on the transition. The funds will be dispensed only when the guard condition of sufficient funds is True. Guard conditions are shown on a state diagram in square brackets by the transition that they are guarding. The transaction that caused your account to change its state was probably the earlier withdrawal. A state diagram can represent a model from the point of view of the system, the account or the customer.

Another example is a word processor. If a document is open, you are able to close it. If no document is open, then Close is not available. After you choose Close once, you cannot choose it again for the same document unless you open that document. A document thus has two states: open and closed.

State transition testing (finite state testing) A black-box test technique using a state transition diagram or state table to derive test cases to evaluate whether the test item successfully executes valid transitions and blocks invalid transitions.

A state transition model has four basic parts:

- The states that the software may occupy (open/closed or funded/insufficient funds).
- The transitions from one state to another (not all transitions are allowed).
- The events that cause a transition (closing a file or withdrawing money).
- The actions that result from a transition (an error message or being given your cash).

Note that in any given state, one event can cause only one action, but that the same event from a different state may cause a different action and a different end state.

We will look first at test cases that execute valid state transitions.

Figure 4.2 shows an example of entering a PIN to a bank account. The states are shown as circles, the transitions as lines with arrows and the events as the text near the transitions. We have not shown the actions explicitly on this diagram, but they would be a message to the customer saying things such as 'Please enter your PIN'.

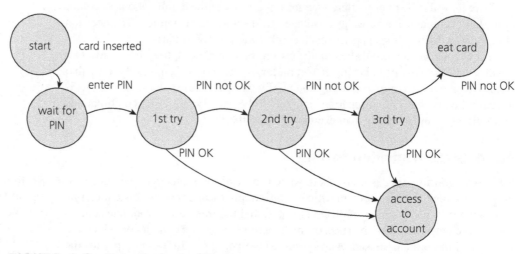

FIGURE 4.2   State diagram for PIN entry

The state diagram shows seven states but only four possible events (Card inserted, Enter PIN, PIN OK and PIN not OK). We have not specified all of the possible transitions here: there would also be a time-out from 'wait for PIN' and from the three tries. The system would go back to the start state after the time had elapsed and would probably eject the card. There would also be a transition from the 'eat card' state back to the start state. We have not specified all the possible events either – there would be a 'cancel' option from 'wait for PIN' and from the three tries, which would also go back to the start state and eject the card. The 'access account' state would be the beginning of another state diagram showing the valid transactions that could now be performed on the account. This state diagram, even though it is incomplete, still gives us information on which to design some useful tests and to explain the state transition technique.

In deriving test cases, we may start with a typical scenario. A sensible first test case here would be the normal situation, where the correct PIN is entered the first time. To be more thorough, we may want to make sure that we cover every state (that is, at least one test goes through each state) or we may want to cover every transition. A second test (to visit every state) would be to enter an incorrect PIN each time, so that the system eats the card. We still have not tested every transition yet. In order to do that, we would want a test where the PIN was incorrect the first time but OK the second time, and another test where the PIN was correct on the third try. These tests are probably less important than the first two.

Note that a transition does not need to change to a different state (although all of the transitions shown above do go to a different state). There could be a transition from 'access account' which just goes back to 'access account' for an action such as 'request balance'.

Test conditions can be derived from the state diagram in various ways. Each state can be noted as a test condition, as can each transition. In the Syllabus, we need to be able to identify the coverage of a set of tests in terms of states or transitions.

Tests can be designed to cover a typical sequence of states, to visit all states, to exercise every transition, to exercise specific transition sequences, or to test invalid transitions (see below).

Going beyond the level expected in the Syllabus, we can also consider transition pairs and triples and so on. Coverage of all individual transitions is also known as 0-switch coverage, coverage of transition pairs is 1-switch coverage, coverage of transition triples is 2-switch coverage, etc. Deriving test cases from the state transition model is a black-box approach. Measuring how much you have tested (covered) is getting close to a white-box perspective. However, state transition testing is regarded as a black-box technique. More information on coverage criteria for state transition testing is covered in the ISTQB Advanced Level Test Analyst Syllabus.

One of the advantages of the state transition technique is that the model can be as detailed or as abstract as you need it to be. Where a part of the system is more important (that is, requires more testing) a greater depth of detail can be modelled. Where the system is less important (requires less testing), the model can use a single state to signify what would otherwise be a series of different states.

Testing for invalid transitions

Deriving tests only from a state diagram or chart (also known as a state graph or chart) is very good for seeing the valid transitions, but we may not easily see the negative tests, where we try to generate invalid transitions. In order to see the total number of combinations of states and transitions, both valid and invalid, a state table is useful.

The state table lists all the states down one side of the table and all the events that cause transitions along the top (or vice versa). Each cell then represents a state-event pair. The content of each cell indicates which state the system will move to when the corresponding event occurs while in the associated state. This will include possible erroneous events – events that are not expected to happen in certain states. These are negative test conditions.

Table 4.10 lists the states in the first column and the possible events across the top row. So, for example, if the system is in State 1, inserting a card will take it to State 2. If we are in State 2, and a valid PIN is entered, we go to State 6 to access the account. In State 2 if we enter an invalid PIN, we go to State 3. We have put a dash in the cells that should be impossible, that is, they represent invalid transitions from that state.

We have put a question mark for two cells, where we enter either a valid or invalid PIN when we are accessing the account. Perhaps the system will take our PIN number as the amount of cash to withdraw? It might be a good test! Most of the other invalid cells would be physically impossible in this example. Invalid (negative) tests will attempt to generate invalid transitions, transitions that should not be possible (but often make good tests when it turns out they are possible).

TABLE 4.10 State table for the PIN example

	Insert card	**Valid PIN**	**Invalid PIN**
S1) Start state	S2	–	–
S2) Wait for PIN	–	S6	S3
S3) 1st try invalid	–	S6	S4
S4) 2nd try invalid	–	S6	S5
S5) 3rd try invalid	–	–	S7
S6) Access account	–	?	?
S7) Eat card	S1 (for new card)	–	–

State transition testing is used for screen-based applications, for example an ATM, and also within the embedded software industry. It is useful for modelling business scenarios which have specific states, or for testing navigation around screens.

A more extensive description of state machines is found in Marick [1994]. State transition testing is also described in Craig and Jaskiel [2002], Copeland [2004], Beizer [1990], Broekman and Notenboom [2003], and Black [2007]. State transition testing is described in ISO/IEC/IEEE 29119-4 [2015], including designing tests and coverage measures.

4.2.5 Use case testing

Use case testing (scenario testing, user scenario testing) A black-box test technique in which test cases are designed to execute scenarios of use cases.

Use case testing is a technique that helps us identify test cases that exercise the whole system on a transaction by transaction basis from start to finish. They are described by Ivar Jacobson in his book *Object-Oriented Software Engineering: A Use Case Driven Approach* [Jacobson 1992]. Information on use cases can also be found at Omg.org in UML 2.5 [2017].

A use case is a description of a particular use of the system by an actor (a human user of the system, external hardware or other components or systems). Each use case describes the interactions the actor has with the subject (i.e. the component or system to which the use case is applied), in order to achieve a specific task (or, at least, produce something of value to the actor). Use cases are a sequence of steps that describe the interactions between the actor and the subject. A use case is a specific way of designing interactions with software items, incorporating requirements for the software functions represented by the use cases.

Each use case specifies some behaviour that a subject can perform in collaboration with one or more actors. The interactions between the actors and the subject may result in changes to the state of the subject. These interactions can be represented graphically by workflows activity diagrams or business process models. They can also be described as a series of steps or even in natural language.

Use cases are defined in terms of the actor, not the system, describing what the actor does and what the actor sees rather than what inputs the system expects and what the system outputs. They often use the language and terms of the business rather than technical terms, especially when the actor is a business user. They serve as the foundation for developing test cases, mostly at the system and acceptance testing levels.

Use cases can uncover integration defects, that is, defects caused by the incorrect interaction between different components. Used in this way, the actor may be something that the system interfaces to such as a communication link or subsystem.

Use cases describe the process flows through a system based on its most likely use. This makes the test cases derived from use cases particularly good for finding defects in the real-world use of the system (that is, the defects that the users are most likely to come across when first using the system). Each use case usually has a mainstream (or most likely) scenario and sometimes additional alternative branches (covering, for example, special cases or exceptional conditions and error conditions, such as system response and recovery from errors in programming, the application and communication). Each use case must specify any preconditions that need to be met for the use case to work. Use cases must also specify postconditions that are observable results and a description of the final state of the system after the use case has been executed successfully.

The PIN example that we used for state transition testing could also be defined in terms of use cases, as shown in Figure 4.3. We show a success scenario and the extensions (which represent the ways in which the scenario could fail to be a success).

For use case testing, we would have a test of the success scenario and one test for each extension. In this example, we may give extension 4b a higher priority than 4a from a security point of view.

System requirements can also be specified as a set of use cases. This approach can make it easier to involve the users in the requirements gathering and definition process.

	Step	Description
Main Success Scenario **A: Actor** **S: System**	1	A: Inserts card
	2	S: Validates card and asks for PIN
	3	A: Enters PIN
	4	S: Validates PIN
	5	S: Allows access to account
Extensions	2a	Card not valid S: Display message and reject card
	4a	PIN not valid S: Display message and ask for re-try (twice)
	4b	PIN invalid 3 times S: Eat card and exit

FIGURE 4.3 Partial use case for PIN entry

Coverage of use case testing can be measured by the percentage of use case behaviours tested divided by the total number of use case behaviours. It is possible to measure coverage of normal behaviour, exceptional and/or error behaviour, or all behaviours. More information on coverage criteria for use case testing is covered in the ISTQB Advanced Level Test Analyst Syllabus.

4.3 WHITE-BOX TEST TECHNIQUES

SYLLABUS LEARNING OBJECTIVES FOR 4.3 WHITE-BOX TEST TECHNIQUES (K2)

FL-4.3.1   Explain statement coverage (K2)

FL-4.3.2   Explain decision coverage (K2)

FL-4.3.3   Explain the value of statement and decision coverage (K2)

In this section we will look in detail at the concept of coverage and how it can be used to measure some aspects of the thoroughness of testing. In order to see how coverage actually works, we will use some code-level examples (although coverage also applies to other levels such as business procedures). In particular, we will show how to measure coverage of statements and decisions, and how to write test cases to extend coverage if it is not 100%.

As mentioned, we will illustrate white-box test techniques that would typically apply at the component level of testing. At this level, white-box techniques focus on the structure of a software component, such as statements, decisions, branches or even distinct paths. These techniques can also be applied at the integration level. At this level, white-box techniques can examine structures such as a call tree, which is a diagram that shows how modules call other modules. These techniques can also be applied at the system level. At this level, white-box techniques can examine structures such as a menu structure, business process or web page structure.

There are also more advanced white-box test techniques at component level, particularly for safety-critical, mission-critical or high-integrity environments to achieve higher levels of coverage. For more information on these techniques see the ISTQB Advanced Level Technical Test Analyst Syllabus.

In this section, look for the definitions of the Glossary terms **decision coverage** and **statement coverage**.

White-box test techniques serve two purposes: coverage measurement and structural test case design. They are often used first to assess the amount of testing performed by tests derived from black-box test techniques, that is, to assess coverage. They are then used to design additional tests with the aim of increasing the coverage.

White-box test techniques used to design tests are a good way of generating additional test cases that are different from existing tests. They can help ensure more breadth of testing, in the sense that test cases that achieve 100% coverage in any measure will be exercising all parts of the software from the point of view of the items being covered.

What is coverage?

Coverage measures the amount of testing performed by a set of tests that may have been derived in a different way, for example using black-box techniques. Wherever we can count things and can tell whether or not each of those things has been tested by some test, then we can measure coverage. The basic coverage measure is:

$$\text{Coverage} = \frac{\text{Number of coverage items exercised}}{\text{Total number of coverage items}} \times 100\%$$

where the coverage item is whatever we have been able to count and see whether a test has exercised or used this item.

A Christmas gift to one of the authors was a map of the world where you can scratch off the countries you have visited. This is a very good analogy for coverage. If I visit a small country, for example Belgium, it seems quite OK to scratch off the whole country. But if I visit the US, Canada, Australia, China or Russia, then do I scratch off the whole country? Even if I have only visited one or a few cities, I can still count the whole country and this seems not quite right. But this would be country coverage. I can count the countries I have visited, divided by the total number of countries in the world, and get a percentage, for example around 18% for visiting 36 countries. However, if you look at the map, it looks like I have covered around 25% of the area (since I have been to the US, Canada, Australia and China). If I were to do area-of-the-map coverage, I would get a higher coverage percentage, but I would not have seen any more of the world. If I now visit St Petersburg in Russia, I increase my country coverage by less than 1%, but increase my area coverage by 12.5%! Why are we talking about this map? Because it highlights some of the same aspects and pitfalls of coverage for components and systems.

There are several dangers (pitfalls or caveats) in using coverage measures:

- 100% coverage does *not* mean 100% tested! Coverage techniques measure only one dimension of a multi-dimensional concept. Country coverage is a higher level than state, county or city coverage.

- Two different test cases may achieve exactly the same coverage but the input data of one may find an error that the input data of the other does not. If you do not execute a line or block of code that contains a bug, you are guaranteed not to see the failures that bug can cause. However, just because you did execute that line or block, does not guarantee that you will see the failures that bug can cause. There may be many different data combinations that exercise the same True/False decision outcome, but some will cause a failure and others will not.

- Coverage looks only at what *has* been written, that is the code itself. It cannot say anything about the software that has *not* been written. If a specified function has not been implemented, black-box test techniques will reveal this. If a function was omitted from the specification, then experience-based techniques may find it. But white-box techniques can only look at a structure which is already there.

- Just because some coverage item has been covered, this does NOT mean that this part of the system is actually doing what it should. Coverage only assesses whether or not you have exercised something, not whether that test passed or failed or whether it was a good test worth running. Coverage says nothing about the quality of either the system or the tests.

So is coverage worth measuring? Yes, coverage can be useful. It is a way of assessing one aspect of thoroughness. But it is best used when you understand exactly what you are measuring, and are aware of the pitfalls, particularly if you are reporting coverage to stakeholders.

Types of coverage

Coverage can be measured based on a number of different structural elements in a system or component. Coverage can be measured at component testing level, integration testing level or at system or acceptance testing levels. For example, at system or acceptance level, the coverage items may be requirements, menu options, screens or typical business transactions. Other coverage measures include things such as database structural elements (records, fields and sub-fields) and files. It is worth checking for any new tools, as the test tool market develops quite rapidly.

At integration level, we could measure coverage of interfaces or specific interactions that have been tested. The call coverage of APIs, modules, objects or procedure calls can also be measured (and is supported by tools to some extent).

There is good tool support for code coverage, that is, for component-level testing. We can measure coverage for each of the black-box test techniques as well:

- Equivalance partitioning: percentage of equivalence partitions exercised (we could measure valid and invalid partition coverage separately if this makes sense).
- Boundary value analysis: percentage of boundaries exercised (we could also separate valid and invalid boundaries if we wished).
- Decision tables: percentage of business rules or decision table columns tested.
- State transition testing: there are a number of possible coverage measures:
  - Percentage of states visited.
  - Percentage of (valid) transitions exercised (this is known as Chow's 0-switch coverage).
  - Percentage of pairs of valid transitions exercised ('transition pairs' or Chow's 1-switch coverage) – and longer series of transitions, such as transition triples, quadruples, etc.
  - Percentage of invalid transitions exercised (from the state table).

The coverage measures for black-box techniques would apply at whichever test level the technique has been used (for example system or component level).

When coverage is discussed by product owners, business analysts, system testers or users, it most likely refers to the percentage of requirements that have been tested by a set of tests. This may be measured by a tool such as a requirements management tool or a test management tool.

However, when coverage is discussed by programmers, it most likely refers to the coverage of code, where the structural elements can be identified using a tool. We will cover statement and decision coverage shortly. However, at this point, note that the word coverage is often misused to mean, 'How many or what percentage of tests have been run?' This is **NOT** what the term coverage refers to. Coverage is the coverage **of** something else **by** the tests. The percentage of tests run should be called test completeness or something similar.

Statements and decision outcomes are both structures that can be measured in code and there is good tool support for these coverage measures. Code coverage is normally done in component and component integration testing, if it is done at all. If someone claims to have achieved code coverage, it is important to establish exactly what elements of the code have been covered, as statement coverage (often what is meant) is significantly weaker than decision coverage or some of the other code coverage measures.

How to measure coverage

For most practical purposes, coverage measurement is something that requires tool support. However, knowledge of the steps typically taken to measure coverage is useful in understanding the relative merits of each technique. Our example assumes an intrusive coverage measurement tool that alters the code by inserting instrumentation:

1 Decide on the structural element to be used, that is, the coverage items to be counted.

2 Count the structural elements or items.

3 Instrument the code.

4 Run the tests for which coverage measurement is required.

5 Using the output from the instrumentation, determine the percentage of elements or items exercised.

Instrumenting the code (step 3) involves inserting code alongside each structural element in order to record when that structural element has been exercised. Determining the actual coverage measure (step 5) is then a matter of analyzing the recorded information.

Coverage measurement of code is best done using tools (as described in Chapter 6) and there are a number of such tools on the market. These tools can help to support increased quality and productivity of testing. They support increased quality by ensuring that more structural aspects are tested, so defects on those structural paths can be found (and fixed, otherwise quality has not increased). They support increased productivity and efficiency by highlighting tests that may be redundant, that is, testing the same structure as other tests, although this is not necessarily a bad thing, since we may find a defect testing the same structure with different data.

In common with all white-box test techniques, code coverage techniques are best used on areas of software code where more thorough testing is required. Safety-critical code, code that is vital to the correct operation of a system, and complex pieces of code are all examples of where white-box techniques are particularly worth applying. For example, some standards for safety-critical systems such as avionics and vehicle control, require white-box coverage for certain types of system. White-box test techniques should normally be used in addition to black-box and experience-based test techniques rather than as an alternative to them.

White-box test design

If you are aiming for a given level of coverage (say 95%) but you have not reached your target (for example you only have 87% so far), then additional test cases can be designed with the aim of exercising some or all of the structural elements not yet reached. This is white-box or structure-based test design. These new tests are then run through the instrumented code and a new coverage measure is calculated. This is repeated until the required coverage measure is achieved (or until you decide that your goal was too ambitious!). Ideally all the tests ought to be run again on the un-instrumented code.

We will look at some examples of structure-based coverage and test design for statement and decision testing below.

4.3.1 Statement testing and coverage

Statement coverage is calculated by:

$$\text{Statement coverage} = \frac{\text{Number of statements exercised}}{\text{Total number of statements}} \times 100\%$$

Studies and experience in the industry have indicated that what is considered reasonably thorough black-box testing may actually achieve only 60% to 75% statement coverage. Typical ad hoc testing is likely to achieve only around 30%, leaving 70% of the statements untested.

Different coverage tools may work in slightly different ways, so they may give different coverage figures for the same set of tests on the same code, although at 100% coverage they should be the same.

We will illustrate the principles of coverage on code. In order to explain our examples, we will use two types of code examples, one a basic pseudo-code – this is not any specific programming language, but should be readable and understandable to you, even if you have not done any programming yourself – and the second is more like javascript. Both give the same control flow. We have omitted the set-up code that is needed to actually run the code, to concentrate on the logic.

For example, consider Code samples 4.1a and 4.1b.

```
READ A
READ B
IF A > B THEN C = 0
ENDIF
```

Code sample 4.1a

```
let a = Number(args[2])
let b = Number(args[3])
if (a > b) {
        c = 0
}
```

Code sample 4.1b

To achieve 100% statement coverage of this code segment just one test case is required, one which ensures that variable A contains a value that is greater than the value of variable B, for example, A = 12 and B = 10. Note that here we are doing structural test *design* first, since we are choosing our input values in order to ensure statement coverage.

Let's look at an example where we measure coverage first. In order to simplify the example, we will regard each line as a statement. Different tools and methods may count different things as statements, but the basic principle is the same however they are counted. A statement may be on a single line, or it may be spread over several lines. One line may contain more than one statement, just one statement or only part of a statement. Some statements can contain other statements inside them. In Code samples 4.2, we have two read statements, one assignment statement and then one IF statement on three lines, but the IF statement contains another statement (print) as part of it.

```
1 READ A
2 READ B
3 C = A + 2*B
4 IF C > 50 THEN
5       PRINT 'Large C'
6 ENDIF
```

Code sample 4.2a

```
1 let a = Number(args[2])
2 let b = Number(args[3])
3 let c = a + 2*b
4 if (c > 50) {
5     console.log('C large')
6 }
```

Code sample 4.2b

Although it is not completely correct, we have numbered each line and will regard each line as a statement. Some tools may group statements that would always be executed together in a basic block which is regarded as a single statement. However, we will just use numbered lines to illustrate the principle of coverage of statements (lines). Let's analyze the coverage of a set of tests on our six-statement program:

TEST SET 1

> Test 1_1: A = 2; B = 3
> Test 1_2: A = 0; B = 25
> Test 1_3: A = 47, B = 1

Which statements have we covered?

- In Test 1_1, the value of C will be 8, so we will cover the statements on lines 1 to 4 and line 6.
- In Test 1_2, the value of C will be 50, so we will cover exactly the same statements as Test 1_1.
- In Test 1_3, the value of C will be 49, so again we will cover the same statements.

Since we have covered five out of six statements, we have 83% statement coverage (with three tests). What test would we need in order to cover statement 5, the one statement that we haven't exercised yet? How about this one:

> Test 1_4: A = 20; B = 25

This time the value of C is 70, so we will print 'Large C' and we will have exercised all six of the statements, so now statement coverage = 100%. Notice that we measured coverage first, and then designed a test to cover the statement that we had not yet covered.

Note that Test 1_4 on its own is more effective (towards our goal of achieving 100% statement coverage) than the first three tests together. Just taking Test 1_4 on its own is also more efficient than the set of four tests, since it has used only one test instead of four. Being more effective and more efficient is the mark of a good test technique.

4.3.2 Decision testing and coverage

A decision is an IF statement, a loop control statement (for example DO–WHILE or REPEAT–UNTIL), or a CASE statement, where there are two or more possible exits or outcomes from the statement. With an IF statement, the exit can either be True or False, depending on the value of the logical condition that comes after IF. With a loop control statement, the outcome is either to perform the code within the loop or not – again a True or False exit. **Decision coverage** is calculated by:

$$\text{Decision coverage} = \frac{\text{Number of decision outcomes exercised}}{\text{Total number of decision outcomes}} \times 100\%$$

Decision coverage
The coverage of decision outcomes. (Note: this is the Glossary definition at publication, but a fuller definition would be: The percentage of decision outcomes that have been exercised by a test suite.)

What feels like reasonably thorough black-box testing may achieve only 40 to 60% decision coverage. Typical ad hoc testing may cover only 20% of the decisions, leaving 80% of the possible outcomes untested. Even if your testing seems reasonably thorough from a functional or black-box perspective, you may have only covered two-thirds or three-quarters of the decisions. Decision coverage is stronger than statement coverage. It 'subsumes' statement coverage – this means that 100% decision coverage always guarantees 100% statement coverage. Any stronger coverage measure may require more test cases to achieve 100% coverage.

Let's go back to Code samples 4.2 again. We saw earlier that just one test case was required to achieve 100% statement coverage. However, decision coverage requires each decision to have had both a True and False outcome. Therefore, to achieve 100% decision coverage, a second test case is necessary where A is less than or equal to B. This will ensure that the decision statement IF A > B has a False outcome. So one test is sufficient for 100% statement coverage, but two tests are needed for 100% decision coverage. Note that 100% decision coverage guarantees 100% statement coverage, but *not* the other way around!

Now let us consider slightly different Code samples shown in Code samples 4.3a and 4.3b.

```
1 READ A
2 READ B
3 C = A - 2*B
4 IF C < 0 THEN
5      PRINT 'C negative'
6 ENDIF
```

Code sample 4.3a

```
1 let a = Number(args[2])
2 let b = Number(args[3])
3 let c = a - 2*b
4 if (c < 0) {
5      console.log('C negative')
6 }
```

Code sample 4.3b

Let us suppose that we already have the following test, which gives us 100% statement coverage for Code samples 4.3.

TEST SET 2

Test 2_1: A = 20; B = 15

Which decision outcomes have we exercised with our test? The value of C is −10, so the condition C < 0 is True, so we will print 'C negative' and we have exercised the True outcome from that decision statement. But we have not exercised the decision outcome of False. What other test would we need to exercise the False outcome and to achieve 100% decision coverage?

Before we answer that question, let's have a look at another way to represent this code. Sometimes the decision structure is easier to see in a control flow diagram (see Figure 4.4).

The dotted line shows where Test 2_1 has gone and clearly shows that we have not yet had a test that takes the False exit from the IF statement.

Let's modify our existing test set by adding another test:

TEST SET 2

Test 2_1: A = 20; B = 15
Test 2_2: A = 10; B = 2

This now covers both of the decision outcomes, True (with Test 2_1) and False (with Test 2_2). If we were to draw the path taken by Test 2_2, it would be a straight line from the read statement down the False exit and through the ENDIF. Note that we could have chosen other numbers to achieve either the True or False outcomes.

4.3.3 The value of statement and decision testing

Coverage is a partial measure of some aspect of the thoroughness of testing; in this section, we have looked at two types of coverage, statement and decision. The value of statement and decision testing is in seeing what new tests are needed in order to achieve a higher level of coverage, whatever dimension of coverage we are looking at. By being more thorough (even in a very limited way), we are leaving less of the component or system completely untested.

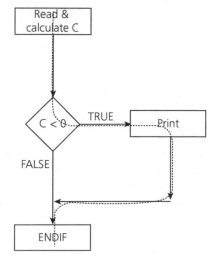

FIGURE 4.4   Control flow diagram for Code samples 4.3

One client decided to measure coverage and found that their supposedly thorough tests only reached 60% decision coverage. They decided to write more tests to increase this to 80%. Although they spent 3 weeks designing and implementing these new tests, they found enough high-severity defects to justify spending that time.

White-box coverage measures and related test techniques are described in ISO/IEC /IEEE 29119-4 [2015]. White-box test techniques are also discussed in Copeland [2003] and Myers [2011]. A good description of the graph theory behind structural testing can be found in Jorgensen [2014], and Hetzel [1988] also shows a structural approach. Pol, Teunissen and van Veenendaal [2001] describes a white-box approach called an algorithm test.

4.4 EXPERIENCE-BASED TEST TECHNIQUES

SYLLABUS LEARNING OBJECTIVES FOR 4.4 EXPERIENCE-BASED TEST TECHNIQUES (K2)

FL-4.4.1   Explain error guessing (K2)

FL-4.4.2   Explain exploratory testing (K2)

FL-4.4.3   Explain checklist-based testing (K2)

In this section we will look at three experience-based techniques, why and when they are useful, and how they fit with black-box test techniques.

Although it is true that testing should be rigorous, thorough and systematic, this is not all there is to testing. There is a definite role for non-systematic techniques, that is, tests based on a person's knowledge, experience, imagination and intuition. The reason is that some defects are hard to find using more systematic approaches, so a good bug hunter can be very creative at finding those elusive defects.

One aspect which is more difficult for experience-based techniques is the measurement of coverage. In order to measure coverage, we need to have some idea of a full set of things that we could possibly test, coverage then being the percentage of that set that we did test. For example, we could look at the coverage of the items in the test charter, a checklist or a set of heuristics. We should also be able to use the traceability of tests to requirements or user stories and look at coverage of those.

In this section, look for the definitions of the Glossary terms **checklist-based testing**, **error guessing** and **exploratory testing**.

4.4.1 Error guessing

Error guessing A test technique in which tests are derived on the basis of the tester's knowledge of past failures, or general knowledge of failure modes.

Error guessing is a technique that is good to be used as a complement to other more formal techniques. The success of error guessing is very much dependent on the skill of the tester, as good testers know where the defects are most likely to lurk. Some people seem to be naturally good at testing. Others are good testers because they have a lot of experience either as a tester or working with a particular system and so are able to pin-point its weaknesses. This is why error guessing, used after more formal techniques have been applied to some extent, can be very effective. In using more formal techniques, the tester is likely to gain a better understanding of the system, what it does and how it works. With this better understanding, they are likely to be better at guessing ways in which the system may not work properly.

There are no rules for error guessing. The tester is encouraged to think of situations in which the software may not be able to cope. Here are some typical things to try: division by zero, blank (or no) input, empty files and the wrong kind of data (for example alphabetic characters where numeric are required). If anyone ever says of a system or the environment in which it is to operate 'That could never happen', it might be a good idea to test that condition, as such assumptions about what will and will not happen in the live environment are often the cause of failures.

Error guessing may be based on:

- How the application has worked in the past.
- What types of mistakes the developers tend to make.
- Failures that have occurred in other applications.

A structured approach to the error-guessing technique is to list possible defects or failures and to design tests that attempt to produce them. These defect and failure lists can be built based on the tester's own experience or that of other people, available defect and failure data, and from common knowledge about why software fails. This way of trying to force specific types of fault to occur is sometimes called an 'attack' or 'fault attack'. See Whittaker [2003].

4.4.2 Exploratory testing

Exploratory testing is a hands-on approach in which testers are involved in minimum planning and maximum test execution. The planning involves the creation of a test charter, a short declaration of the scope of a short (one- to two-hour) time-boxed test effort, the objectives and possible approaches to be used.

> **Exploratory testing**
> An approach to testing whereby the testers dynamically design and execute tests based on their knowledge, exploration of the test item and the results of previous tests.

The test design and test execution activities are performed in parallel, typically without formally documenting the test conditions, test cases or test scripts. The tests are informal, because they are not pre-defined or documented in advance in detail (although a test charter is most often written in advance). This does not mean that other, more formal testing techniques will not be used. For example, the tester may decide to use BVA, but will think through and test the most important boundary values without necessarily writing them down. Some notes will be written while the exploratory testing is going on, so that a report can be produced afterwards.

One typical way to organize and manage exploratory testing is to have sessions, hence this is also known as session-based testing. Each session is time-boxed, for example with a firm time limit of 90 minutes. A test charter will give a list of test conditions (sometimes referred to as objectives for the test session), but the testing does not have to conform completely to that charter, particularly if new areas of high risk are discovered in the session. The test session is completely dedicated to the testing, without extraneous interruptions.

Test logging is undertaken as test execution is performed, documenting (at a high level) the key aspects of what is tested, any defects found and any thoughts about possible further testing, possibly using test session sheets. A key aspect of exploratory testing is learning: learning by the tester about the software, its use, its strengths and its weaknesses. As its name implies, exploratory testing is about exploring, finding out about the software, what it does, what it does not do, what works and what does not work. The tester is constantly making decisions about what to test next and where to spend the (limited) time.

This is an approach that is most useful when there are no or poor specifications and when time is severely limited. It can also serve to complement other, more formal testing, helping to establish greater confidence in the software. In this way, exploratory testing can be used as a check on the formal test process by helping to ensure that the most serious defects have been found.

Exploratory testing is described in Kaner, Bach and Petticord [2002] and Copeland [2003]. Other ways of testing in an exploratory way (attacks) are described by Whittaker [2003].

4.4.3 Checklist-based testing

Checklist-based testing is testing based on experience, but that experience has been summarized and documented in a checklist. Testers use the checklist to design, implement and execute tests based on the items or test conditions found in the checklist. The checklist may be based on:

Checklist-based testing An experience-based test technique whereby the experienced tester uses a high-level list of items to be noted, checked, or remembered, or a set of rules or criteria against which a product has to be verified.

- experience of the tester
- knowledge, for example what is important for the user
- understanding of why and how software fails.

When using a checklist, the tester may modify it by adding new questions or things to check, or may just use what is already there. An experienced tester may be the one who writes the first version of the checklist as a way to help less experienced testers do better testing.

Checklists can be general, or more likely, aimed at particular areas such as different test types and levels. For example, a checklist for functional testing would be quite different from one aimed at testing non-function quality attributes.

If different people use the same checklist, it is more likely that there will a degree of consistency in what is tested. However, the actual tests executed may be quite different, since the checklist is only mentioning high-level items. This variability, even while using the same checklist, may help to uncover more defects and achieve different levels of coverage (if that is measured), even though it is less repeatable due to human creativity (which is a good thing).

CHAPTER REVIEW

Let's review what you have learned in this chapter.

From Section 4.1 (categories of test techniques), you should be able to give reasons why black-box, white-box, and experience-based approaches are useful, and be able to explain the characteristics and differences between these types of techniques. You should be able to list the factors that influence the selection of the appropriate test technique for a particular type of problem, such as the type of system, risk, customer requirements, models for use case modelling, requirements models or testing knowledge. You should know the Glossary terms **black-box test technique**, **coverage**, **experience-based test technique**, **test technique** and **white-box test technique**.

From Section 4.2, you should be able to write test cases from given software models using equivalence partitioning (EP), Boundary Value Analysis (BVA), decision table testing and state transition testing. You should understand and be able to apply each of these four techniques, understand what level and type of testing could use each technique and how coverage can be measured for each of them. You should also understand the concept and benefits of use case testing. You should know the Glossary terms **boundary value analysis**, **decision table testing**, **equivalence partitioning**, **state transition testing** and **use case testing**.

From Section 4.3, you should be able to describe the concept and importance of code coverage. You should be able to explain the concepts of statement and decision coverage and understand that these concepts can also be used at test levels other than component testing (such as business procedures at system test level). You should be able to write test cases from given control flows using statement testing and decision testing, and you should be able to assess statement and decision coverage for completeness. You should know the Glossary terms **coverage**, **decision coverage** and **statement coverage**.

From Section 4.4, you should be able to explain the reasons for writing test cases based on intuition, experience and knowledge about common defects and you should be able to compare experience-based techniques with black-box test techniques. You should know the Glossary terms **checklist-based testing**, **error guessing** and **exploratory testing**.

SAMPLE EXAM QUESTIONS

Question 1 Which of the following statements about checklist-based testing is true?

a. A checklist contains test conditions and detailed test cases and procedures.

b. A checklist can be used for functional testing, but not for non-functional testing.

c. Checklists should always be used exactly as written and should not be modified by the tester.

d. Checklists may be based on experience of why and how software fails.

Question 2 In a competition, ribbons are awarded as follows: less than 12 metres, no ribbon, a yellow ribbon up to 25 metres, a red ribbon up to 35 metres, and a blue ribbon for further than that.

What distances (in metres) would be chosen using BVA?

a. 0, 11, 12, 25, 26, 35, 36.

b. 11, 12, 13, 29, 30, 31, 40.

c. 7, 18, 32, 39.

d. 0, 12, 13, 26, 27, 36, 37.

Question 3 Which statement about tests based on increasing statement or decision coverage is true?

a. Increasing statement coverage may find defects where other tests have not taken both true and false outcomes.

b. Increasing statement coverage may find defects in code that was exercised by other tests.

c. Increasing decision coverage may find defects where other tests have not taken both true and false outcomes.

d. Increasing decision coverage may find defects in code that was exercised by other tests.

Question 4 Why are both black-box and white-box test techniques useful?

a. They find different types of defect.

b. Using more techniques is always better.

c. Both find the same types of defect.

d. Because specifications tend to be unstructured.

Question 5 What is a key characteristic of white-box test techniques?

a. They are mainly used to assess the structure of a specification.

b. They are used both to measure coverage and to design tests to increase coverage.

c. They are based on the skills and experience of the tester.

d. They use a formal or informal model of the software or component.

Question 6 Which of the following would be an example of decision table testing for a financial application, applied at the system-test level?

a. A table containing rules for combinations of inputs to two fields on a screen.

b. A table containing rules for interfaces between components.

c. A table containing rules for mortgage applications.

d. A table containing rules for basic arithmetic to two decimal places.

Question 7 Which of the following could be a coverage measure for state transition testing?

V All states have been reached.

W The response time for each transaction is adequate.

X Every transition has been exercised.

Y All boundaries have been exercised.

Z Specific sequences of transitions have been exercised.

a. X, Y and Z.

b. V, X, Y and Z.

c. W, X and Y.

d. V, X and Z.

Question 8 Postal rates for light letters are $0.25 up to 10g, $0.35 up to 50g plus an extra $0.10 for each additional 25g up to 100g.

Which test inputs (in grams) would be selected using equivalence partitioning (EP)?

a. 8, 42, 82, 102.

b. 4, 15, 65, 92, 159.

c. 10, 50, 75, 100.

d. 5, 20, 40, 60, 80.

Question 9 Which of the following could be used to assess the coverage achieved for black-box test techniques?

V Decision outcomes exercised.

W Partitions exercised.

X Boundaries exercised.

Y State transitions exercised.

Z Statements exercised.

a. V, W, Y or Z.

b. W, X or Y.

c. V, X or Z.

d. W, X, Y or Z.

Question 10 Which of the following would white-box test techniques be most likely to be applied to?

1) Boundaries between mortgage interest rate bands.

2) An invalid transition between two different arrears statuses.

3) The business process flow for mortgage approval.

4) Control flow of the program to calculate repayments.

a. 2, 3 and 4.

b. 2 and 4.

c. 3 and 4.

d. 1, 2 and 3.

Question 11 Use case testing is useful for which of the following?

P Designing acceptance tests with users or customers.

Q Making sure that the mainstream business processes are tested.

R Finding defects in the interaction between components.

S Identifying the maximum and minimum values for every input field.

T Identifying the percentage of statements exercised by a sets of tests.

a. P, Q and R.

b. Q, S and T.

c. P, Q and S.

d. R, S and T.

Question 12 Which of the following statements about the relationship between statement coverage and decision coverage is correct?

a. 100% decision coverage is achieved if statement coverage is greater than 90%.

b. 100% statement coverage is achieved if decision coverage is greater than 90%.

c. 100% decision coverage always means 100% statement coverage.

d. 100% statement coverage always means 100% decision coverage.

Question 13 Why are experience-based test techniques good to use?

a. They can find defects missed by black-box and white-box test techniques.

b. They do not require any training to be as effective as formal techniques.

c. They can be used most effectively when there are good specifications.

d. They will ensure that all of the code or system is tested.

Question 14 If you are flying with an economy ticket, there is a possibility that you may get upgraded to business class, especially if you hold a gold card in the airline's frequent flier program. If you do not hold a gold card, there is a possibility that you will get bumped off the flight if it is full and you check in late. This is shown in Figure 4.5. Note that each box (that is, statement) has been numbered.

Three tests have been run:

Test 1:   Gold card holder who gets upgraded to business class.

Test 2:   Non-gold card holder who stays in economy.

Test 3:   A person who is bumped from the flight.

What is the statement coverage of these three tests?

a. 60%.

b. 70%.

c. 80%.

d. 90%.

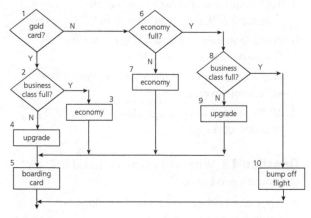

FIGURE 4.5   Control flow diagram for flight check-in

Question 15 Consider the control flow shown in Figure 4.6. In this example, if someone is a member, then they get a 10% discount, but only on items with an ItemCode of 25 or less. The following tests have already been run:

Test 1: Name is a member, ItemCode = 50

Test 2: Name is not a member, ItemCode = 27

FIGURE 4.6   Control flow diagram for Question 15

What is the statement coverage and decision coverage of these tests?

a. Statement coverage = 100%, Decision coverage = 100%.

b. Statement coverage = 100%, Decision coverage = 50%.

c. Statement coverage = 75%, Decision coverage = 100%.

d. Statement coverage = 100%, Decision coverage = 75%.

Question 16 When choosing which technique to use in a given situation, which factors should be taken into account?

U Previous experience of types of defects found in this or similar systems.

V The existing knowledge of the testers.

W Regulatory standards that apply.

X The type of test execution tool that will be used.

Y The work products available.

Z Previous experience in the development language.

a. V, W, Y and Z.

b. U, V, W and Y.

c. U, X and Y.

d. V, W and Y.

Question 17 Given the state diagram in Figure 4.7, which test case is the minimum series of valid transitions to cover every state?

a. SS – S1 – S2 – S4 – S1 – S3 – ES.

b. SS – S1 – S2 – S3 – S4 – ES.

c. SS – S1 – S2 – S4 – S1 – S3 – S4 – S1 – S3 – ES.

d. SS S1 S4 S2 S1 S3 ES.

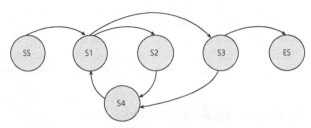

FIGURE 4.7 State diagram for PIN entry

EXERCISES

Exercises based on the techniques covered in this chapter are given in this section. Worked solutions are given in the next section.

Equivalence Partitioning/Boundary Value Analysis exercise

Scenario: If you take the train before 9:30 am or in the afternoon after 4:00 pm until 7:30 pm (the rush hour), you must pay full fare. A saver ticket is available for trains between 9:30 am and 4:00 pm, and after 7:30 pm.

What are the partitions and boundary values to test the train times for ticket types? Which are valid partitions and which are invalid partitions? What are the boundary values? (A table may be helpful to organize your partitions and boundaries.) Derive test cases for the partitions and boundaries.

Are there any questions you have about this requirement? Is anything unclear?

Decision table exercise

Scenario: If you hold an over 60s rail card, you get a 34% discount on whatever ticket you buy. If you are travelling with a child (under 16), you can get a 50% discount on any ticket if you hold a family rail card, otherwise you get a 10% discount. You can only hold one type of rail card.

Produce a decision table showing all the combinations of fare types and resulting discounts and derive test cases from the decision table.

State transition exercise

Scenario: A website shopping basket starts out as empty. As purchases are selected, they are added to the shopping basket. Items can also be removed from the shopping basket. When the customer decides to check out, a summary of the items in the basket and the total cost are shown, for the customer to say whether this is OK or not. If the contents and price are OK, then you leave the summary display and go to the payment system. Otherwise you go back to shopping (so you can remove items if you want).

a. Produce a state diagram showing the different states and transitions. Define a test, in terms of the sequence of states, to cover all transitions.

b. Produce a state table. Give an example test for an invalid transition.

Statement and decision testing exercise

Note that statement and decision testing are no longer K3, as they were in the previous Syllabus, but this exercise should help you to understand the technique a bit better anyway!

Scenario: A vending machine dispenses either hot or cold drinks. If you choose a hot drink (for example tea or coffee), it asks if you want milk (and adds milk if required), then it asks if you want sugar (and adds sugar if required), then your drink is dispensed.

a. Draw a control flow diagram for this example. (Hint: regard the selection of the type of drink as one statement.)

b. Given the following tests, what is the statement coverage achieved? What is the decision coverage achieved?

Test 1: Cold drink.
Test 2: Hot drink with milk and sugar.

c. What additional tests would be needed to achieve 100% statement coverage? What additional tests would be needed to achieve 100% decision coverage?

EXERCISE SOLUTIONS

EP/BVA exercise

The first thing to do is to establish exactly what the boundaries are between the full fare and saver fare. Let's put these in a table to organize our thoughts:

Scheduled departure time	≤ 9:29 am	9:30 am – 4:00 pm	4:01 pm – 7:30 pm	≥ 7:31 pm
Ticket type	full	saver	full	saver

We have assumed that the boundary values are: 9:29 am, 9:30 am, 4:00 pm, 4:01 pm, 7:30 pm and 7:31 pm. By setting out exactly what we think is meant by the specification, we may highlight some ambiguities or, at least, raise some questions. This is one of the benefits of using the technique! For example:

'When does the morning rush hour start? At midnight? At 11:30 pm the previous day? At the time of the first train of the day? If so, when is the first train? 5:00 am?'

This is a rather important omission from the specification. We could make an assumption about when it starts, but it would be better to find out what is correct.

- If a train is due to leave at exactly 4:00 pm, is a saver ticket still valid?

- What if a train is due to leave before 4:00 pm but is delayed until after 4:00 pm? Is a saver ticket still valid? (That is, if the actual departure time is different from the scheduled departure time.)

Our table above has helped us to see where the partitions are. All of the partitions in the table above are valid partitions. It may be that an invalid partition would be a time that no train was running, for example before 5:00 am, but our specification did not mention that! However it would be good to show this possibility also. We could be a bit more formal by listing all valid and invalid partitions and boundaries in a table, as we described in Section 4.3.1, but in this case it does not actually add a lot, since all partitions are valid.

Here are the test cases we can derive for this example:

Test case reference	Input	Expected outcome
1	Depart 4:30 am	Pay full fare
2	Depart 9:29 am	Pay full fare
3	Depart 9:30 am	Buy saver ticket
4	Depart 11:37 am	Buy saver ticket
5	Depart 4:00 pm	Buy saver ticket
6	Depart 4:01 pm	Pay full fare
7	Depart 5:55 pm	Pay full fare
8	Depart 7:30 pm	Pay full fare
9	Depart 7:31 pm	Buy saver ticket
10	Depart 10:05 pm	Buy saver ticket

Note that test cases 1, 4, 7 and 10 are based on equivalence partition values; test cases 2, 3, 5, 6, 8 and 9 are based on boundary values. There may also be other information about the test cases, such as preconditions, that we have not shown here.

Decision table exercise

The fare types mentioned are an over 60s rail card, a family rail card and whether you are travelling with a child or not. With three conditions or causes, we have eight columns in our decision table below.

Causes (inputs)	R1	R2	R3	R4	R5	R6	R7	R8
over 60s rail card?	Y	Y	Y	Y	N	N	N	N
family rail card?	Y	Y	N	N	Y	Y	N	N
child also travelling?	Y	N	Y	N	Y	N	Y	N
Effects (outputs)								
Discount (%)	X/?/50%	X/?/34%	34%	34%	50%	0%	10%	0%

When we come to fill in the effects, we may find this a bit more difficult. For the first two rules, for example, what should the output be? Is it an X because holding more than one rail card should not be possible? The specification does not actually say what happens if someone does hold more than one card, that is, it has not specified the output, so perhaps we should put a question mark in this column. Of course, if someone does hold two rail cards, they probably would not admit this, and perhaps they would claim the 50% discount with their family rail card if they are travelling with a child, so perhaps we should put 50% for Rule 1 and 34% for Rule 2 in this column. Our notation shows that we do not know what the expected outcome should be for these rules!

This highlights the fact that our natural language (English) specification is not very clear as to what the effects should actually be. A strength of this technique is that it forces greater clarity. If the answers are spelled out in a decision table, then it is clear what the effect should be. When different people come up with different answers for the outputs, then you have an unclear specification!

The word 'otherwise' in the specification is ambiguous. Does 'otherwise' mean that you always get at least a 10% discount or does it mean that if you travel with a child and an over 60s card but not a family card you get 10% and 34%? Depending on what assumption you make for the meaning of 'otherwise', you will get a different last row in your decision table.

Note that the effect or output is the same (34%) for both Rules 3 and 4. This means that our third cause (whether or not a child is also travelling) actually has no influence on the output. These columns could therefore be combined with 'do not care' as the entry for the third cause. This rationalizing of the table means we will have fewer columns and therefore fewer test cases. The reduction in test cases is based on the assumption we are making about the factor having no effect on the outcome, so a more thorough approach would be to include each column in the table.

Here is a rationalized table, where we have shown our assumptions about the first two outcomes and we have also combined Rules 6 and 8 above, since having a family rail card has no effect if you are not travelling with a child.

Causes (inputs)	R1	R2	R3	R5	R6	R7
over 60s rail card?	Y	Y	Y	N	N	N
family rail card?	Y	Y	N	Y	–	N
child also travelling?	Y	N	–	Y	N	Y
Effects (outputs)						
Discount (%)	50%	34%	34%	50%	0%	10%

Here are the test cases that we derive from this table. (If you did not rationalize (or collapse) the table, then you will have eight test cases rather than six.) Note that you would not necessarily test each column, but the table enables you to make a decision about which combinations to test and which not to test this time.

Test case reference	Input	Expected outcome
1	S. Wilkes, with over 60s rail card and family rail card, travelling with grandson Josh (age 11)	50% discount for both tickets
2	Mrs M. Davis, with over 60s rail card and family rail card, travelling alone	34% discount
3	J. Rogers, with over 60s rail card, travelling with his wife	34% discount (for J. Rogers only, not his wife)
4	S. Gray, with family rail card, travelling with her daughter Betsy	50% discount for both tickets
5	Miss Congeniality, no rail card, travelling alone	No discount
6	Joe Bloggs with no rail card, travelling with his 5-year-old niece	10% discount for both tickets

Note that we may have raised some additional issues when we designed the test cases. For example, does the discount for a rail card apply only to the traveller or to someone travelling with them? Here we have assumed that it applies to all travellers for the family rail card, but to the individual passenger only for the over 60s rail card.

State transition exercise

The state diagram is shown in Figure 4.8. The initial state (S1) is when the shopping basket is empty. When an item is added to the basket, it goes to state (S2), where there are potential purchases. Any additional items added to the basket do not change the state (just the total number of things to purchase). Items can be removed, which does not change the state unless the total items ordered goes from 1 to 0. In this case, we go back to the empty

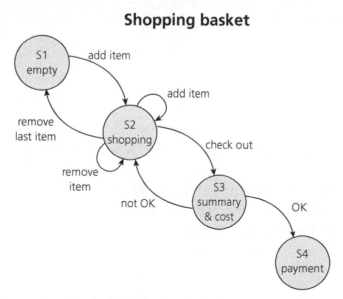

Shopping basket

FIGURE 4.8 State diagram for shopping basket

basket (S1). When we want to check out, we go to the summary state (S3) for approval. If the list and prices are approved, we go to payment (S4); if not, we go back to the shopping state (possibly to remove some items to reduce the total price we have to pay). There are four states and seven transitions.

Note that S1 is our start state for this example and S4 is the end state – this means that we are not concerned with any event that happens once we get to State S4.

Here is a test to cover all transitions. Note that the end state from one step or event is the start state for the next event, so these steps must be done in this sequence.

State	Event (action)
S1	Add item
S2	Remove (last) item
S1	Add item
S2	Add item
S2	Remove item
S2	Check out
S3	Not OK
S2	Check out
S3	OK
S4	Payment

Although our example is not interested in what happens from State 4, there would be other events and actions once we enter the payment process that could be shown by another state diagram (for example check validity of the credit card, deduct the amount, email a receipt, etc.).

The corresponding state table is:

State or event	Add item	Remove item	Remove last item	Check out	Not OK	OK
S1 Empty	S2	–	–	–	–	–
S2 Shopping	S2	S2	S1	S3	–	–
S3 Summary	–	–	–	–	S2	S4
S4 Payment	–	–	–	–	–	–

All of the boxes that contain '–' (dash) are invalid transitions in this example. Example negative tests would include:

- Attempt to add an item from the summary and cost state (S3).
- Try to remove an item from the empty shopping basket (S1).
- Try to enter OK while in the shopping state (S2).

Statement and decision testing exercise

The control flow diagram is shown in Figure 4.9. Note that drawing a control diagram here illustrates that white-box testing can also be applied to the structure of general processes, not just to computer algorithms. Flowcharts are generally easier to understand than text when you are trying to describe the results of decisions taken on later events.

On Figure 4.10, we can see the route that Tests 1 and 2 have taken through our control flow graph. Test 1 has gone straight down the left-hand side to select a cold drink. Test 2 has gone to the right at each opportunity, adding both milk and sugar to a hot drink.

Every statement (represented by a box on the diagram) has been covered by our two tests, so we have 100% statement coverage.

We have not taken the No Exit from either the 'milk?' or 'sugar?' decisions, so there are two decision outcomes that we have not tested yet. We did test both of the outcomes from the 'hot or cold?' decision, so we have covered four out of six decision outcomes. Decision coverage is 4/6 or 67% with the two tests.

No additional tests are needed to achieve statement coverage, as we already have 100% coverage of the statements.

One additional test is needed to achieve 100% decision coverage:

Test 3: Hot drink, no milk, no sugar.

This test will cover both of the 'No' decision outcomes from the milk and sugar decisions, so we will now have 100% decision coverage.

FIGURE 4.9 Control flow diagram for drinks dispenser

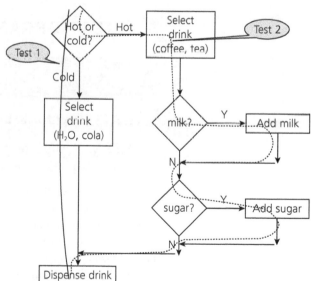

FIGURE 4.10 Control flow diagram showing coverage of tests

CHAPTER FIVE

Test management

Testing is a complex activity. It can be a distinct sub-project within the larger software development, maintenance or integration project. It usually accounts for a substantial proportion of the overall project budget. Therefore we must understand how we should manage the testing we do.

In this chapter, we cover essential topics for test management in six sections. The first relates to how to organize the testers and the testing. The second concerns the estimation, planning and strategizing of the test effort. The third addresses test progress monitoring, test reporting and test control. The fourth explains configuration management and its relationship to testing. The fifth covers the central topic of risk and how testing affects and is affected by product and project risks. The sixth and final section discusses the management of defects.

5.1 TEST ORGANIZATION

SYLLABUS LEARNING OBJECTIVES FOR 5.1 TEST ORGANIZATION (K2)

FL-5.1.1   Explain the benefits and drawbacks of independent testing (K2)

FL-5.1.2   Identify the tasks of a test manager and tester (K1)

In this section, We'll talk about organizing a test effort within a project. We'll look at the value of independent testing, and discuss the potential benefits and risks associated with independent testing. We'll examine the various types of different team members we might want on a test team. And we'll familiarize ourselves with the typical tasks performed by test managers and testers.

As we go through this section, keep your eyes open for the Glossary terms **tester**, and **test manager**.

5.1.1 Independent testing

In Chapter 1 we talked about independent testing from the perspective of individual tester psychology. In this chapter, we'll look at the organizational and managerial implications of independence.

Testing tasks may be done by people with a specific testing role, for example with tester as part of their job title, but testers are definitely not the only people who do testing. Developers, business analysts, users and customers also do testing tasks for different reasons and at different times. Even those who are full-time testers may do a variety of different tasks at different times. But if lots of people do testing, why have people dedicated to it? One reason is that the view of a different person, especially one who is trained to look for problems, can be much more effective at finding those problems. Many organizations, especially in safety-critical areas, have separate teams of independent testers to capitalize on this effect. As we saw in Chapter 1 Section 1.5, independence can overcome cognitive bias.

If there is a separate test team, approaches to organizing it vary, as do the places in the organizational structure where the test team fits. Since testing is an assessment of quality, and since that assessment may not always be perceived as positive, many organizations strive to create an organizational climate where testers can deliver an independent, objective assessment of quality.

Levels of independence

When thinking about how independent the test team is, recognize that independence is not an either/or condition, but a continuum.

At one end of the continuum lies the absence of independence, where the developer performs testing on their own code within the development team. Of course, every good developer does do some testing of their own code, but this should not be the ONLY testing!

Moving toward independence, you find an integrated tester or group of testers working alongside the developers, but still within and reporting to the development manager. For example, developers may test each other's code after testing their own, or a tester on an Agile team may help developers and do some independent testing within the team. Pair programming is one way of having another pair of eyes on the code as it is being developed, whether it is two developers pairing, or a developer and a tester.

A further level of independence would be to have a team of testers who are independent and outside the development team, reporting to project management or business management.

Sometimes there are testers or teams of testers with special skills or responsibilities within an organization; such specialists may also be outside the development organization, which would be the other end of the independence continuum. For example, there may be a tester or team that specializes in performance or security testing.

In fully independent testing, you might see a separate test team reporting into the organization at a point equal to the development or project team or at a higher level. You might find specialists in the business domain (such as users of the system), specialists in technology (such as database experts), and specialists in testing (such as security testers or performance test experts) in a separate test team, as part of a larger independent test team, or as part of a contracted outsourced test team.

Potential benefits of independence

Let's examine the potential benefits and risks of independence, starting with the benefits.

An independent tester can often see more, different defects than a tester working within a development team – or a tester who is by profession a developer. While business analysts, marketing staff, designers and developers bring their own assumptions to the specification and implementation of the item under test, an independent tester brings a different set of assumptions to testing and to reviews, which often helps expose hidden defects and problems related to the group's way of thinking, as we discussed in Chapter 3. An independent tester brings a sceptical attitude of professional pessimism, a sense that, if there's any doubt about the observed behaviour, they should ask: 'Is this a defect?'

At the team level, an independent test team reporting to a senior or executive manager may enjoy (once they earn it) more credibility in the organization than a test manager or tester who is part of the development team. An independent tester who reports to senior management may be able to report his or her results honestly and without concern for reprisals that might result from pointing out problems in co-workers' or, worse yet, the manager's work. An independent test team often has a separate budget, which helps ensure the proper level of money is spent on tester training, testing tools, test equipment and so forth. In addition, in some organizations, testers in an independent test team may find it easier to have a career path that leads up into more senior roles in testing.

Potential drawbacks of test independence

Independent test teams are not risk-free. It is possible for the testers and the test team to become isolated. This can take the form of interpersonal isolation from the developers, the designers, and the project team itself. It can also take the form of isolation from the broader view of quality and the business objectives, for example, an obsessive focus on defects, often accompanied by a refusal to accept business prioritization of defects. This leads to communication problems, feelings of alienation and antipathy, a lack of identification with and support for the project goals, spontaneous blame festivals and political backstabbing.

Even well-integrated test teams can suffer problems. Other project stakeholders might come to see the independent test team (rightly or wrongly) as a bottleneck and a source of delay.

Some developers abdicate their responsibility for quality, saying, 'Well, we have this test team now, so why do I need to unit test my code?'

Independent testers may not have all of the information that they need about the test object, since they may be outside the development organization itself (where often much information is communicated informally). This leads to them being less effective than they should or could be.

Independence is not a replacement for familiarity. Although an independent view sees things that those closer to it miss, those who know the code or the test object best may be able to see some things that the independent tester would miss because of their limited knowledge. It is not a case of independence is always best, but of getting the best balance between independence and familiarity.

Independence varies

Due to a desire for the benefits of an independent test team, companies sometimes establish them, only to break them up again later. Why does that happen? A common cause is the failure of the test manager to effectively manage the risks of independence listed above. Some test teams succumb to the temptation to adopt a 'No can do' attitude, coming up with reasons why the project should bend to their needs rather than each side being flexible so as to enable project success. Testers take to acting as enforcers of process or as auditors, without a proper management mandate and support. Resentments and pressures build, until at last the organization decides that the independent test team causes more problems than it solves. It is especially important for testers and test managers to understand the mission they serve and the reasons why the organization wants an independent test team. Often, the entire test team must realize that, whether they are part of the project team or independent, they exist to provide a service to the project team.

There is no one right approach to organizing testing. For each project, you must consider whether to use an independent test team, based on the project, the application domain and the levels of risk, among other factors. As the size, complexity and criticality of the project increases, it is important to have independence in later levels of testing (like integration test, system test and acceptance test), though some testing is often best done by other people such as project managers, quality managers, developers, business and domain experts or infrastructure or IT operations experts.

In most projects, there will be multiple test levels; the amount of independence in testing varies between levels as well (as it should). Often more independence is most effective at the higher levels, for example system and user acceptance testing.

The type of development life cycle also influences the level of independence of testing. In Agile development, a tester may provide some independence as part of the development team and may (also) be part of an independent team performing independent testing at higher levels. Product owners may perform acceptance testing to validate user stories at the end of each iteration.

5.1.2 Tasks of a test manager and tester

We have seen that the location of testers or of a test team within a project organization can vary widely. Similarly, there is wide variation in the roles that people within testing play. Some of these roles occur frequently, some infrequently. Two roles that are found within many organizations are those of the **test manager** and the **tester**, though the same people may play both roles at various points during the project. The activities and tasks performed by these two roles will vary, depending on the organization, the project and product context, and the skills of the individuals. Let's take a look at the work typically done in these roles, starting with the test manager.

Test manager tasks

A test manager tends to be the person tasked with overall responsibility for the test process and successful leadership of the test activities. The test manager role may be performed by someone who holds this as their full-time position (a professional test manager), or it might be done by a quality assurance manager, project manager or a development manager. Regarding the last two people on this list, warning bells about independence should be ringing in your head now, in addition to thoughts about how we can ensure that such non-testers gain the knowledge and outlook needed to manage testing. The test manager tasks may also be done by a senior tester. Whoever is playing the role, expect them to plan, monitor and control the testing work.

A test manager may be a single person trying to ensure that all testing is done as well as it can be, or a test manager may have one or more teams of people reporting to them (for example in larger organizations). Sometimes the person at the top of the hierarchy would be called a test coordinator or test coach, and the individual teams may be led by a test leader or lead tester. In any case, the test manager's role is to manage the testing!

Typical tasks of the test manager role may include the following:

- At the outset of the project, in collaboration with the other stakeholders, devise the test objectives, organizational test policies (if not already in place), and test strategies.

Test manager The person responsible for project management of testing activities and resources, and evaluation of a test object. The individual who directs, controls, administers, plans and regulates the evaluation of a test object.

Tester A skilled professional who is involved in the testing of a component or system.

- Plan the test activities, based on the test objectives and risks, and the context of the organization and the project. This may involve selecting the test approaches, estimating time, effort and cost for testing, acquiring resources, defining test levels, types and test cycles and planning defect management.

- Write and update over time any test plan(s).

- Coordinate the test plan(s) with other project stakeholders, project managers, product owners and anyone else who may affect or be affected by the project or the testing.

- Share the testing perspective with other project activities, such as integration planning, especially where third-party suppliers are involved.

- Lead, guide and monitor the analysis, design, implementation and execution of the tests, monitor test progress and results, and check the status of exit criteria (or definition of done).

- Prepare and deliver test progress reports and test summary reports, based on information gathered from the testers.

- Adapt the test planning based on test results and progress (whether documented in test progress or summary reports or not) and take any actions necessary for test control.

- Support setting up the defect management system and adequate configuration management of the testware, and traceability of the tests to the test basis.

- Produce suitable metrics for measuring test progress and evaluating the quality of the testing and the product (test object).

- Recognize when test automation is appropriate and, if it is, plan and support the selection and implementation of tools to support the test process, including setting a budget for tool selection (and possible purchase, lease and support and training of the team), allocating time and effort for pilot projects and providing continuing support in the use of the tool(s). (See Chapter 6 for more on tool support for testing.)

- Decide about the implementation of test environment(s) and ensure that they are put into place before test execution and managed during test execution.

- Promote and advocate the testers, the test team and the test profession within the organization.

- Develop the skills and careers of testers, through training, performance evaluations, coaching and other activities, such as lunch-time discussions or presentations.

Although this is a list of typical activities of a test manager, the tasks may be carried out by people who are not labelled as a test manager. For example, in Agile development, the Agile team may perform some of these tasks, especially those to do with day-to-day testing within the team. Test managers who are outside an individual development team, who work with several teams or the whole organization, may be called a test coach. See Black [2009] for more on managing the test process.

Tester tasks

As with test managers, projects should include testers at the outset. In the planning and preparation of the testing, testers should review and contribute to test plans, as well as analyzing, reviewing and assessing requirements and design specifications.

They may be involved in or even be the primary people identifying test conditions and creating test designs, test cases, test procedure specifications and test data, and may automate or help to automate the tests. They often set up the test environments or assist system administration and network management staff in doing so.

In sequential life cycles, as test execution begins, the number of testers often increases, starting with the work required to implement tests in the test environment. They may play such a role on all test levels, even those not under the direct control of the test group; for example they might implement unit tests which were designed by developers. Testers execute and log the tests, evaluate the results and document problems found. They monitor the testing and the test environment, often using tools for this task, and often gather performance metrics. Throughout the testing life cycle, they review each other's work, including test specifications, defect reports and test results.

In Agile development, testers are involved in every iteration or sprint, performing a wide variety of testing tasks on whatever is being developed at the time, so they are continuously involved throughout. They may be reviewing user stories and identifying test conditions, implementing the tests, running them and reporting on results.

Testers may have specializations such as test analysis, test design, specific test types (especially non-functional testing), or test automation. Such specialists may take the role of tester at different test levels and at different times. For example, the person doing the testing tasks at component or component integration level is often the developer (but see caveats about independence in Section 5.1.1). At system testing or system integration testing, an independent test team may do the testing activities. In acceptance testing, the test tasks may be done by business analysts, subject matter experts, users or product owners. At operational acceptance testing, operations and/ or system administration staff may be performing the tester tasks.

Typical tasks of the tester may include the following:

- Reviewing and contributing to test plans from the tester perspective.
- Analyzing, reviewing and assessing requirements, user stories and acceptance criteria, specifications and models (that is, the test basis) for testability and to detect defects early.
- Identifying and documenting test conditions and test cases, capturing traceability between test cases, test conditions and the test basis to assist in checking the thoroughness of testing (coverage), the impact of failed tests and the impact on the tests of changes in the test basis.
- Designing, setting up and verifying test environments(s), coordinating with system administration and network management.
- Designing and implementing test cases and test procedures, including automated tests where appropriate.
- Acquiring and preparing test data to be used in the tests.
- Creating a detailed test execution schedule (for manual tests).
- Executing the tests, evaluating the results and documenting deviations from expected results as defect reports.
- Using appropriate tools to help the test process.
- Automating tests as needed (for technical test specialists), as supported by a test automation engineer or expert or a developer. (See Chapter 6 for more on test automation.)

- Evaluating non-functional characteristics such as performance efficiency, reliability, usability, security, compatibility and portability.

- Reviewing tests developed by others, including other testers, business analysts, developers or product owners. Part of a tester's role is to help educate others about doing better testing.

Defining the skills test staff need

This section is outside what is required by the Syllabus, but we include it as useful and practical advice anyway!

Doing testing properly requires more than defining the right positions and number of people for those positions. Good test teams have the right mix of skills based on the tasks and activities they need to carry out, and people outside the test team who are in charge of test tasks need the right skills, too.

People involved in testing need basic professional and social qualifications such as literacy, the ability to prepare and deliver written and verbal reports, the ability to communicate effectively and so on. Going beyond that, when we think of the skills that testers need, three main areas come to mind:

- **Application or business domain:** A tester must understand the intended behaviour, the problem the system will solve, the process it will automate and so forth, in order to spot improper behaviour while testing, and recognize the 'must-work' functions and features.

- **Technology:** A tester must be aware of issues, limitations and capabilities of the chosen implementation technology, in order to effectively and efficiently locate problems and recognize the 'likely-to-fail' functions and features.

- **Testing:** A tester must know the testing topics discussed in this book, and often more advanced testing topics, in order to effectively and efficiently carry out the test tasks assigned.

The specific skills in each area and the level of skill required vary by project, organization, application and the risks involved.

The set of testing tasks and activities are many and varied, and so too are the skills required, so we often see specialization of skills and separation of roles. For example, due to the special knowledge required in the areas of testing, technology and business domain, respectively, test automation experts may handle automating the regression tests, developers may perform component and integration tests and users and operators may be involved in acceptance tests.

We have long advocated pervasive testing, the involvement of people throughout the project team in carrying out testing tasks. Let's close this section, though, on a cautionary note. Software and system companies (for example producers of shrink-wrapped software and consumer products) typically overestimate the technology knowledge required to be an effective tester. Businesses that use information technology (for example banks and insurance companies) typically overestimate the business domain knowledge needed.

All types of projects tend to underestimate the testing knowledge required. We have seen a project fail in part because people without proper testing skills tested critical components, leading to the disastrous discovery of fundamental architectural problems later. Most projects can benefit from the participation of professional testers, as amateur testing alone will usually not suffice.

5.2 TEST PLANNING AND ESTIMATION

> **SYLLABUS LEARNING OBJECTIVES FOR 5.2 TEST PLANNING AND ESTIMATION (K3)**
>
> FL-5.2.1 Summarize the purpose and content of a test plan (K2)
>
> FL-5.2.2 Differentiate between various test strategies (K2)
>
> FL-5.2.3 Give examples of potential entry and exit criteria (K2)
>
> FL-5.2.4 Apply knowledge of prioritization, and technical and logical dependencies, to schedule test execution for a given set of test cases (K3)
>
> FL-5.2.5 Identify factors that influence the effort related to testing (K1)
>
> FL-5.2.6 Explain the difference between two estimation techniques: the metrics-based technique and the expert-based technique (K2)

In this section, we'll talk about a complicated trio of test topics: plans, estimates and strategies. Plans, estimates and strategies depend on a number of factors, including the level, targets and objectives of the testing we are setting out to do. Writing a plan, preparing an estimate and selecting test strategies tend to happen concurrently and ideally during the planning period for the overall project, though we must be ready to revise them as the project proceeds and we gain more information.

Let's look closely at how to prepare a test plan, examining issues related to planning for a project, for a test level, for a specific test type and for test execution. We'll discuss selecting test strategies and ways to establish adequate exit criteria for testing. In addition, we'll look at various tasks related to test execution that need planning. We'll examine typical factors that influence the effort related to testing and see two different estimation techniques: metrics-based and expert-based.

Look out for the Glossary terms **entry criteria**, **exit criteria**, **test approach**, **test estimation**, **test plan**, **test planning** and **test strategy** in this section.

5.2.1 The purpose and content of test plan

While people tend to have different definitions of what goes in a **test plan**, for us a test plan is the project plan for the testing work to be done. It is not a test design specification, a collection of test cases or a set of test procedures; in fact, most of our test plans do not address that level of detail.

Why do we write test plans? We have three main reasons: to guide our thinking, to communicate to others and to help manage future changes.

First, writing a test plan guides our thinking. We find that if we can explain something in words, we understand it. If we cannot explain it, there's a good chance we don't understand. Writing a test plan forces us to confront the challenges that await us and focus our thinking on important topics. In Chapter 2 of Fred Brooks' brilliant

> **Test plan**
> Documentation describing the test objectives to be achieved and the means and the schedule for achieving them, organized to coordinate testing activities.

and essential book on software engineering management, *The Mythical Man-Month*, he explains the importance of careful estimation and planning for testing as follows:

> *Failure to allow enough time for system test, in particular, is peculiarly disastrous. Since the delay comes at the end of the schedule, no one is aware of schedule trouble until almost the delivery date [and] delay at this point has unusually severe ... financial repercussions. The project is fully staffed, and cost-per-day is maximum [as are the associated opportunity costs]. It is therefore very important to allow enough system test time in the original schedule.*

Brooks [1995]

This is particularly applicable to sequential development life cycles (as many were back in 1995). Agile development was designed to address some of these problems, but it does not obviate the need for system testing, so the advice is still relevant.

We find that using a template when writing test plans helps us remember the important challenges. You can use the template and examples shown in ISO/IEC/IEEE 29119-3 [2013], use someone else's template or create your own template over time.

Test planning The activity of establishing or updating a test plan.

Second, the **test planning** process and the plan itself serve as vehicles for communicating with other members of the project team, testers, peers, managers and other stakeholders. This communication allows the test plan to influence the project team and allows the project team to influence the test plan. This is especially important in the areas of organization-wide testing policies and motivations; test scope, objectives, and critical areas to test; project and product risks, resource considerations and constraints; and the testability of the item under test.

You can accomplish this communication through circulation of one or two test plan drafts and through review meetings. Such a draft may include many notes such as the following examples:

> *[To Be Determined: Jennifer: Please tell me what the plan is for releasing the test items into the test lab for each cycle of system test execution?]*
> *[Dave – please let me know which version of the test tool will be used for the regression tests of the previous increments.]*

As you document the answers to these kinds of questions, the test plan becomes a record of previous discussions and agreements between the testers and the rest of the project team. Thus test planning is an ongoing activity performed throughout the product's life cycle (and beyond into maintenance).

Third, the test plan helps us manage change. During early stages of the project, as we gather more information, we revise our plans. As the project evolves and situations change, we adapt our plans. Written test plans give us a baseline against which to measure such revisions and changes. Furthermore, updating the plan at major milestones helps keep testing aligned with project needs. As we run the tests, we make final adjustments to our plans based on the results. You might not have the time – or the energy – to update your test plans every time a variance occurs, as some projects can be quite dynamic. A simple approach is described in Black [2009] Chapter 6, for documenting variances from the test plan. You can implement it using a database or spreadsheet. You can include these change records in a periodic test plan update, as part of a test status report, or as part as an end of project test summary.

We have found that it is better to write multiple test plans in some situations. For example, when we manage both integration and system test levels, those two test execution periods may occur at different points in time and will have different objectives.

For some systems projects, a hardware test plan and a software test plan will address different techniques and tools, as well as different audiences. However, since there might be overlap between these test plans, a master test plan that addresses the common elements can reduce the amount of redundant documentation.

What to do with your brain while planning tests

Writing a good test plan is easier than writing a novel, but both tasks require an organized approach and careful thought. In fact, since a good test plan is kept short and focused, unlike some novels, some might argue that it is harder to write a good test plan. Let's look at some of the planning tasks you need to carry out.

At a high level, you need to consider the purpose served by the testing work. In terms of the overall organizational needs, this purpose is referred to variously as the test team's mission or the organization's testing policy. A test plan is influenced by many factors; as well as test policy and the organization's test strategy, the development life cycle and methods being used for development, and the availability of resources. In terms of the specific project, understanding the purpose of testing means knowing the answers to questions such as:

● What is in scope and what is out of scope for this testing effort?

● What are the test objectives?

● What are the important project and product risks? (More on risks in Section 5.5.)

● What is the overall approach of testing in this project?

● How will test activities be integrated and coordinated into the software life cycle activities?

● How do we decide what to test, what people and other resources are needed to perform test activities, and how test activities will be carried out?

● What constraints affect testing (for example budget limitations, hard deadlines, etc.)?

● What is most critical for this product and project?

● Which aspects of the product are more (or less) testable?

● What should be the overall test execution schedule and how should we decide the order in which to do test analysis, test design, implementation, execution and evaluation of specific tests, either on specific dates or in the context of an iteration? (Product and planning risks, discussed later in this chapter, will influence the answers to these questions.)

● What metrics will be used for test monitoring and control and how will they be gathered and analyzed?

● What is the budget for all test activities?

● What should be the level of detail and structure for test documentation? (Templates or example documents or work products are helpful for this.)

You should then select strategies which are appropriate to the purpose of testing (more on the topic of selecting strategies in Section 5.2.2).

In addition, you need to decide how to split the testing work into various levels, as discussed in Chapter 2 (for example component, integration, system and acceptance). If that decision has already been made, you need to decide how to best fit your testing work in the level you are responsible for with the testing work done in those other test levels. During the analysis and design of tests, you will want to reduce gaps and overlap between levels and, during test execution, you will want to coordinate between the levels. Such details dealing with inter-level coordination are often addressed in the master test plan.

In addition to integrating and coordinating between test levels, you should also plan to integrate and coordinate all the testing work to be done with the rest of the project. For example, what items must be acquired for the testing? Are there ongoing supply issues, such as with imitation bank notes (that is, simulated bank notes) for a financial application such as an ATM? When will the developers complete work on the component or system under test? What operations support is required for the test environment? What kind of information must be delivered to the maintenance team at the end of testing?

Moving down into the details, what makes a plan a plan (rather than a statement of principles, a laundry list of good ideas or a collection of suggestions) is that the author specifies in it who will do what when and (at least in a general way) how. Resources are required to carry out the work. There are often hard decisions that require careful consideration and building a consensus across the team, including with the project manager.

The entire testing process, from planning through to completion, produces information, some of which you will need to document. How precisely should testers write the test designs, cases and procedures? How much should they leave to the judgement of the tester during test execution, and what are the reproducibility issues associated with this decision? What kinds of templates can testers use for the various documents they will produce? How do those documents relate to one another? If you intend to use tools for tasks such as test design or execution, as discussed in Chapter 6, you will need to understand how the models or automated tests will integrate with manual testing, and plan who will be responsible for automation design, implementation and support. There may be a separate test automation plan, but this needs to be coordinated with other test plans.

Some information you will need to gather in the form of raw data and then distil. What metrics to do you intend to use to monitor, control and manage the testing? Which of those metrics, and perhaps other metrics, will you use to report your results? We'll look more closely at possible answers to those questions in Section 5.3, but a good test plan provides answers early in the project.

5.2.2 Test strategy and test approach

A **test strategy** is the general way in which testing will happen within each of the levels of testing, independent of project, across the organization. The **test approach** is the name the ISTQB gives to the implementation of the test strategy on a specific project. Since the test approach is specific to a project, you should define and document the approach in the test plans, refining and providing further detail in the test designs.

Deciding on the test approach involves careful consideration of the testing objectives, the project's goals and overall risk assessment. These decisions provide the starting point for planning the test process, for selecting the test design techniques and test types to be applied, and for defining the entry and exit criteria. In your decision-making on the approach, you should take into account the project, product and organization context, issues related to risks, hazards and safety, the available resources, the team's level of skills, the technology involved, the nature of the system under test, considerations related to whether the system is custom-built or assembled from commercial off-the-shelf components (COTS), the organization's test objectives and any applicable regulations.

Test strategy (organizational test strategy) Documentation that expresses the generic requirements for testing one or more projects run within an organization, providing detail on how testing is to be performed, and is aligned with the test policy.

Test approach The implementation of the test strategy for a specific project.

The choice of test approaches or strategies is one powerful factor in the success of the test effort and the accuracy of the test plans and estimates. This factor is under the control of the testers and test managers. Of course, having choices also means that you can make mistakes, so we'll go into more detail about how to pick the right test strategies in a minute. First, though, let's survey the major types of test strategies that are commonly found.[1]

- **Analytical:** In this strategy, tests are determined by analyzing some factor, such as requirements (or other test basis) or risk. For example, the risk-based strategy involves performing a risk analysis using project documents and stakeholder input, then planning, estimating, designing and prioritizing the tests based on risk. We will talk more about risk analysis later in this chapter. Another analytical test strategy is the requirements-based strategy, where an analysis of the requirements specification forms the basis for planning, estimating and designing tests. Analytical test strategies have in common the use of some formal or informal analytical technique, usually during the requirements and design stages of the project.

- **Model-based:** In this strategy, tests are designed based on some model of the test object. For example, you can build mathematical models for loading and response for e-commerce servers, and test based on that model. If the behaviour of the system under test conforms to that predicted by the model, the system is deemed to be working. Model-based test strategies have in common the creation or selection of some formal or informal model for critical system behaviours, usually during the requirements and design stages of the project. Examples also include business process models, state models, for example state transition diagrams, etc., or reliability grown models.

- **Methodical:** In this strategy, a pre-defined and fairly stable list of test conditions is used. For example, you might have a checklist that you have put together over the years that suggests the major areas that testing should cover, or you might follow an industry standard for software quality, such as ISO/IEC 25010 [2011], for your outline of major test areas. You then methodically design, implement and execute tests following this outline. Methodical test strategies have in common the adherence to a pre-planned, systematized approach. This may have been developed in-house, assembled from various concepts developed in-house and gathered from outside, or adapted significantly from outside ideas, and may have an early or late point of involvement for testing. Some examples include: working through a list (that is, taxonomy) of typical defects, or working through a list of desired quality characteristics, such as company-wide look-and-feel standards for websites and mobile apps.

- **Process- or standard-compliant:** In this strategy, an external standard or set of rules is used to analyze, design and implement tests. For example, you might adopt the standard ISO/IEC/IEEE 29119-3 [2013] for your testing, or you may use TMMi (Test Maturity Model integration, www.tmmi.org) to assess your current testing and improve it. More information about TMMi can be found in van Veenendaal and Wells [2012]. Alternatively, process- or standard-compliant strategies have in common reliance upon an externally developed approach to

---

[1] The catalogue of testing strategies that has been included in the ISTQB Foundation Syllabus grew out of an email discussion between Rex Black, Ross Collard, Kathy Iberle and Cem Kaner. We thank them for their thought provoking comments.

testing, often with little (if any) customization. They may have an early or late point of involvement for testing. For example, some organizations need to conform to safety-critical or financial regulations which may include processes for identifying tests in a rigorous way from the test basis.

● **Directed (or consultative):** In this strategy, stakeholders or experts (technology or business domain experts) may direct the testing according to their advice and guidance. For example, you might ask the users or developers of the system to tell you what to test or even rely on them to do the testing. Consultative or directed strategies have in common the reliance on a group of non-testers to guide or perform the testing effort, and typically emphasize the later stages of testing simply due to the lack of recognition of the value of early testing. This strategy may be helpful when the developing organization is a new start-up without a lot of testing knowledge or expertise. For example, an outside expert may advise on security testing.

● **Regression-averse:** In this strategy, the most important factor is to ensure that the system's performance does not deteriorate or get worse when it is changed and enhanced. To protect existing functionality, automated regression tests would be extensively used, as well as standard test suites and reuse of existing tests and test data. For example, you might try to automate all the tests of system functionality so that, whenever anything changes, you can re-run every test to ensure nothing has broken. Regression-averse strategies have in common a set of procedures – usually automated – that allow them to detect regression defects. A regression-averse strategy may involve automating functional tests prior to release of the function, in which case it requires early testing, but sometimes the testing is almost entirely focused on testing functions that have already been released, which is in some sense a form of post-release test involvement.

● **Reactive (or dynamic):** In this strategy, the tests react and evolve based on what is found while test execution occurs, rather than being designed and implemented before test execution starts. For example, you might create a lightweight set of testing guidelines that focus on rapid adaptation or known weaknesses in software. Reactive strategies, using exploratory testing, have in common concentrating on finding as many defects as possible during test execution and adapting to the realities of the system under test as it is when delivered, and they typically emphasize the later stages of testing. See, for example, the attack-based approach of Whittaker [2002] and Whittaker and Thompson [2003] and the exploratory approach of Kaner, Bach and Petticord [2002].

Some of these strategies are more preventive, others more dynamic. For example, analytical test strategies involve up-front analysis of the test basis and tend to identify problems in the test basis prior to test execution. This allows the early, cheap removal of defects. That is a strength of preventive approaches.

Reactive test strategies focus on the test execution period. Such strategies allow the location of defects and defect clusters that might have been hard to anticipate until you have the actual system in front of you. That is a strength of reactive approaches.

Rather than see the choice of strategies, particularly the preventive or reactive strategies, as an either/or situation, we'll let you in on the worst kept secret of testing (and many other disciplines). There is no one best way. We suggest that you adopt whatever test strategies make the most sense for your particular test approach, and feel free to borrow and blend.

How do you know which strategies to pick or blend for the best chance of success? There are many factors to consider, but let's highlight a few of the most important:

- **Risks:** Testing is about risk management, so consider the risks and the level of risk. For a well-established application that is evolving slowly, regression is an important risk, so regression-averse strategies make sense. For a new application, a risk analysis may reveal different risks if you pick a risk-based analytical strategy.

- **Skills:** Strategies must not only be chosen, they must also be executed. So you have to consider the skills that your testers possess and lack. A standard-compliant strategy is a smart choice when you lack the time and skills in your team to create your own approach.

- **Objectives:** Testing must satisfy the needs of stakeholders to be successful. If the objective is to find as many defects as possible with a minimal amount of up-front time and effort invested – for example, at a typical independent test lab – then a dynamic or reactive strategy makes sense.

- **Regulations:** Sometimes you must satisfy not only stakeholders, but also regulators. In this case, you may need to devise a methodical test strategy that satisfies these regulators that you have met all their requirements.

- **Product:** Some products such as weapons systems and contract development software tend to have well-specified requirements. This leads to synergy with a requirements-based analytical strategy.

- **Business:** Business considerations and business continuity are often important. If you can use a legacy system as a model for a new system, you can use a model-based strategy.

We mentioned above that a good team can sometimes triumph over a situation where materials, process and delaying factors are ranged against its success. However, talented execution of an unwise strategy is the equivalent of going very fast down a motorway in the wrong direction. Therefore, you must make smart choices in terms of testing strategies. Furthermore, you must choose testing strategies with an eye toward the factors mentioned earlier, the schedule, budget and feature constraints of the project and the realities of the organization and its politics.

5.2.3 Entry criteria and exit criteria (definition of ready and definition of done)

Two important things to think about when determining the approach and planning the testing are: how do we know we are ready to start a given test activity, and how do we know we are finished (with whatever testing we are concerned with)? At what point can you safely start a particular test level? When are you confident that it is complete? The factors to consider in such decisions are called entry and exit criteria or in Agile development, definition of ready and definition of done (DoD).

Typical **entry criteria** include the following:

- Availability of testable requirements, user stories and/or models, for example when following a model-based testing strategy, that is, the test basis is available.
- Availability of test items that have met the exit criteria for any previous test levels.
- Availability of the test environment.

> **Entry criteria**
> (definition of ready)
> The set of conditions for officially starting a defined task.

- Availability of necessary test tools and any other materials needed.
- Availability of test data and other necessary resources.
- Availability of staff for testing tasks.
- Availability of the component or system to be tested, in a state where tests can be done, that is, availability of the test object.

Why are entry criteria important? If everything needed for testing to go ahead is in place before you start, the testing will go much more smoothly. The problems of getting started with the testing often turn out to be that something needed is not actually ready or in place. Then the testing process gets the blame for the delays. If entry criteria, which are the preconditions for testing, are enforced, or at least thought about beforehand, everything is more likely to go better. If not, you are increasing risk, introducing delays and additional costs, and making life more difficult for yourself.

Typical **exit criteria** include the following:

> **Exit criteria**
> (completion criteria, test completion criteria, definition of done) The set of conditions for officially completing a defined task.

- **Tests:** the number planned, prepared, run, passed, failed, blocked, skipped etc. are acceptable.
- **Coverage:** the extent to which the test basis (for example requirements, user stories, acceptance criteria), risk, functionality, supported configurations, and the software code have been tested (that is, achieved a defined level of coverage) – or have not.
- **Defects:** the number known to be present, the arrival rate, the number estimated to remain, the number resolved and the number of unresolved defects are within an agreed limit.
- **Quality:** the status of the important quality characteristics for the system, for example reliability, performance efficiency, usability, security and other relevant quality characteristics are adequate.
- **Money:** the cost of finding the next defect in the current level of testing compared to the cost of finding it in the next level of testing (or in production).
- **Schedule:** the project schedule implications of starting or ending testing.
- **Risk:** the undesirable outcomes that could result from shipping too early (such as latent defects or untested areas), or too late (such as loss of market share).

When writing exit criteria, we try to remember that a successful project or iteration is a balance of quality, budget, schedule and feature considerations. This is important in each sprint and is important in other development life cycles when exit criteria are applied at the end of the project.

Why are exit criteria important? Knowing what your goals are is important in any human endeavour. If we do not think about 'How will we know we are done' beforehand, then we may stop before we have done enough testing (increasing risk) or we might keep testing when we have done enough (not likely but possible, and this would be wasteful).

In practice, testing is often stopped rather than finished, because time pressure seems to hold the trump card for everything else. But if (or rather when) this happens, if you do have documented exit criteria, you can make the risks more visible to stakeholders and managers by showing what has not yet been completed in the testing. You may not win the argument for doing more testing at the time, but you will have good information to explain next time why the exit criteria are important, especially when/if there are undesirable consequences to not meeting them this time. We also want a 'Stop testing now!' decision to be made with knowledge of all the factors, not just basing that decision on a calendar date.

5.2.4 Test execution schedule

Part of test management is the management of tests. Once test cases and test procedures have been designed and implemented (some as automated tests), they may be assembled into test suites for convenience of running sets of tests together. A schedule for the execution of the test suites should be based on a number of factors, including the priorities of the tests (from risk analysis), technical or logical dependencies of tests or test suites and the type of tests, for example confirmation tests after defects have been fixed, or regression tests. These factors need to be balanced with a sensible and efficient sequence of executing the tests.

For example, it may be that several high-priority tests are dependent on a single low-priority test to set up essential data or starting conditions. In that case, the low-priority test should be executed before the high-priority tests, even when risk priority is the most important factor.

The same logic may apply where tests are dependent on other tests. Actually, this is one reason why tests should ideally be designed to be independent of any other tests. Independent tests can be run in any order.

In Agile development, rapid feedback from tests is key to efficient working of the team, but this means that the test execution schedule is biased toward confirmation tests and short tests, which can be run quickly. This also shows why it is important to be able to identify (or tag) tests so that they can be assembled into different test suites for different execution schedules, something that is particularly important for automated tests.

It is more likely to be the tester or the team rather than the test manager who is making the test execution schedule, but whoever does it, they need to balance the trade-off between efficiency, priority of the tests and the objective of the test execution at the time.

This learning objective is a K3 in the Syllabus, which means that you need to be able to produce a test execution schedule, taking priorities and dependencies into account. See the exercise at the end of this chapter, and the mock exam in Chapter 7.

5.2.5 Factors influencing the test effort

In this section, we'll look at **test estimation**, first describing how to go about estimating testing, what it will involve and what it can cost, and then looking at factors that influence the test effort, many of which are significant for testing even though they are not part of what we are estimating when we estimate testing.

Estimating what testing will involve and what it will cost

The testing work to be done can often be seen as a subproject within the larger project. We can adapt fundamental techniques of estimation for testing. We could start with a work-breakdown structure that identifies the stages, activities and tasks.

Starting at the highest level, we can break down a testing project into major activities using the test process identified in the ISTQB Syllabus (and described in Chapter 1 Section 1.4.2): test planning, test monitoring and control, test analysis, test design, test implementation, test execution and test completion. Within each activity, we identify tasks and perhaps subtasks. To identify the activities and tasks, we work both forward

Test estimation
The calculated approximation of a result related to various aspects of testing, (for example, effort spent, completion date, costs involved, number of test cases, etc.), which is usable even if input data may be incomplete, uncertain or noisy.

and backward. When we say we work forward, we mean that we start with the planning activities and then move forward in time step-by-step, asking 'Now, what comes next?'

Working backward means that we consider the risks that we identified during risk analysis (which we'll discuss in Section 5.5). For those risks which you intend to address through testing, ask yourself, 'What activities and tasks are required in each stage to carry out this testing?' Let's look at an example of how you might work backward.

Suppose that you have identified performance as a major area of risk for your product. Performance testing is an activity in test execution. You now estimate the tasks involved with running a performance test, how long those tasks will take and how many times you will need to run the performance tests.

Now, those tests did not just appear out of thin air: someone had to develop them. Performance test development entails activities in test analysis, design and implementation. You now estimate the tasks involved in developing a performance test, such as writing test scripts and creating test data.

Typically, performance tests need to be run in a special test environment that is designed to look like the production or field environment, at least in those ways which would affect response time and resource utilization. Performance test environment acquisition and configuration is an activity in the test implementation activity. You now estimate tasks involved in acquiring and configuring such a test environment, such as simulating performance based on the production environment design to look for potential bottlenecks, getting the right hardware, software and tools and setting up that hardware, software and tools. Performance tests need special tools to generate load and check response. The acquisition and implementation of such tools also needs to be planned (more on tools in Chapter 6).

It may be possible to use virtualization for your test environment and performance testing tools; this seems to be an attractive idea, since it should save money as you do not have to acquire your own environment or tools. However, the use of virtual environments and using the tools in those environments still needs careful planning.

Not everyone knows how to use performance testing tools or to design performance tests. Performance testing training or staffing is a task in the test planning activity. Depending on the approach you intend to take, you now estimate the time required to identify and hire a performance test professional or to train one or more people in your organization to do the job.

Finally, in many cases a detailed test plan is written for performance testing, due to its differences from other test types. Performance testing planning is a task in test planning. You now estimate the time required to draft, review and finalize a performance test plan.

When you are creating your work-breakdown structure, remember that you will want to use it for both estimation (at the beginning) and monitoring and control (as the project continues). To improve the accuracy of the estimate and enable more precise control, make sure that you subdivide the work finely enough. This means that tasks should be short in duration, say one to three days. If they are much longer – say two weeks – then you run the risk that long and complex subtasks are hiding within the larger task, only to be discovered later. This can lead to nasty surprises during the project.

Factors that affect the test effort

Testing is a complex endeavour on many projects and a variety of factors can influence it. When creating test plans and estimating the testing effort and schedule, you must keep these factors in mind or your plans and estimates will deceive you at the beginning of the project and betray you at the middle or end.

The test strategies or approaches you pick will have a major influence on the testing effort, as we discussed in Section 5.2.2. In this section, let's look at factors related to the product, the development process, the people involved and the results of testing.

Product characteristics

The characteristics of the product that we are testing have a major impact on how we will test it:

● The risks associated with the product. A high-risk product needing a lot of testing will suffer much more severe impacts if testing is not estimated correctly, especially if it is under-estimated.

● The quality of the test basis. We want sufficient product documentation so that the testers can figure out what the system is, how it is supposed to work and what correct behaviour looks like. In other words, adequate and high-quality information about the test basis will help us do a better, more efficient job of defining the tests.

● The size of the product. A larger product leads to increases in the size of the project and the project team. This will also increase the difficulty of predicting and managing the projects and the team. This leads to the disproportionate rate of collapse of large projects.

● The requirements for quality characteristics such as usability, reliability, security, performance etc. also influences the testing effort. These test types can be expensive and time-consuming.

● The complexity of the product domain. Examples of complexity considerations include:

   – The difficulty of comprehending and correctly handling the problem the system is being built to solve, for example avionics and oil exploration software.
   – The use of innovative technologies, especially those long on hyperbole and short on proven track records.
   – The need for intricate and perhaps multiple test configurations, especially when these rely on the timely arrival of scarce software, hardware and other supplies.
   – The prevalence of stringent security rules, strictly regimented processes or other regulations.

● The geographical distribution of the team, especially if the team crosses time zones (as many outsourcing efforts do).

● The required level of detail for test documentation. While good project documentation is a positive factor, it is also true that having to produce detailed documentation, such as meticulously specified test cases, results in delays. During test execution, having to maintain such detailed documentation requires lots of effort, as does working with fragile test data that must be maintained or restored frequently during testing.

● Requirements for legal and regulatory compliance. If you are working in a regulated industry, the time and effort taken to meet those regulatory requirements can be significant.

Development process characteristics

The life cycle and development process in use has an impact on how the test effort is spent. Testing is quite different in Agile development compared to a sequential development life cycle, and other aspects of development also influence testing:

- The stability and maturity of the organization. Mature organizations tend to have better requirements, architecture and unit tests, thus saving test effort later in the life cycle.

- The development life cycle model in use. The life cycle model itself is an influential process factor, as the V-model tends to be more fragile in the face of late change while incremental models such as Agile development tend to have high regression testing costs.

- The test approach. Choosing the right approach is important for good testing, as we have seen. With a less than ideal approach, testing will take longer and take more effort than is necessary.

- The tools used. Tools are supposed to increase efficiency and reduce time spent on some tasks, so test tools, especially those that reduce the effort associated with test execution which is on the critical path for release, should decrease execution time for tests. Of course, other factors about automation may be far more significant, as we will see in Chapter 6. On the development side, debugging tools and a dedicated debugging environment (as opposed to debugging in the test environment) also reduce the time required to complete testing.

- The test process. A test process that is well-understood, with testers trained to perform the activities and tasks they need to do in the most effective and efficient way is the optimum. Test process maturity is another factor, since more mature testing will be more efficient and effective.

- Time pressure. This is another factor to be considered. Pressure should not be an excuse to take unwarranted risks. However, it is a reason to make careful, considered decisions and to plan and re-plan intelligently throughout the process, which is another hallmark of mature processes.

People characteristics

People execute the process, and people factors are as important or more important than any other. Indeed, even when many troubling things are true about a project, an excellent team can often make good things happen on the project and in testing. Important people factors include:

- The skills and experience of the people involved. The skills of individuals and the team as a whole are important, as well as the alignment of those skills with the project's needs. Domain knowledge is likely to be more relevant when the problem being solved is complex, thus requiring specific knowledge on the part of the tester to operate the software and to determine correct versus incorrect behaviour.

- Team cohesion and leadership. Since a project team is a team, solid relationships, reliable execution of agreed-upon commitments and responsibilities and a determination to work together toward a common goal are important. This is especially important for testing, where so much of what we test, use and produce either comes from, relies upon or goes to people outside the testing group. Because of the importance of trusting relationships and the lengthy learning curves involved in software and system engineering, the stability of the project team is an important people factor, too.

Test results

The test results themselves are important in the total amount of test effort during test execution:

- The number and severity of defects found. Wouldn't testing be easy if we never found any defects? Initial tests would just run with no problems, and there would be no need for any tests to be repeated. However, in the real world, the more defects there are and the more severe those defects, the greater the impact on the testing and the test estimates.

- The amount of rework required. Delivery of good quality software at the start of test execution and quick, solid defect fixes during test execution prevents delays in the test execution process. A defect, once identified, should not have to go through multiple cycles of fix/retest/re-open, at least not if the initial estimate is going to be held to. Good design of the test object should make changes easier. For example, good modular design may have a low-level function called by a number of higher-level functions. If a change is made in the low-level function, the functions calling it should work without being changed (if correctly designed).

You probably noticed from this list that we included a number of factors outside the scope and control of the test manager. Indeed, events that occur before or after testing can bring these factors about. For this reason, it is important that testers, especially test managers, be attuned to the overall context in which they operate. Some of these contextual factors result in specific project risks for testing, which should be addressed in the test plan. Project risks are discussed in more detail in Section 5.5.

5.2.6 Test estimation techniques

There are two techniques for estimation covered by the ISTQB Foundation Syllabus. One involves consulting the people who will do the work and other people with expertise on the tasks to be done (expert-based). The other involves analyzing metrics from past projects and from industry data (metrics-based). Let's look at each in turn.

Asking the individual contributors and experts involves working with experienced staff members to develop a work-breakdown structure for the project. With that done, you work together to understand, for each task, the effort, duration, dependencies and resource requirements. The idea is to draw on the collective wisdom of the team to create your test estimate. Using project management software or a whiteboard and sticky notes, you and the team can then predict the testing end date and major milestones. This technique is often called bottom-up estimation, because you start at the lowest level of the hierarchical breakdown in the work-breakdown structure (the task) and let the duration, effort, dependencies and resources for each task add up across all the tasks. This is the expert-based technique.

Analyzing metrics can be as simple or sophisticated as you make it. The simplest approach is to ask, 'How many testers do we typically have per developer on a project?' A somewhat more reliable approach involves classifying the project in terms of size (small, medium or large) and complexity (simple, moderate or complex) and then seeing on average how long projects of a particular size and complexity combination have taken in the past. Another simple and reliable approach we have used is to look at the average effort per test case in similar past projects and to use the estimated number of test cases to estimate the total effort. Sophisticated approaches involve building mathematical models in a spreadsheet or other tool that look at historical or industry averages for certain key parameters – number of tests run by a tester per day, number of defects found by a tester per day, etc. – and then plugging in those parameters to predict duration and effort for key tasks or activities on your project. The tester-to-developer ratio is an example of a top-down estimation technique, in that the entire estimate is derived at the project level, while the parametric technique is bottom-up, at least when it is used to estimate individual tasks or activities.

We prefer to start by drawing on the team's wisdom to create the work-breakdown structure and a detailed bottom-up estimate. We then apply models and rules of thumb to check and adjust the estimate bottom-up and top-down using past history. This approach tends to create an estimate that is both more accurate and more defensible than either technique by itself.

Even the best estimate must be negotiated with management. Negotiating sessions exhibit amazing variety, depending on the people involved. However, there are some classic negotiating positions. It is not unusual for the test manager to try to sell the management team on the value added by the testing or to alert management to the potential problems that would result from not testing enough. It is not unusual for management to look for smart ways to accelerate the schedule or to press for equivalent coverage in less time or with fewer resources. In between these positions, you and your colleagues can reach compromise, if the parties are willing. Our experience has been that successful negotiations about estimates are those where the focus is less on winning and losing and more about figuring out how best to balance competing pressures in the realms of quality, schedule, budget and features.

In Agile development, planning poker is an example of the expert-based technique; team members estimate based on their own experience of the effort needed to deliver and test a feature. Burndown charts are an example of the metrics-based technique, since the effort being spent is captured and reported and used to feed into the team's velocity to determine the amount of work the team can do in the next iteration. This is actually monitoring of the current sprint in order to use the results to help predict and estimate the effort needed for the following sprint. The ISTQB Foundation Level Agile Tester Extension Syllabus has more on estimation of testing in Agile development.

In sequential life cycle models, a technique such as Wideband Delphi estimation is an example of expert-based estimation, since groups of engineers provide estimates which are then aggregated together.

Defect removal models are examples of metrics-based techniques. Data is gathered from previous projects about the number of defects and the time to remove them; this provides a basis for future similar projects. More information about these are given in the ISTQB Advanced Level Test Manager Syllabus.

5.3 TEST MONITORING AND CONTROL

> **SYLLABUS LEARNING OBJECTIVES FOR 5.3 TEST MONITORING AND CONTROL (K2)**
>
> FL-5.3.1 **Recall metrics used for testing (K1)**
>
> FL-5.3.2 **Summarize the purposes, contents and audiences for test reports (K2)**

In this section, we'll review techniques and metrics that are commonly used for monitoring test implementation and execution. We'll focus especially on the use and interpretation of such test metrics for reporting, controlling and analyzing the test effort, including those based on defects and those based on test data. We'll also look at options for reporting test status using such metrics and other information.

As you read, remember to watch for the Glossary terms **test control**, **test monitoring**, **test progress report** and **test summary report**.

Test monitoring is concerned with gathering data and information about test activities; **test control** is using that information to guide or control the remaining testing. We will look briefly at test control in this introduction, then consider various metrics that could be gathered, and finally discuss how information should be communicated in test reports.

Projects do not always unfold as planned. In fact, any human endeavour more complicated than a family picnic is likely to vary from plan. Risks become occurrences. Stakeholder needs evolve. The world around us changes. When plans and reality diverge, we must act to bring the project back under control, and testing is no exception.

In some cases, the test findings themselves are behind the divergence; for example, suppose the quality of the test items proves unacceptably bad and delays test progress. In other cases, testing is affected by outside events; for example, testing can be delayed when the test items show up late or the test environment is unavailable. Test control is about guiding and corrective actions to try to achieve the best possible outcome for the project.

The specific corrective or guiding actions depend, of course, on what we are trying to control. Consider the following hypothetical examples of test control actions:

- A portion of the software under test will be delivered late, after the planned test start date. Market conditions dictate that we cannot change the release date. Test control might involve re-prioritizing the tests so that we start testing against what is available now.

- For cost reasons, performance testing is normally run on weekday evenings during off-hours in the production environment. Due to unanticipated high demand for your products, the company has temporarily adopted an evening shift that keeps the production environment in use 18 hours a day, five days a week. Test control might involve rescheduling the performance tests for the weekend.

- The item being tested had previously met its entry (or exit) criteria, but since the criteria were evaluated, the test item has changed due to defects found and resulting rework. Control actions may include re-evaluating the entry (or exit) criteria.

> **Test monitoring** A test management activity that involves checking the status of testing activities, identifying any variances from the planned or expected status and reporting status to stakeholders.
>
> **Test control** A test management task that deals with developing and applying a set of corrective actions to get a test project on track when monitoring shows a deviation from what was planned.

While these examples show test control actions that affect testing, the project team might also have to take some actions that affect others on the project. For example, suppose that the test completion date is at risk due to a high number of defect fixes that fail confirmation testing in the test environment. In this case, test control might involve requiring the developers making the fixes to thoroughly retest the fixes prior to checking them in to the code repository for inclusion in a test build.

5.3.1 Metrics used in testing

The purpose of metrics in testing

Having developed our plans, defined our test strategies and approaches, and estimated the work to be done, we must now track our testing work as we carry it out. Test monitoring can serve various purposes during the project, including the following:

- Give the test team and the test manager feedback on how the testing work is going, allowing opportunities to guide and improve the testing and the project. This would be done by collecting time and cost data about progress versus the planned schedule and budget.

- Provide the project team with visibility about the test results and the quality of the test object.

- Measure the status of the testing, test coverage and test items against the exit criteria to determine whether the test work is done, and to assess the effectiveness of the test activities with respect to the objectives.

- Gather data for use in estimating future test efforts, including the adequacy of the test approach.

Especially for small projects, the test manager or a delegated person can gather test progress monitoring information manually using documents, spreadsheets and simple databases. When working with large teams, distributed projects and long-term test efforts, we find that the efficiency and consistency of data collection is aided by the use of automated tools (see Chapter 6).

Common test metrics

We will show some examples of using metrics in testing and conclude this section with a list of other common test metrics.

In Figure 5.1, columns A and B show the test ID and the test case or test suite name. The state of the test case is shown in column C ('Warn' indicates a test that resulted in a minor failure). Column D shows the tested configuration, where the codes A, B and C correspond to test environments described in detail in the test plan. Columns E and F show the defect (or bug) ID number (from the defect tracking database) and the risk priority number of the defect (ranging from 1, the highest risk, to 25, the least risky). Column G shows the initials of the tester who ran the test. Columns H to L capture data for each test related to dates, effort and duration (in hours). We have metrics for planned and actual effort and dates completed which would allow us to summarize progress against the planned schedule and budget. This spreadsheet can also be summarized in terms of the percentage of tests which have been run and the percentage of tests which have passed and failed.

Figure 5.1 might show a snapshot of test progress during the test execution period, or perhaps even at test closure if it were deemed acceptable to skip some of the tests.

	Test ID	Test Suite/Case	Status	System Config	Bug ID	Bug RPN	Run By	Plan Date	Act Date	Plan Effort	Actual Effort	Test Duration	Comment
1			System Test Case Summary										
2			Cycle One										
3													
6													
7	1.000	*Functionality*											
8	1.001	File	Fail	A	701	1	LTW	1/8	1/8	4	6	6	
9	1.002	Edit	Fail	A	709	1	LTW	1/9	1/10	4	8	8	
10					710	5							
11					718	3							
12					722	4							
13	1.003	Font	Pass	B			IHB	1/10	1/10	4	4	4	
14	1.004	Tables	Warn	B	708	15	IHB	1/8	1/9	4	5	5	
15	1.005	Printing	Skip					1/10		4			Out of runway
16		**Suite Summary**						**1/10**	**1/10**	**20**	**23**	**23**	
17													
18	2.000	*Performance/Stress*											
19	2.001	Solaris Server	Warn	A,B,C	701	1	EM	1/10	1/13	4	8	24	Replan 1/11
20	2.002	NT Server	Fail	A,B,C	724	2	EM	1/11	1/14	4	4	24	Replan 1/12
21					713	2							
22					725	1							
23	2.003	Linux Server	Skip					1/12		4			Out of runway
24		**Suite Summary**						**1/12**	**1/14**	**12**	**12**	**48**	
25													
26	3.000	*Error Handling/Recovery*											
27	3.001	Corrupt File	Fail	A	701	1	LTW	1/8	1/9	4	8	8	
28					706	2							
29					707	4							
30					709	1							
31					710	5							
32					713	2							
33	3.002	Server Crash	Fail	A	712	6	LTW	1/9	1/10	4	6	6	
34					713	2							
35					717	1							
36		**Suite Summary**						**1/9**	**1/10**	**8**	**14**	**14**	
37													
38	4.000	*Localization*											
39	4.001	Spanish	Skip										
40	4.002	French	Skip										
41	4.003	Japanese	Skip										
42	4.004	Chinese	Skip										
43		**Suite Summary**						**1/0**	**1/0**	**0**	**0**	**0**	

FIGURE 5.1 Test case summary worksheet

During the analysis, design and implementation of the tests, such a worksheet would show the state of the tests in terms of their state of development.

In addition to test case status, it is also common to monitor test progress during the test execution period by looking at the number of defects found and fixed. Figure 5.2 shows a graph that plots the total number of defects opened and closed over the course of the test execution so far.

It also shows the planned test period end date and the planned number of defects that will be found. Ideally, as the project approaches the planned end date, the total number of defects opened will settle in at the predicted number and the total number of defects closed will converge with the total number opened. These two outcomes tell us that we have found enough defects to feel comfortable that we have finished, that we have no reason to think many more defects are lurking in the product and that all known defects have been resolved.

Charts such as Figure 5.2 can also be used to show failure rates or defect density. When reliability is a key concern, we might be more concerned with the frequency with which failures are observed than with how many defects are causing the failures. In organizations that are looking to produce ultra reliable software, they may plot the

Integration and System Test Execution
System Quality Problems Analysis

Predicted number of bugs IST will
find by planned project end date, 3/21

Exploratory testing yields
more than usual number
of bugs on most Fridays

Thanksgiving

Confirmation testing of fixed bugs in
each new release makes the total
closed curve jump on Mondays
and Tuesdays

Date Opened/Closed

Key Milestones
Integration Test Entry 10/7   Integration Test Exit 2/14
System Test Entry 10/21   System Test Exit 3/21

Total Opened
Total Closed
N.B. Closed counts include deferred bugs

FIGURE 5.2   Total defects opened and closed chart

number of unresolved defects normalized by the size of the product, either in thousands of source lines of code (KSLOC), function points (FP) or some other metric of code size. Once the number of unresolved defects falls below some predefined threshold – for example, three per million lines of code – then the product may be deemed to have met the defect density exit criteria.

Measuring test progress based on defects found and fixed is common and useful, if used with care. Avoid using defect metrics alone, as it is possible to achieve a flat defect find rate and to fix all the known defects by stopping any further testing, by deliberately impeding the reporting of defects and by allowing developers to reject, cancel or close defect reports without any independent review.

That said, test progress monitoring techniques vary considerably depending on the preferences of the testers and stakeholders, the needs and goals of the project, regulatory requirements, time and money constraints and other factors.

Common metrics for test progress monitoring include:

- The percentage of planned work done in test case preparation (or percentage of planned test cases implemented).
- The percentage of planned work done in test environment preparation.
- Metrics relating to test execution, such as the number of test cases run and not run, the number of test cases passed or failed, or/and the number of test conditions passed or failed.
- Metrics relating to defects, such as defect density, defects found and fixed, failure rate and confirmation test results.
- The extent of test coverage achieved, measured against requirements, user stories, acceptance criteria, risks, code, configurations or other areas of interest.

- The status of the testing (including analysis, design and implementation) compared to various test milestones, that is, task completion, resource allocation and usage, and effort.
- The economics of testing, such as the costs and benefits of continuing test execution in terms of finding the next defect or running the next test.

As a complementary monitoring technique, you might assess the subjective level of confidence the testers have in the test items. However, avoid making important decisions based on subjective assessments alone, as people's impressions have a way of being inaccurate and coloured by bias.

5.3.2 Purpose, contents and audiences for test reports

The purpose of test reports

Test monitoring is about gathering detailed test data; reporting test progress is about effectively communicating our findings to other project stakeholders. As with test progress monitoring, in practice there is wide variability observed in how people report test progress, with the variations driven by the preferences of the testers and stakeholders, the needs and goals of the project, regulatory requirements, time and money constraints and limitations of the tools available for test progress reporting. Often variations or summaries of the metrics used for test progress monitoring, such as Figure 5.1 and Figure 5.2, are used for test progress reporting, too. Regardless of the specific metrics, charts and reports used, test progress reporting is about helping project stakeholders understand the results of a test period, especially as it relates to key project goals and whether (or when) exit criteria were satisfied.

In addition to notifying project stakeholders about test results, test progress reporting is often about enlightening and influencing them. This involves analyzing the information and metrics available to support conclusions, recommendations and decisions about how to guide the project forward or to take other actions. For example, we might estimate the number of defects remaining to be discovered, present the costs and benefits of delaying a release date to allow for further testing, assess the remaining product and project risks and offer an opinion on the confidence the stakeholders should have in the quality of the system under test.

You should think about test progress reporting during test planning, since you will often need to collect specific metrics during and at the end of a test period to generate the test progress reports in an effective and efficient fashion. The specific data you will want to gather will depend on your specific reports, but common considerations include the following:

- How will you assess the adequacy of the test objectives for a given test level and whether those objectives were achieved?
- How will you assess the adequacy of the test approaches taken and whether they support the achievement of the project's testing goals?
- How will you assess the effectiveness of the testing with respect to these objectives and approaches?

For example, if you are doing risk-based testing, one main test objective is to subject the important product risks to the appropriate extent of testing. Table 5.1 shows an example of a chart that would allow you to report your test coverage and

TABLE 5.1 Risk coverage by defects and tests

Product risk areas	Unresolved defects		Test cases to be run		
	Number	%	Planned	Actual	%
Performance, load, reliability	304	28	3,843	1,512	39
Robustness, operations, security	234	21	1,032	432	42
Functionality, data, dates	224	20	4,744	2,043	43
Use cases, user interfaces, localization	160	15	498	318	64
Interfaces	93	8	193	153	79
Compatibility	71	6	1,787	939	53
Other	21	2	760	306	40
	1,107	*100*	*12,857*	*5,703*	*44*

unresolved defects against the main product risk areas you identified in your risk analysis. If you are doing requirements-based testing, you could measure coverage in terms of requirements or functional areas instead of risks.

The content of test reports

Test progress report
(test status report)
A test report produced at regular intervals about the progress of test activities against a baseline, risks and alternatives requiring a decision.

Test summary report
(test report)
A test report that provides an evaluation of the corresponding test items against exit criteria.

The Syllabus discusses two types of test report: a **test progress report** and a **test summary report**. Both reports contain a lot of information in common; the main difference is that test progress reports are used at regular intervals throughout the project, during test activities, and would result in test control actions; the test summary report is in a sense the final test progress report for the whole project, and is prepared at the end of a test activity or test level. For example, a test summary report could also be used in a retrospective.

Because test progress reports are reporting on more dynamic information, there are some things which are included in this report that are no longer relevant for a test summary report, including:

- The current status of the test activities and progress against the test plan.
- Factors that are currently impeding the progress of the testing.
- The testing planned for the next period, to be including in the next test progress report.
- The quality of the test object as currently assessed by the testing.

When exit criteria are met, the test manager issues the test summary report. Such a report, created either at a key milestone or at the end of a test level, describes the results of a given test level. In addition to including the kind of charts and tables shown earlier (but now at the end of the time period being monitored), you might discuss important events (especially problematic ones) that occurred during testing, the objectives of testing and whether they were achieved, the test approach, strategies followed, how well they worked and the overall effectiveness of the test effort. The test summary report draws on the test progress reports over the duration of the project or test level, particularly the last one.

The contents of both test progress reports and test summary reports may include the following:

- A summary of the testing performed.
- Information about what occurred during the period the report covers.
- Deviations from plan, with regard to the schedule, duration or effort of test activities.
- The status of the testing and of product (test object) quality with respect to the exit criteria or definition of done.
- The factors that have blocked or continue to block progress.
- Relevant metrics, such as those relating to defects, test cases, test coverage, test activity progress, and resource consumption, as described in Section 5.3.1.
- Residual risks (see Section 5.5).
- Reusable test work products produced.

Not every test report will contain all this information (for example a quick software update), and some may include additional information (for example for a complex project with many stakeholders or under legal and regulatory requirements). The content of the report depends on the project, organizational requirements and the software development life cycle. For example, in Agile development, test progress reporting may be incorporated into task boards, defect summaries and burndown charts, which may be discussed during a daily stand-up meeting. For more about test reports in Agile projects, see the ISTQB-AT Foundation Level Agile Tester Extension Syllabus.

The audience for test reports and the effect on the report

In addition to the factors already mentioned that influence the content of a test report (either progress or summary), each test report should be tailored for the intended audience of the report. For example, a test summary report which is intended for the CEO and other high-level management should be short and concise, with overview summaries of the main points. It may contain a summary of defects of high and other priority levels and the percentage of tests passed, but information about budget and schedule would be of more importance to them. A test progress report which is intended for testers and developers would include detailed information about defect types and trends, such as we saw in Figure 5.2.

The standard ISO/IEC/IEEE 291119-3 [2013] gives structures and examples of test progress reports and what they call test completion reports (test summary reports).

5.4 CONFIGURATION MANAGEMENT

SYLLABUS LEARNING OBJECTIVE FOR 5.4 CONFIGURATION MANAGEMENT (K2)

FL-5.4.1   Summarize how configuration management supports testing (K2)

In this brief section, we'll look at how configuration management relates to and supports testing. The only Glossary term is **configuration management**.

Configuration management is a topic that often perplexes new practitioners, but, if you ever have the bad luck to work as a tester on a project where this critical activity is handled poorly, you will never forget how important it is. Briefly put, configuration management is in part about determining clearly what the items are that make up the software or system. These items include source code, test scripts, third-party software (including tools that support testing), hardware, data and both development and test documentation. Configuration management is also about making sure that these items are managed carefully, thoroughly and attentively throughout the entire project and product life cycle.

Configuration management has a number of important implications for testing. For one thing, it allows the testers to manage their testware and test results using the same configuration management mechanisms, as if they were as valuable as the source code and documentation for the system itself – which of course they are.

For another thing, configuration management supports the build process, which is essential for delivery of a test release into the test environment. It is critical to have a solid, reliable way of delivering test items that work and are the proper version.

Last but not least, configuration management allows us to map what is being tested to the underlying files and components that make it up. This is absolutely critical. For example, when we report defects, we need to report them *against* something, something which is configuration controlled or version controlled. If it is not clear what we found the defect in, the developers will have a very tough time of finding the defect in order to fix it. For the kind of test reports discussed earlier to have any meaning, we must be able to trace the test results back to what exactly we tested.

Configuration management for testing may involve ensuring the following:

- All test items of the test object are uniquely identified, version controlled, tracked for changes and related to each other, that is, what is being tested.

- All items of testware are uniquely identified, version controlled, tracked for changes, related to each other and related to a version of the test item(s) so that traceability can be maintained throughout the test process.

- All identified work products and software items are referenced unambiguously in test documentation.

Ideally, when testers receive an organized, version-controlled test release from a change-managed source code repository, it is accompanied by release notes which contain all the information shown.

While our description was brief, configuration management is a topic that is as complex as test environment management. Advanced planning is critical to making this work. During the project planning stage, and perhaps as part of your own test plan, make sure that configuration management procedures and tools are selected. As the project proceeds, the configuration process and mechanisms must be implemented, and the key interfaces to the rest of the development process should be documented. Come test execution time, this will allow you and the rest of the project team to avoid nasty surprises like testing the wrong software, receiving uninstallable builds and reporting unreproducible defects against versions of code that do not exist anywhere but in the test environment.

Configuration management A discipline applying technical and administrative direction and surveillance to identify and document the functional and physical characteristics of a configuration item, control changes to those characteristics, record and report change processing and implementation status, and verify compliance with specified requirements.

5.5 RISKS AND TESTING

SYLLABUS LEARNING OBJECTIVES FOR 5.5 RISK AND TESTING (K2)

FL-5.5.1   Define risk level by using likelihood and impact (K1)

FL-5.5.2   Distinguish between project and product risks (K2)

FL-5.5.3   Describe, by using examples, how product risk analysis may influence the thoroughness and scope of testing (K2)

This section covers a topic that we believe is critical to testing: risk. Let's look closely at risks, the possible problems that might endanger the objectives of the project stakeholders. We will discuss how to determine the level of risk using likelihood and impact. We will see that there are risks related to the product and risks related to the project, and look at typical risks in both categories. Finally, and most important, we'll look at various ways that risk analysis and risk management can help us plot a course for solid testing

As you read this section, make sure to attend carefully to the Glossary terms **product risk**, **project risk**, **risk**, **risk level** and **risk-based testing**.

5.5.1 Definition of risk

Risk is a word we all use loosely, but what exactly is risk? Simply put, it is the possibility of a negative or undesirable outcome. In the future, a risk has some likelihood between 0% and 100%; it is a possibility, not a certainty. In the past, however, either the risk has materialized and become an outcome or issue or it has not; the likelihood of a risk in the past is either 0% or 100%.

> **Risk** A factor that could result in future negative consequences.

The likelihood of a risk becoming an outcome is one factor to consider when thinking about the **risk level** associated with its possible negative consequences. The more likely the outcome is, the worse the risk. However, likelihood is not the only consideration.

> **Risk level** (risk exposure) The qualitative or quantitative measure of a risk defined by impact and likelihood.

For example, most people are likely to catch a cold in the course of their lives, usually more than once. The typical healthy individual suffers no serious consequences. Therefore the overall level of risk associated with colds is low for this person. But the risk of a cold for an elderly person with breathing difficulties would be high. The potential consequences or impact is an important consideration affecting the level of risk, too.

Remember that in Chapter 1 we discussed how system context, and especially the risk associated with failures, influences testing. Here, we'll get into more detail about the concept of risks, how they influence testing and specific ways to manage risk.

5.5.2 Product and project risks

We can classify risks into project risks (factors relating to the way the work is carried out, that is, the test project) and product risks (factors relating to what is produced by the work, that is, the thing we are testing). We will look at product risks first.

Product risks

You can think of a **product risk** as the possibility that the system or software might fail to satisfy some reasonable customer, user or stakeholder expectation. Unsatisfactory software might omit some key function that the customers specified, the users required or the stakeholders were promised. It might be unreliable and frequently fail to behave normally. It might fail in ways that cause financial or other damage to a user or the company that user works for. It might have problems with data integrity and data quality, such as data migration issues, data conversion problems, data transport problems and violations of data standards such as field and referential integrity. It might have problems related to a particular quality characteristic. The problems might not involve functionality, but rather security, reliability, usability, maintainability or performance. This type of quality attribute-related risk is sometimes referred to as a 'quality risk'. Generally, the software could fail to perform its intended functions, dissatisfying users and customers. If you can write a test for it, it's a product risk.

Here are some example product risks:

- Software might not perform its intended functions according to the specification.

- Software might not perform its intended functions according to user, customer, and/or stakeholder needs or expectations (which is usually different from the first!).

- A particular computation may be performed incorrectly in some circumstances.

- A loop control structure may be coded incorrectly.

- Response times may be inadequate for a high-performance transaction processing system.

- User experience (UX) feedback might not meet product expectations.

Project risks

We just discussed risks to product quality. However, testing is an activity like the rest of the project and thus it is subject to risks that endanger the project. To deal with the **project risks** that apply to testing, we can use the same concepts we apply to identifying, prioritizing and managing product risks, which we will discuss in Section 5.3.3.

Remembering that a risk is the possibility of a negative outcome, what project risks affect testing? There are direct risks such as the late delivery of the test items to the test team or availability issues with the test environment. There are also indirect risks such as excessive delays in repairing defects found in testing or problems with getting professional system administration support for the test environment.

Of course, these are merely four examples of project risks; many others can apply to your testing effort. To discover these risks, ask yourself and other project participants and stakeholders: 'What could go wrong on the project to delay or invalidate the test plan, the test strategy and the test estimate? What are unacceptable outcomes of testing or in testing? What are the likelihoods and impacts of each of these risks?' This process is very much like the risk analysis process for products. Checklists and examples can help you identify test project risks [Black 2004].

The Syllabus gives a good list of project risks in different categories. We list them here along with some examples and ways to deal with them.

Project issues:

- Delays may occur in delivery, task completion or satisfaction of exit criteria or definition of done. For example, logistics or product quality problems may block tests: These can be mitigated through careful planning, good defect triage and management, and robust test design.

- Inaccurate estimates, reallocation of funds to higher priority projects, or general cost cutting across the organization may result in inadequate funding.

- Late changes may result in substantial rework. For example, excessive change to the product may invalidate test results or require updates to test cases, expected results and environments. These can be mitigated through good change control processes, robust test design and lightweight test documentation. When severe defects occur, transference of the risk by escalation to management is often in order.

Organizational issues:

- Skills, training and staff may not be sufficient. For example, shortages of people, skills or training may lead to problems with communicating and responding to test results, unrealistic expectations of what testing can achieve, and needlessly complex project or team organization.

- Personnel issues may cause conflict and problems, affecting work. For example, if two people do not get along, working against each other rather than toward a common goal (it happens), this is demoralizing to the whole team as well as degrading the quality of everyone's work.

- Users, business staff or subject matter experts may not be available due to conflicting business priorities.

Political issues:

- Testers may not communicate their needs and/or the test results adequately. For example, high-level managers may not realize the need for ongoing support, time and effort for test automation after an initial start, if testers and automators do not communicate the need for this.

- Developers and/or testers may fail to follow up on information found in testing and reviews (for example not improving development and testing practices).

- There may be an improper attitude toward, or expectations of, testing (for example not appreciating the value of finding defects during testing).

Technical issues:

- Requirements or user stories may not be clear enough or well enough defined. For example, ambiguous, conflicting or unprioritized requirements, an excessively large number of requirements given other project constraints, high system complexity and quality problems with the design, the code or the tests mean that the system will take longer to develop and may not meet customer expectations. The best cure for this is clear unambiguous requirements.

- The requirements may not be met, given existing constraints. For example, a requirement may want the app to be able to check the user's bank balance to see if they can pay for what they are ordering, but the bank software does not allow it.

- The test environment may not be ready on time or may not be adequate. For example, insufficient or unrealistic test environments may yield misleading results, including false positives and false negatives. One option is to transfer the risks to management by explaining the limits on test results obtained in limited environments. Mitigation, sometimes complete alleviation, can be achieved by outsourcing tests such as performance tests that are particularly sensitive to proper test environments, or by using virtualization.

- Data conversion, migration planning and their tool support may be late.

- Weaknesses in the development process may impact the consistency or quality of project work products such as design, code, configurations, test data and test cases. For example, test items may not install in the test environment. This can be mitigated through smoke (or acceptance) testing prior to starting other testing or as part of a nightly build or continuous integration. Having a defined uninstall process is a good contingency plan.

- Poor defect management and similar problems may result in accumulated defects and other technical debt.

Supplier issues:

- A third party may fail to deliver a necessary product or service or go bankrupt.

- Contractual issues may cause problems to the project. For example, problems with underlying platforms or hardware, failure to consider testing issues in the contract, or failure to properly respond to the issues when they arise can quickly add up to serious delays as well as time-consuming negotiations with a supplier. The best way to mitigate this is to ensure that the contract is solid to begin with, and have the technical details reviewed by testers or a test manager.

Project risks do not just affect testing of course, they also affect development. In some organizations, project managers are responsible for dealing with all project risks, but sometimes test managers are given responsibility for test-related project risks (as well as product risks).

There may be other risks that apply to your project and not all projects are subject to the same risks. See Chapter 2 of Black [2009], Chapters 6 and 7 of Black [2004] and Chapter 3 of Craig and Jaskiel [2002] for a discussion on managing project risks during testing and in the test plan.

Finally, don't forget that test items can also have risks associated with them. For example, there is a risk that the test plan will omit tests for a functional area or that the test cases do not exercise the critical areas of the system.

5.5.3 Risk-based testing and product quality

Risk management

Dealing with risks within an organization is known as risk management, and testing is one way of managing aspects of risk. For any risk, product or project, you have four typical options:

- **Mitigate:** Take steps in advance to reduce the likelihood (and possibly the impact) of the risk.

- **Contingency:** Have a plan in place to reduce the impact should the risk become an outcome.

- **Transfer:** Convince some other member of the team or project stakeholder to reduce the likelihood or accept the impact of the risk.

- **Ignore:** Do nothing about the risk, which is usually a smart option only when there's little that can be done or when the likelihood and impact are low.

There is another typical risk management option, buying insurance, which is not usually pursued for project or product risks on software projects, though it is not unheard of.

Risk management activities include:

- Identifying and analyzing (and re-evaluating on a regular basis) what can go wrong.

- Determining the priority of risks, which risks are the most important to deal with.

- Implementing actions to mitigate those risks, to reduce their likelihood or impact or both.

- Making contingency plans to deal with risks if they do happen.

We can deal with test-related risks to the project and product by applying some straightforward, structured risk management techniques. The first step is to assess or analyze risks early in the project. Like a big ocean liner, projects, especially large projects, require steering well before the iceberg is in plain sight. By using a test plan, you can remind yourself to consider and manage risks during the planning activity.

Risk-based testing

Risk-based testing is the idea that we can organize our testing efforts in a way that reduces the residual level of product risk when the system is delivered. Risk-based testing uses risk to prioritize and emphasize the appropriate tests during test execution, but it is about more than that. Risk-based testing starts early in the project, identifying risks to system quality and using that knowledge of risk to guide testing planning, specification, preparation and execution. Risk-based testing involves both mitigation (testing to provide opportunities to reduce the likelihood of defects, especially high-impact defects) and contingency (testing to identify work-arounds to make the defects that do get past us less painful). Risk-based testing also involves measuring how well we are doing at finding and removing defects in critical areas, as was shown in Table 5.1. Risk-based testing can also involve using risk analysis to identify proactive opportunities to remove or prevent defects through non-testing activities and to help us select which test activities to perform.

> **Risk-based testing**
> Testing in which the management, selection, prioritization and use of testing activities and resources are based on corresponding risk types and risk levels.

Mature test organizations use testing to reduce the risk associated with delivering the software to an acceptable level [Beizer 1990, Hetzel 1988]. In the middle of the 1990s, a number of testers, including us, started to explore various techniques for risk-based testing. In doing so, we adapted well-accepted risk management concepts to software testing. Applying and refining risk assessment and management techniques are discussed in Black [2004] and Black [2009]. For two alternative views, see Chapter 11 of Pol, Teunissen and van Veenendaal [2002] and Chapter 2 of Craig and Jaskiel [2002]. The origin of the risk-based testing concept can be found in Chapter 1 of Beizer [1990] and Chapter 2 of Hetzel [1988].

Risk analysis

Risk-based testing starts with product risk analysis. One technique for risk analysis is a close reading of the requirements specification, user stories, design specifications, user documentation and other items. Another technique is brainstorming with many of the project stakeholders. Another is a sequence of one-to-one or small group sessions with the business and technology experts in the company. Some people use all these techniques when they can. To us, a team-based approach that involves the key stakeholders and experts is preferable to a purely document-based approach, as team approaches draw on the knowledge, wisdom and insight of the entire team to determine what to test and how much.

While you could perform the risk analysis by asking, 'What should we worry about?' usually more structure is required to avoid missing things. One way to provide that structure is to look for specific risks in particular product risk categories. You could consider risks in the areas of functionality, localization, usability, reliability, performance and supportability. Alternatively, you could use the quality characteristics and sub-characteristics from ISO/IEC 25010 [2011] (introduced in Chapter 2), as each sub-characteristic that matters is subject to risks that the system might have troubles in that area. You might have a checklist of typical or past risks that should be considered. You might also want to review the tests that failed and the bugs that you found in a previous release or a similar product. These lists and reflections serve to jog the memory, forcing you to think about risks of particular types, as well as helping you structure the documentation of the product risks.

When we talk about specific risks, we mean a particular kind of defect or failure that might occur. For example, if you were testing the calculator utility that is bundled with Microsoft Windows, you might identify incorrect calculation as a specific risk within the category of functionality. However, this is too broad. Consider incorrect addition. This is a high-impact kind of defect, as everyone who uses the calculator will see it. It is unlikely, since addition is not a complex algorithm. Contrast that with an incorrect sine calculation. This is a low-impact kind of defect, since few people use the sine function on the Windows calculator. It is more likely to have a defect, though, since sine functions are hard to calculate.

It's worth making the point here that in early risk analysis, we are making educated guesses. Some of those guesses will be wrong. Make sure that you plan to re-assess and adjust your risks at regular intervals in the project and make appropriate course corrections to the testing or the project itself.

One common problem people have when organizations first adopt risk-based testing is a tendency to be excessively alarmed by some of the risks once they are clearly articulated. Don't confuse impact with likelihood or vice versa. You should manage risks appropriately, based on likelihood and impact. Triage the risks by understanding how much of your overall effort can be spent dealing with them.

It's very important to maintain a sense of perspective, a focus on the point of the exercise. As with life, the goal of risk-based testing should not be, but cannot practically be, a risk-free project. What we can accomplish with risk-based testing is the marriage of testing with best practices in risk management to achieve a project outcome that balances risks with quality, features, budget and schedule.

Assigning a risk level

After identifying the risk items, you and, if applicable, the stakeholders, should review the list to assign the likelihood of problems and the impact of problems associated with each one. There are many ways to go about this assignment of likelihood and impact. You can do this with all the stakeholders at once. You can have the business people determine impact and the technical people determine likelihood, and then merge the determinations. Either way, the reason for identifying risks first and then assessing their level, is that the risks are relative to each other.

The scales used to rate likelihood and impact vary. Some people rate them high, medium and low. Some use a 1–10 scale. The problem with a 1–10 scale is that it is often difficult to tell a 2 from a 3 or a 7 from an 8, unless the differences between each rating are clearly defined. A five-point scale (very high, high, medium, low and very low) tends to work well.

Given two classifications of risk levels, likelihood and impact, we have a problem. We need a single, aggregate risk rating to guide our testing effort. As with rating scales, practices vary. One approach is to convert each risk classification into a number and then either multiply (or add) the numbers to calculate a risk priority number. For example, suppose a particular risk has a high likelihood and a medium impact. The risk priority number would then be 6 (2 times 3).

Mitigation options

Armed with a risk priority number, we can now decide on the various risk mitigation options available to us. Do we use formal training for developers or analysts, rely on cross-training and reviews or assume they know enough? Do we perform extensive testing, cursory testing or no testing at all? Should we ensure unit testing and system testing coverage of this risk? These options and more are available to us.

As you go through this process, make sure you capture the key information in a document. We are not fond of excessive documentation but this quantity of information simply cannot be managed in your head. We recommend a lightweight table like the one shown in Table 5.2, which we usually capture in a spreadsheet.

TABLE 5.2 A risk analysis template

Product risk	Likelihood	Impact	Risk priority number	Mitigation
Risk category 1				
Risk 1				
Risk 2				
Risk n				

Concluding thoughts on risk

To summarize, the results of product risk analysis are used for the following purposes:

- To determine the test techniques to be used.
- To determine the particular levels and types of testing to be performed (for example functional testing, security testing, performance testing).
- To determine the extent of testing to be carried out for the different levels and types of testing.

- To prioritize testing in order to find the most critical defects as early as possible.
- To determine whether any activities in addition to testing could be employed to reduce risk, such as providing training in design and testing to inexperienced developers.

Let's finish this section with two quick tips about product risk analysis. First, remember to consider both likelihood and impact. While it might make you feel like a hero to find lots of defects, testing is also about building confidence in key functions. We need to test the things that probably will not break, but would be catastrophic if they did.

Second, we re-iterate that in early risk analysis, we are making educated guesses. Make sure that you follow up and revisit the risk analysis at key project milestones. For example, if you are following a V-model, you might perform the initial analysis during the requirements phase, then review and revise it at the end of the design and implementation phases, as well as prior to starting unit test, integration test and system test. We also recommend revisiting the risk analysis during testing. You might find you have discovered new risks or found that some risks were not as risky as you thought and increased your confidence in the risk analysis. In Agile development, revisiting the risk analysis at the start of every sprint is a good idea.

5.6 DEFECT MANAGEMENT

SYLLABUS LEARNING OBJECTIVES FOR 5.6 DEFECT MANAGEMENT (K3)

FL-5.6.1   **Write a defect report covering defects found during testing (K3)**

Let's wind down this chapter on test management with an important subject: how we can document and manage the defects that occur during testing. One of the objectives of testing is to find defects, which reveal themselves as discrepancies between actual and expected outcomes. When we observe a defect, we need to log the details. Proper test management involves establishing appropriate actions to investigate and dispose of defects. This includes tracking defects from initial discovery and classification through to resolution, confirmation testing and ultimate disposition, with the defects following a clearly established set of rules and processes for defect management and classification. We'll look at what topics we should cover when reporting defects. At the end of this section, you will be ready to write a thorough defect report.

The only Syllabus term in this section is **defect management**.

What are defect reports for?

When running a test, you might observe actual results that vary from expected results. This is not a bad thing – one of the major goals of testing is to find problems. Different organizations have different names to describe such situations. Commonly, they are called incidents, bugs, defects, problems or issues.

To be precise, we sometimes draw a distinction between an incident or anomaly on the one hand and defects or bugs on the other. An incident or anomaly is any situation where the system exhibits questionable behaviour, and a defect is some problem, imperfection or deficiency in the item we are testing.

Causes of defects include misconfiguration or failure of the test environment, corrupted test data, bad tests, incorrect expected results and tester mistakes. In some cases, the policy is to classify as a defect anything that arises from a test design, the test environment or anything else which is under formal configuration management. Bear in mind the possibility that a questionable behaviour is not necessarily a true defect. We log these defects so that we have a record of what we observed and can follow it up and track what is done to correct it, whether or not it turns out to be a problem in the work product we are testing or something else. This is **defect management**.

While it is most common to find defect logging or defect reporting processes and tools in use during formal, independent testing, you can also log, report, track and manage defects found during development and reviews. In fact, this is a good idea, because it gives useful information on the extent to which early (and cheaper) defect detection and removal activities are happening.

Of course, we also need some way of reporting, tracking and managing defects that occur in the field or after deployment of the system. While many of these defects will be user error or some other behaviour not related to a problem in system behaviour, some percentage of defects do escape from quality assurance and testing activities. The defect detection percentage (DDP), which compares field defects with test defects, can be a useful metric of the effectiveness of the test process.

Here is an example of a DDP formula that would apply for calculating DDP for the last level of testing prior to release to the field:

$$DDP = \frac{\text{defects (testers)}}{\text{defects (testers)} + \text{defects (field)}}$$

It is most common to find defects reported against the code or the system itself. However, we have also seen cases where defects are reported against requirements and design specifications, user and operator guides and tests. Often, it aids the effectiveness and efficiency of reporting, tracking and managing defects when the defect tracking tool provides an ability to vary some of the information captured depending on what the defect was reported against.

In some projects, a very large number of defects are found. Even on smaller projects where 100 or fewer defects are found, you can easily lose track of them unless you have a process for reporting, classifying, assigning and managing the defects from discovery to final resolution.

> **Defect management**
> The process of recognizing and recording defects, classifying them, investigating them, taking action to resolve them and disposing of them when resolved.

Objectives for defect reports

A defect report contains a description of the misbehaviour that was observed and classification of that misbehaviour. As with any written communication, it helps to have clear goals in mind when writing. Typical objectives for such reports include the following:

- To provide developers, managers and others with detailed information about the behaviour observed (the adverse event), that is, the defect. This will enable them to identify specific effects, to isolate the problem with a minimal reproducing test, and to correct the defect(s) as needed or to otherwise resolve the problem.

- To support test managers in the analysis of trends in aggregate defect data, either for understanding more about a particular set of problems or tests, or for understanding and reporting the overall level of system quality. This will enable them to track the quality of the work product and the impact on the testing. For example, if a lot of defects are being reported, the testers will do less testing, since their time is taken with writing defect reports. This also means that more confirmation tests will be needed.

- To enable defect reports to be analyzed over a project, and even across projects, to give information and ideas that can lead to development and test process improvements.

When writing a defect report, it helps to have the readers in mind, too. The developers need the information in the report to find and fix the defects. Before that happens, though, the defects should be reviewed and prioritized so that scarce testing and developer resources are spent fixing and confirmation testing the most important defects. Since some defects may be deferred – perhaps to be fixed later or perhaps, ultimately, not to be fixed at all – we should include work-arounds and other helpful information for help-desk or technical support teams. Finally, testers often need to know what their colleagues are finding so that they can watch for similar behaviour elsewhere and avoid trying to run tests that will be blocked.

How to write a good defect report: some tips

A good defect report is a technical document. In addition to being clear for its goals and audience, any good report grows out of a careful approach to researching and writing the report. We have some rules of thumb that can help you write a better defect report.

Use a careful, attentive approach to running your tests. You never know when you are going to find a problem. If you are pounding on the keyboard while gossiping with office mates or daydreaming about a movie you just saw, you might not notice strange behaviours. Even if you see the defect, how much do you really know about it? What can you write in your defect report?

Intermittent or sporadic symptoms are a fact of life for some defects and it is always discouraging to have a defect report bounced back as irreproducible. It's a good idea to try to reproduce symptoms when you see them. We have found three times to be a good rule of thumb. If a defect has intermittent symptoms, we would still report it, but we would be sure to include as much information as possible, especially how many times we tried to reproduce it and how many times it did in fact occur.

You should also try to isolate the defect by making carefully chosen changes to the steps used to reproduce it. In isolating the defect, you help guide the developer to the problematic part of the system. You also increase your own knowledge of how the system works, and how it fails.

Think outside the box. Some test cases focus on boundary conditions, which may make it appear that a defect is not likely to happen frequently in practice. We have found that it's a good idea to look for more generalized conditions that cause the failure to occur, rather than simply relying on the test case. This helps prevent the infamous defect report rejoinder, 'No real user is ever going to do that'. It also cuts down on the number of duplicate reports that get filed.

As there is often a lot of testing going on with the system during a test period, there are lots of other test results available. Comparing an observed problem against other test results and known defects is a good way to find and document additional information that the developer is likely to find very useful. For example, you might check for similar symptoms observed with other defects, the same symptom observed with defects that were fixed in previous versions or similar (or different) results seen in tests that cover similar parts of the system.

Many readers of defect reports, managers especially, will need to understand the priority and severity of the defect. The impact of the problem on the users, customers and other stakeholders is important. Most defect tracking systems have a title or summary field and that field should mention the impact, too.

Choice of words definitely matters in defect reports. You should be clear and unambiguous. You should also be neutral, fact-focused and impartial, keeping in mind the testing-related interpersonal issues discussed in Chapter 1 and earlier in this chapter. Finally, keeping the report concise helps keep people's attention and avoids the problem of losing them in the details.

As a last rule of thumb for defect reports, we recommend that you use a review process for all reports filed. It works if you have the lead tester review reports and we have also allowed testers, at least experienced ones, to review other testers' reports. Reviews are proven quality assurance techniques and defect reports are important project deliverables.

What goes in a defect report?

A defect report describes some situation, behaviour or event that occurred during testing that was not as it should be, or that requires further investigation. In many cases, a defect report consists of one or two screens full of information gathered by a defect tracking tool and stored in a database.

A defect report filed during dynamic testing typically includes the following:

- An identifier.
- A title and short summary of the defect being reported.
- Date of the defect report, issuing organization, the date and time of the failure, the name of the tester, that is, the author of the defect report (and perhaps the reviewer of the test).
- Identification of the test item (configuration item being tested), the test environment and any additional information about the configuration of the software, system or environment.
- The development life cycle activity(s) or sprint in which the defect was observed.
- A description of the defect to enable reproduction and resolution, such as the steps to reproduce and the isolation steps tried.
- The expected and actual results of the test.
- The scope or degree of impact (severity) of the defect on the interests of stakeholder(s).
- Urgency/priority to fix.
- State of the defect report (for example open, deferred, duplicate, waiting to be fixed, awaiting confirmation testing, re-opened, closed).
- Conclusions, recommendations and approvals.
- Global issues, such as other areas that may be affected by a change resulting from the defect.

- Change history, such as the sequence of actions taken by project team members with respect to the defect, to isolate, repair and confirm it as fixed. These fields should mention the inputs given and outputs observed, the different ways you could – and could not – make the problem recur, and the impact.
- References, including the test case that revealed the problem, and references to specifications or other work products that provide information about correct behaviour.

Sometimes testers classify the scope, severity and priority of the defect, though sometimes managers or a bug triage committee handle that role.

If you are using a defect management tool, some of the information will be automatically generated, such as the time and date of the report, the ID number, the report author and the initial state (open).

An example defect report can be found in ISO/IEC/IEEE 29119-3 [2013].

As the defect is managed to resolution, managers might assign a level of priority to the report. The change control board or bug triage committee might document the risks, costs, opportunities and benefits associated with fixing or not fixing the defect. The developer, when fixing the defect, can capture the root cause, the time or development stage where it was introduced and the time or testing activity that identified it, and removed it (which may be different to when it was identified).

After the defect has been resolved, managers, developers or others may want to capture conclusions and recommendations. Throughout the life cycle of the defect report, from discovery to resolution, the defect tracking system should allow each person who works on the defect report to enter status and history information.

What happens to defect reports after you file them?

As we mentioned earlier, defect reports are managed through a life cycle from discovery to resolution. The defect report life cycle is often shown as a state transition diagram (see Figure 5.3). While your defect tracking system may use a different life cycle, let's take this one as an example to illustrate how a defect report life cycle might work.

In the defect report life cycle shown in Figure 5.3, all defect reports move through a series of clearly identified states after being reported. Some of these state transitions occur when a member of the project team completes some assigned task related to closing a defect report. Some of these state transitions occur when the project team decides not to repair a defect during this project, leading to the deferral of the defect report. Some of these state transitions occur when a defect report is poorly written or describes behaviour which is actually correct, leading to the rejection of that report.

Let's focus on the path taken by defect reports which are ultimately fixed. After a defect is reported, a peer tester or test manager reviews the report. If successful in the review, the defect report becomes opened, so now the project team must decide whether or not to repair the defect. If the defect is to be repaired, a developer is assigned to repair it.

Once the developer believes the repairs are complete, the defect report returns to the tester for confirmation testing. If the confirmation test fails, the defect report is re-opened and then re-assigned. Once the tester confirms a good repair, the defect report is closed. No further work remains to be done on this defect.

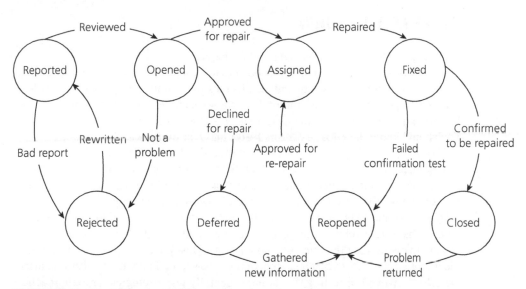

FIGURE 5.3   Defect report life cycle

In any state other than rejected, deferred or closed, further work is required on the defect prior to the end of this project. In such a state, the defect report has a clearly identified owner. The owner is responsible for transitioning the defect into an allowed subsequent state. The arrows in the diagram show these allowed transitions.

In a rejected, deferred or closed state, the defect report will not be assigned to an owner. However, certain real world events can cause a defect report to change state even if no active work is occurring on the defect report. Examples include the recurrence of a failure associated with a closed defect report and the discovery of a more serious failure associated with a deferred defect report.

Ideally, only the owner can transition the defect report from the current state to the next state and ideally the owner can only transition the defect report to an allowed next state. Most defect tracking systems support and enforce the defect life cycle and life cycle rules. Good defect tracking systems allow you to customize the set of states, the owners and the transitions allowed to match your actual workflows. And, while a good defect tracking system is helpful, the actual defect workflow should be monitored and supported by project and company management.

CHAPTER REVIEW

Let's review what you have learned in this chapter.

From Section 5.1, you should now be able to explain the basic ideas of test organization. You should know why independent testing is important, but also be able to analyze the potential benefits and problems associated with independent test teams. You should be able to recall the tasks that a tester and a test manager will carry out. You should know the Glossary terms **tester** and **test manager**.

From Section 5.2, you should now understand the fundamentals of test planning and estimation. You should know the reasons for writing test plans and be able to explain how test plans relate to projects, test levels, test objectives and test activities. You should be able to write a test execution schedule based on priority and dependencies. You should be able to explain the justification behind various entry and exit criteria that might relate to projects, test levels and or test objectives. You should be able to distinguish the purpose and content of test plans from that of test design specifications, test cases and test procedures. You should know the factors that affect the effort involved in testing, including especially test strategies (and approaches) and how they affect testing. You should be able to explain how metrics, expertise and negotiation are used for estimating. You should know the Glossary terms **entry criteria**, **exit criteria**, **test approach**, **test estimation**, **test plan**, **test planning** and **test strategy**.

From Section 5.3, you should be able to explain the essentials of test progress monitoring and control. You should know the common metrics that are captured, logged and used for monitoring, as well as ways to present these metrics. You should be able to explain a typical test progress report and test summary report. You should know the Glossary terms **test control**, **test monitoring**, **test progress report** and **test summary report**.

From Section 5.4, you should now understand the basics of configuration management that relate to testing, and how it helps us do our testing work better. You should know the Glossary term **configuration management**.

From Section 5.5, you should now be able to explain how risk is related to testing. You should know that a risk is a potential undesirable or negative outcome and that most of the risks we are interested in relate to the achievement of project objectives. You should know about likelihood and impact as factors that determine the importance of a risk. You should be able to compare and contrast risks to the product (and its quality) and risks to the project itself and know typical risks to the product and project. You should be able to describe how to use risk analysis and risk management for testing and test planning. You should know the Glossary terms **product risk**, **project risk**, **risk**, **risk level** and **risk-based testing**.

From Section 5.6, you should now understand defect logging and be able to use defect management on your projects. You should know the content of a defect report, be able to write a high quality report based on test results and manage that report through its life cycle. You should know the Glossary term **defect management**.

SAMPLE EXAM QUESTIONS

Question 1 What is a potential drawback of independent testing?

a. Independent testing is likely to find the same defects as developers.

b. Developers may lose a sense of responsibility for quality.

c. Independent testing may find more defects.

d. Independent testers may be too familiar with the system.

Question 2 Which of the following is among the typical tasks of a test manager?

a. Develop system requirements, design specifications and usage models.

b. Handle all test automation duties.

c. Keep tests and test coverage hidden from developers.

d. Gather and report test progress metrics.

Question 3 According to the ISTQB Glossary, what do we mean when we call someone a test manager?

a. A test manager manages a team of junior testers.

b. A test manager plans and controls testing activities.

c. A test manager sets up test environments.

d. A test manager creates a detailed test execution schedule.

Question 4 What is the primary difference between the test plan, the test design specification and the test procedure specification?

a. The test plan describes one or more levels of testing, the test design specification identifies the associated high-level test cases and a test procedure specification describes the actions for executing a test.

b. The test plan is for managers, the test design specification is for developers and the test procedure specification is for testers who are automating tests.

c. The test plan is the least thorough, the test procedure specification is the most thorough and the test design specification is midway between the two.

d. The test plan is finished in the first third of the project, the test design specification is finished in the middle third of the project and the test procedure specification is finished in the last third of the project.

Question 5 Which of the following factors is an influence on the test effort involved in most projects?

a. Geographical separation of tester and developers.

b. The departure of the test manager during the project.

c. The quality of the information used to develop the tests.

d. Unexpected long-term illness by a member of the project team.

Question 6 A business domain expert has given advice and guidance about the way the testing should be carried out and a technology expert has recommended using a checklist of common types of defect. Which two test strategies are being used?

a. Analytical and Process compliant.

b. Reactive and Methodical.

c. Directed and Methodical.

d. Regression-averse and Analytical.

Question 7 Consider the following exit criteria which might be found in a test plan:

  I. No known customer-critical defects.
  II. All interfaces between components tested.
 III. 100% code coverage of all units.
 IV. All specified requirements satisfied.
  V. System functionality matches legacy system for all business rules.

Which of the following statements is true about whether these exit criteria belong in an acceptance test plan?

a. All statements belong in an acceptance test plan.

b. Only statement I belongs in an acceptance test plan.

c. Only statements I, II and V belong in an acceptance test plan.

d. Only statements I, IV and V belong in an acceptance test plan.

Question 8 According to the ISTQB Glossary, what is a test approach?

a. The implementation of the test strategy for a specific project.

b. Documentation that expresses the generic requirements for testing one or more projects within an organization providing detail on how testing is to be performed.

c. Documentation describing the test objectives to be achieved and the means and the schedule for achieving them, organized to coordinate testing activities.

d. The set of interrelated activities comprising of test planning, test monitoring and control, test analysis, test design, test implementation, test execution and test completion.

Question 9 Which of the following metrics would be most useful to monitor during test execution?

a. Percentage of test cases written.

b. Number of test environments remaining to be configured.

c. Number of defects found and fixed.

d. Percentage of requirements for which a test has been written.

Question 10 What would appear in a test progress report that would not be included in a test summary report?

a. Summary of testing performed.

b. The status of the test activities against the test plan.

c. Factors that have blocked or continue to block progress.

d. Reusable test products produced.

Question 11 In a defect report, the tester makes the following statement: 'The payment processing subsystem fails to accept payments from American Express cardholders, which is considered a must-work feature for this release.' This statement is likely to be found in which of the following sections?

a. Scope or degree of impact of the defect.

b. Identification of the test item.

c. Summary of the defect.

d. Description of the defect.

Question 12 During an early period of test execution, a defect is located, resolved and passed its confirmation test, but is seen again later during subsequent test execution. Which of the following is a testing-related aspect of configuration management that is most likely to have broken down?

a. Traceability.

b. Configuration item identification.

c. Configuration control.

d. Test documentation management.

Question 13 You are working as a tester on a project to develop a point-of-sales system for grocery stores and other similar retail outlets. Which of the following is a product risk for such a project?

a. The arrival of a more reliable competing product on the market.

b. Delivery of an incomplete test release to the first cycle of system test.

c. An excessively high number of defect fixes fail during confirmation testing.

d. Failure to accept allowed credit cards.

Question 14 What is a risk?

a. A bad thing that has happened to the product or the project.

b. A bad thing that might happen.

c. Something that costs a lot to put right.

d. Something that may happen in the future.

Question 15 You are writing a test plan and are currently completing a section on risk. Which of the following is most likely to be listed as a project risk?

a. Unexpected illness of a key team member.

b. Excessively slow transaction processing time.

c. Data corruption under network congestion.

d. Failure to handle a key use case.

Question 16 You and the project stakeholders develop a list of product risks and project risks during the planning stage of a project. What else should you do with those lists of risks during test planning?

a. Determine the extent of testing required for the product risks and the mitigation and contingency actions required for the project risks.

b. Obtain the resources needed to completely cover each product risk with tests and transfer responsibility for the project risks to the project manager.

c. Execute sufficient tests for the product risks, based on the likelihood and impact of each product risk and execute mitigation actions for all project risks.

d. No further risk management action is required at the test planning stage.

Question 17 The following are ways to estimate test effort:

1. Burndown charts.
2. Wideband Delphi.
3. Expert opinion.
4. Previous experience.
5. Planning poker.
6. Similar project data.

Which of these are an example of a metrics-based technique?

a. 3, 4 and 5.
b. 1, 5 and 6.
c. 2, 3 and 4.
d. 1, 2 and 5.

Question 18 In a defect report, the tester makes the following statement: 'At this point, I expect to receive an error message explaining the rejection of this invalid input and asking me to enter a valid input. Instead the system accepts the input, displays an hourglass for between one and five seconds and finally terminates abnormally, giving the message, "Unexpected data type: 15. Click to continue".' This statement is likely to be found in which of the following sections of a defect report?

a. Summary.
b. Impact.

c. Item pass/fail criteria.
d. Defect description.

Question 19 There are five tests to be executed. A high-priority test has been scheduled as the third in the sequence of five, rather than the first. Which of the following would NOT be a good reason for this?

a. The high priority test has a logical dependency on the two tests run before it.

b. All tests are the same priority and this is the most efficient sequence.

c. The tests scheduled before it are more likely to pass so this will take less time and give feedback more quickly.

d. The first three tests have the same priority so it does not matter what order they are run in.

Question 20 Exit criteria have been agreed at the start of the project, but it is now clear that they will not all be met before the release date next week. What should the test manager NOT say to those who want to release next week anyway?

a. These exit criteria were agreed for a very good reason, to avoid this situation. It is essential that all exit criteria are met before we release.

b. It is not my role to make that decision, so if you go ahead and release next week anyway, I will carefully monitor the effects and will report the results to high-level management.

c. Have all project stakeholders, business owners and the product owner been informed of the risks of releasing next week, and do they all understand and accept them? (Sign on this paper stating this.)

d. What are the most critical exit criteria, and can we get agreement from all stakeholders about which are absolutely necessary and which could be compromised this time?

EXERCISES

Test execution schedule exercise

You have been asked to develop a test execution schedule for the second release of a customer data management application. The first release only allowed basic customer records to be added. This second one contains 5 new features and 2 bug fixes, together with the new features' priorities (1 is highest) and the defect severity levels, in the table below.

TABLE 5.3 Exercise: Test execution schedule

Priority	Feature/Fix	Test order
1	Delete inactive customer record	
2	De-activate customer	
3	Edit extra data items	
4	Edit basic data	
5	Link customer records (for example in the same company)	
5	Provide extra data items when record added	

What would be the BEST test execution sequence for this release?

Defect report exercise

Assume you are testing a maintenance release which will add a new supported model to a browser-based application that allows car dealers to order custom-configured cars from the maker. You are working with a selected number of dealers who are performing beta testing. When they find problems, they send you an email describing the failure. You use that email to create a defect report in your defect management system.

You receive the following email from one of the dealers:

I entered an order for a Racinax 917X in midnight violet. During the upload, I got an 'unexpected return value' error message. I then checked the order and it was in the system. I think the internet connection might have gone down for a moment as we found out later that there was a power surge elsewhere in the building at around that time.

Write a defect report based on this email and note any elements of such a report which might not be available based on this email alone.

Note that this scenario, including the name of the car model, is entirely fictitious.

EXERCISE SOLUTIONS

Test execution schedule exercise

Below we show the solution, with the tests listed in the test order. The justifications are shown below the table.

TABLE 5.4   Solution: Test execution schedule

Priority	Feature/Fix	Test order
2	De-activate customer	1
1	Delete inactive customer record	2
5	Provide extra data items when record added	3
3	Edit extra data items	4
4	Edit basic data	5
5	Link customer records (for example in the same company)	6

The highest priority is to Delete an inactive customer, but first we must have an inactive customer, so we run De-activate customer first. This is a functional dependency.

The next highest priority is to Edit extra data items, but again, we need to have some extra data items in order to do this, another functional dependency.

The final two are independent, so the priority 4 test is run before the priority 5 test.

Defect report exercise

Here is an example of a defect report:

Test defect report identifier: This would be assigned by the defect tracking tool.

Summary: System returns confusing error message if internet connectivity is interrupted.

Defect description:
  Steps to reproduce

1. Entered an order for a Racinax 917X in midnight violet.

2. During the order upload, the system displayed an 'unexpected return value' error message.

3. Verified that, in spite of the error message, the order was in the system.

Suspected cause Given that a brief interruption in the internet connection may have occurred during order transmission due to the power surge, the suspected cause of the failure is a lack of robust handling of slow or unreliable internet connections.

Impact assessment The message in step 2 is not helpful to the user, because it gives the user no clues about what to do next. A user encountering the message described in step 2 might decide to re-enter the order, which in this case would result in a redundant order.
Some car dealerships will have unreliable internet connections, with the frequency of connection loss depending on location, wireless infrastructure available in the dealership, type of internet connection hardware used in the dealers' computers, and other such factors. Therefore we can expect that some number of defects such as this will occur in widespread use. (Indeed, this beta test defect proves that this is a likely event in the real world.) Since a careless or rushed dealer might decide to resubmit the order based on the error message, this will result in redundant orders, which will cause significant loss of profitability for the dealerships and the salespeople themselves.

This report addresses the inputs, the expected results, the actual results, the difference between the expected and actual results, and the procedure steps in which the tester identified the unexpected results. Here is some additional information needed to improve the report:

- The failure needs to be reproduced at least two more times. By doing the failure replication in the test environment, the tester will be able to control whether or not the internet connection goes down during the order and for how long the connection is down.

- Is the problem in any way specific to the Racinax 917X model and/or the colour? Isolation of the failure is needed, and then the report can be updated.

- Is the problem in any way specific to power surges? We would guess not but checking with different types of connections (during the isolation and replication discussed above) would make sense. If it proves independent of the type of connection, we would know that the problem is more general than just for power surges.

- The defect report should also include information about the date and time of the test, the beta test environment and the name of the beta tester and the tester entering the defect.

CHAPTER SIX
Tool support for testing

You may be wishing that you had a magic tool that would automate all of the testing for you. If so, you will be disappointed. However, there are a number of very useful tools that can bring significant benefits. In this chapter, we will see that there is tool support for many different aspects of software testing. We will see that success with tools is not guaranteed, even if an appropriate tool is acquired – there are also risks in using tools. There are some special considerations mentioned in the Syllabus for test execution tools and test management tools.

6.1 TEST TOOL CONSIDERATIONS

SYLLABUS LEARNING OBJECTIVES FOR 6.1 TEST TOOL CONSIDERATIONS (K2)

FL-6.1.1   Classify test tools according to their purpose and the test activities they support (K2)

FL-6.1.2   Identify benefits and risks of test automation (K1)

FL-6.1.3   Remember special considerations for test execution and test management tools (K1)

As we go through this section, watch for the Syllabus terms **data-driven testing**, **keyword-driven testing**, **performance testing tool**, **test automation**, **test execution tool** and **test management tool**. You will find these terms and their definitions, taken from the ISTQB Glossary, in this chapter, in the Glossary and online.

In this section, we will describe the various tool types in terms of their general functionality, rather than going into lots of detail. The reason for this is that, in general, the types of tool will be fairly stable over a longer period, even though there will be new vendors in the market, new and improved tools, and even new types of tool in the coming years.

We will also discuss both the benefits and the risks of using tools to run or execute tests. We will outline special considerations for test execution tools and for test management tools, the most popular types of test tools.

We will not mention any open source or commercial tools in this chapter. If we did, this book would date very quickly! Tool vendors are acquired by other vendors, change their names, and change the names of the tools quite frequently, so we will not mention the names of any tools or vendors.

There are a number of ways in which tools can be used to support testing activities:

- To start with the most visible use, we can use tools directly in testing. This includes test execution tools and test data preparation tools.

- We can use tools to help us manage the testing process. This includes tools that manage requirements, test cases, test procedures, automate test scripts, test results, test data and defects, as well as tools that assist with reporting and monitoring test execution progress.

- We can use tools as part of exploration, investigation and evaluation. For example, we can use tools to monitor file activity for an application.

- We can use tools in a number of other ways, in the form of any tool that aids in testing. This would include spreadsheets when used to manage test assets or progress, or as a way to document manual or automated tests.

6.1.1 Test tool classification

In this section, we will look first at how tools can be classified, starting with tool objectives or purposes. Then we will look at tools that support various aspects of testing: management of testing and testware, static testing, test design and implementation, test execution and logging, performance measurement and dynamic analysis, and finally tool support for specialized testing needs.

Tool classification

What are we trying to achieve with tools? What are the motivations? As you can imagine, these vary depending on the activity, but common objectives or purposes for the use of tools include the following:

- We might want to improve the efficiency of our test activities by automating repetitive tasks or by automating activities that would otherwise require significant resources to do manually. For example, the execution of regression tests is repetitive and takes significant time and effort to do manually.

- We might want to improve the efficiency of our testing by providing support for manual test activities throughout the test process. For example, tools can help in noting our findings while doing exploratory testing. See Chapter 1, Section 1.1.4 for more on the test process.

- We might want to improve the quality of test activities by achieving more consistency and reproducibility. For example, tools can help to reproduce failures more accurately and with more information. When a defect is fixed, the exact same test should be run again, otherwise you cannot be sure that the defect was correctly fixed. This requires both consistency and reproducibility.

- We might need to carry out activities that simply cannot be done manually, but which can be done via automated tools. For example, large-scale performance testing can only be achieved using tools; it is highly unfeasible to get thousands of users to test your system manually.

- We might want to increase the reliability of our testing. For example, automation of large data comparisons, simulating user behaviour, or repeating large numbers of tests (which can lead to mistakes due to tedium of the work, if it is done by people).

How are tools classified?

Tools can be classified in different ways. One is by their purpose (as above), or they can be classified by licencing model (commercial or open source), by price and/or by technology used. In this chapter, tools are classified by the testing activities or areas that are supported by a set of tools, for example, tools that support management activities, tools to support static testing, etc.

There is not necessarily a one-to-one relationship between a type of tool described here and a tool offered by a commercial tool vendor or an open source tool. Some tools perform a very specific and limited function and support only one test activity (sometimes called a point solution), but many of the tools provide support for a number of different functions (tool suites or families of tools). For example, a test management tool may provide support for managing testing (progress monitoring), configuration management of testware, defect management, and requirements management and traceability; another tool may provide both coverage measurement and test design support.

Tools versus people

There are some things that people can do much better or easier than a computer can do. For example, when you see a friend in an unexpected place, say in an airport, you can immediately recognize their face. This is an example of pattern recognition that people are very good at, but it is not easy to write software that can recognize a face.

There are other things that computers can do much better or more quickly than people can do. For example, can you add up 20 three-digit numbers quickly? This is not easy for most people to do, so you are likely to make some mistakes even if the numbers are written down. A computer does this accurately and very quickly. As another example, if people are asked to do exactly the same task over and over, they soon get bored and then start making mistakes.

The point is that it is a good idea to use computers to do things that computers are really good at and that people are not very good at. Tool support is very useful for repetitive tasks – the computer doesn't get bored and will be able to exactly repeat what was done before. Because the tool will be fast, this can make those activities much more efficient and more reliable. The tools can also do things that might over-load a person, such as comparing the contents of a large data file or simulating how the system would behave.

Tools that affect their own results

A tool that measures some aspect of software may be intrusive. This means that the tool may have unexpected side effects in the software under test. For example, a tool that measures timings for performance testing needs to interact very closely with that software in order to measure it. A performance tool will set a start time and a stop time for a given transaction in order to measure the response time, for example. But the act of taking that measurement, that is, storing the time at those two points, could actually make the whole transaction take slightly longer than it would do if the tool was not measuring the response time. Of course, the extra time is very small, but it is still there. This effect is called the 'probe effect'.

Another example of the probe effect occurs with coverage tools. In order to measure coverage, the tool must first identify all of the structural elements that might be exercised to see whether a test exercises it or not. This is called instrumenting the code. The tests are then run through the instrumented code so that the tool can tell (through the instrumentation) whether or not a given branch (for example) has been exercised. But the instrumented code is not the same as the real code – it also includes the instrumentation code. In theory, the code is the same, but in practice, it isn't. Because different coverage tools work in slightly different ways, you may get a slightly different coverage measure on the same program because of the probe effect. For example, different tools may count branches in different ways, so the percentage of coverage would be compared to a different total number of branches. The response time of the instrumented code may also be significantly worse than the code without instrumentation. (There are also non-intrusive coverage tools that observe the blocks of memory containing the object code to get a rough measurement without instrumentation, for example for embedded software.)

One further example of the probe effect is when a debugging tool is used to try to find a particular defect. If the code is run with the debugger, then the bug disappears; it only reappears when the debugger is turned off, thereby making it much more difficult to find. These are sometimes known as "Heisen-bugs" (after Heisenberg's uncertainty principle).

Tool classification categories

In the descriptions of the tools below, we will indicate the tools that are more likely to be used by developers, for example during component testing and component integration testing, by showing (D) (for Developer) after the tool type. For example, coverage measurement tools are most often used in component testing, but performance testing tools are more often used at system testing, system integration testing and acceptance testing.

Note that for the Foundation Certificate exam, you only need to recognize the different types of tools; you do not need to understand in any detail what they do (or know how to use them). We will briefly describe what the tools do (more detail than in the Syllabus) to help you identify the different types of tool.

Tool support for management of testing and testware

What does test management mean? It could be the management of tests or it could be managing the testing process. The tools in this broad category provide support for either or both of these. The management of testing applies over the whole of the software development life cycle, so a test management tool could be among the first to be used in a project. A test management tool may also manage the tests, which would begin early in the project and would then continue to be used throughout the project and also after the system had been released. In practice, test management tools are typically used by specialist testers or test managers at system or acceptance test level.

Test management tools and application lifecycle management (ALM) tools

Test management tools provide features that cover both the management of testing, such as progress reports and keeping track of testing activities, and the management of testware, such as logging of test results and keeping track of test environments needed for tests. There are some tools that provide support for only one activity (for example defect management tools); other tools or tool suites may provide support for all test management activities. Special considerations for test management tools are discussed in Section 6.1.3.

Application lifecycle management (ALM) tools manage not only testing but also development and deployment. With a focus on communication, collaboration and task tracking, they are popular in Agile development.

Test management tool A tool that provides support to the test management and control part of a test process. It often has several capabilities, such as testware management, scheduling of tests, the logging of results, progress tracking, incident management and test reporting.

(Note that the Glossary definition mentions incident management, but the Syllabus covers defect management.)

The information from test management tools (and ALM tools) can be used to monitor the testing process and decide what actions to take (test control), as described in Chapter 5. The tool also gives information about the component or system being tested (the test object). Test management tools help to gather, organize and communicate information about the testing on a project.

Requirements management tools

Are requirements management tools really testing tools? Some people may say they are not, but they do provide some features that are very helpful to testing. Because tests are based on requirements, the better the quality of the requirements, the easier it will be to write tests from them. It is also important to be able to trace tests to requirements and requirements to tests, as we saw in Chapter 2. Note that requirements means any source of what the system should do, such as user stories.

Defect management tools

This type of tool is also known as a defect tracking tool, an incident management tool, a bug tracking tool or a bug management tool. However not all of the things tracked are actually defects or bugs. There may also be perceived problems, anomalies (that aren't necessarily defects) or enhancement requests; this is why they are sometimes referred to as incidents and incident management tools. Also, what is normally recorded is information about the failure (not the defect) that was generated during testing; information about the defect that caused that failure would come to light when someone (for example a developer) begins to investigate the failure.

Defect reports go through a number of stages, from initial identification and recording of the details, through analysis, classification, assignment for fixing, fixed, re-tested and closed, as described in Chapter 5. Defect management tools make it much easier to keep track of the defects and their status over time.

Configuration management tools

An example: A test group began testing the software, expecting to find the usual fairly high number of problems. But to their surprise, the software seemed to be much better than usual this time. Very few defects were found. Before they celebrated the great quality of this release, they just made an additional check to see if they had the right version and discovered that they were actually testing the version from two months earlier (which had been debugged) with the tests for that earlier version. It was nice to know that this was still OK, but they were not actually testing what they thought they were testing or what they should have been testing.

Configuration management tools are not strictly testing tools either, but good configuration management is critical for controlled testing, as was described in Chapter 5. We need to know exactly what it is that we are supposed to test, such as the exact version of all of the things that belong in a system. It is possible to perform configuration management activities without the use of tools, but the tools make life a lot easier, especially in complex environments. The same tool may be used for testware as well as for software items. Testware also has different versions and is changed over time. It is important to run the correct version of the tests as well, as our example shows.

Continuous integration tools (D)

The (D) after this (and other types of tools) indicates that these tools are more likely to be used by developers.

Incremental and iterative development life cycles require frequent builds, and continuous integration tools are an essential part of the Agile toolkit. Continuous integration is the practice of integrating new or changed code with the existing code repository very frequently, at least daily but sometimes dozens of times a day or more. Unit tests are most often automatically run when a new build is made (when a developer commits his or her change), so any defects found can be corrected immediately. The result of the integration is a system that is tested and could in principle be deployed to users at any time.

If the deployment is automated, then it is called continuous delivery, but there might still be some final human approval before it is released. If deployment is automatic (with no final human approval), then it is called continuous deployment. Continuous integration, delivery and deployment are the basis for DevOps, where code changes are delivered to users in an automated delivery pipeline.

These tools are continuous because the integration of the code components happens so often, and is automatic (without human intervention), whenever the new build is triggered by a developer. This type of tool is included here because it includes tests, which are managed in the continuous integration tool.

Tool support for static testing

The tools described in this section support the testing activities described in Chapter 3.

Tools that support reviews

The value of different types of review was discussed in Chapter 3. For a very informal review, where one person looks at another's work product and gives a few comments about it, a tool such as this might just get in the way. However, when the review process is more formal, when many people are involved, or when the people involved are in different geographical locations, then tool support becomes far more beneficial.

It is possible to keep track of all the information for a review process using spreadsheets and text documents, but a review tool that is designed for the purpose is more likely to do a better job. For example, one thing that should be monitored for each review is that the reviewers have not gone over the work product too quickly, that is, that the checking rate (number of pages checked per hour) was close to that recommended for that review cycle. A review tool could automatically calculate the checking rate and flag exceptions. The review tools can normally be tailored for the particular review process or type of review being done.

Static analysis tools (D)

Static analysis tools are normally used by developers as part of the development and component testing process. The key aspect is that the code (or other artefact) is not executed or run. Of course, the tool itself is executed, but the source code we are interested in is the input data to the tool.

Static analysis tools are an extension of compiler technology, in fact some compilers do offer static analysis features. It's worth checking what is available from existing compilers or development environments before looking at acquiring a more sophisticated static analysis tool.

Static analysis can also be carried out on things other than software code, for example, static analysis of requirements or static analysis of websites to assess for proper use of accessibility tags or the following of HTML standards.

Static analysis tools for code can help the developers to understand the structure of the code and can also be used to enforce coding standards.

Tool support for test design and specification

The tools described in this section support the testing activities described in Chapter 4. These tools help to create maintainable test designs, test cases, test procedures and test data.

Test design tools

Test design tools help to construct test cases, or at least test inputs (part of a test case). If an automated oracle is available, then the tool can also construct the expected result, so it can actually generate test cases, rather than just test inputs.

Tests that are designed using a tool need to have a starting point to derive the tests from. This could be requirements from a requirements management tool, which may identify valid and invalid boundary values for an input field, for example. Tests can also be derived from elements on a screen, to ensure that each element is exercised by a test, for example buttons, input fields or pull-down lists. Tests can also be derived from a model of the system, as in model-based testing (see below). Coverage tools may identify the tests needed to extend white-box coverage.

There are two problems with test design tools. First, although it is relatively easy to generate test inputs, automatically generating the correct expected result is more challenging. Sometimes an oracle is available (for example valid boundary conditions), other times only a partial oracle (generating some aspect but not all detail of an expected result), and most often no oracle other than 'The system is still running'.

The second problem is having too many tests and needing to find a way of identifying the most important tests to run. Cutting down an unmanageable number of tests can be done by risk analysis (see Chapter 5).

Model-based testing tools

Tools that generate test inputs or test cases from stored information that represents some kind of model of the system or software are called model-based testing tools. Such tools may be based on a state diagram, to implement state transition testing, for example.

Model-based testing tools work by generating tests (inputs or test cases) automatically based on what is stored about the model used to describe the system behaviour. If the system is changed, only the model is updated, and the new tests are then generated automatically.

More information about Model-Based Testing (MBT) is available in the ISTQB Foundation Level Model-Based Tester Extension Syllabus and qualification.

Test data preparation tools

Setting up test data can be a significant effort, especially if an extensive range or volume of data is needed for testing. Test data preparation tools help in this area. They may be used by developers, but they may also be used during system or acceptance testing. They are particularly useful for performance and reliability testing, where a large amount of realistic data is needed.

The most sophisticated tools can deal with a range of files and database formats. These tools are also useful for anonymizing data to conform to data protection rules.

Test-driven development (TDD) tools (D)

Test-driven development (TDD) is a software development approach started as part of EXtreme Programming, which had a great influence on Agile development. The idea behind TDD is that tests are written first, before code, because if you think about how you will test something, you are anticipating what could go wrong; when you then write the code, it is more likely to cope with problems.

TDD tools provide a framework for writing and running tests. The tests that are developed in TDD are basically unit tests; these are not sufficient testing for the component being developed, but they are a good starting point. Other levels of testing are still needed, that is, integration, system and acceptance testing.

Acceptance test-driven development (ATDD) and behaviour-driven development (BDD) tools

Tools to develop system-level tests before developing the system itself are becoming increasingly popular. ATDD is a way of capturing requirements by writing acceptance tests in conjunction with users. This approach is also called Specification by Example, as in Adzic [2011]. BDD is focused on system behaviour and functionality, and is normally done by the development team. Tools to support ATDD /BDD usually have syntax (rules), like a natural language, that need to be followed. An example of this syntax is the 'Given/When/Then' format: 'Given <some condition>, When <something is done>, Then <some result should happen>'. Another format is 'As a <role, for example customer>, In order to <achieve something, for example buy a product>, I want to <do something, for example place an order from my phone>'.

The ATDD/BDD tools support this domain language for specifying the tests, and also enable those tests to be generated and run.

Tools may cover both test design/implementation and test execution/logging. Both TDD and ATDD/BDD tools enable the tests specified in the tools to be run, so they cover test execution as well as test design and implementation. In addition, some other test design and integration tools, for example MBT tools, provide outputs directly to test execution and logging tools. These tools were described in this section, but also provide support for the test activities described below.

Tool support for test execution and logging

Test execution tools

When people think of a testing tool, it is usually a test execution tool that they have in mind, a tool that can run tests. This type of tool is also referred to as a test running tool. Some tools of this type offer a way to get started by capturing or recording manual tests; hence they are also known as capture/playback tools, capture/replay tools or record/playback tools. The analogy is with recording a television programme and playing it back. However, the tests are not something which is played back just for someone to watch!

Test execution tool
A test tool that executes tests against a designated test item and evaluates the outcomes against expected results and postconditions.

Test execution tools use a scripting language to drive the tool. The scripting language is actually a programming language. Testers who wish to use a test execution tool directly may need to use programming skills to create and modify the scripts, although some newer tools provide a higher-level interface for testers. The advantage of programmable scripting is that tests can repeat actions (in loops) for different data values (test inputs), they can take different routes depending on the outcome of a test (for example if a test fails, go to a different set of tests) and they can be called from other scripts giving modular structure to the set of tests.

When people first encounter a test execution tool, they tend to use it to capture (or record) tests, which sounds really good when you first hear about it. However, the approach breaks down when you try to replay the captured tests. This approach does not scale up for large numbers of tests, as described in Section 6.1.3. The main reason for this is that a captured script is very difficult to maintain because:

- It is closely tied to the flow and interface presented by the GUI (graphical user interface).
- It may rely on the circumstances, state and context of the system at the time the script was recorded. For example, a script will capture a new order number assigned by the system when a test is recorded. When that test is played back, the system will assign a different order number and reject subsequent requests that contain the previously captured order number.
- The test input information is hard-coded, that is, it is embedded in the individual script for each test.

Any of these things can be overcome by modifying the scripts, but then we are no longer just recording and playing back! If it takes more time to update a captured test than it would take to run the same test again manually, the scripts tend to be abandoned and the tool becomes 'shelf-ware'.

There are better ways to use test execution tools to make them work well and actually deliver the benefits of unattended automated test running. There are at least five levels of scripting and also different comparison techniques. Data-driven testing is an advance over captured scripts, but keyword-driven testing gives significantly more benefits. See Fewster and Graham [1999], Buwalda *et al.* [2001], Graham and Fewster [2012], Gamba and Graham [2018] and Section 6.2.3.

There are many different ways to use a test execution tool and the tools themselves are continuing to gain new useful features. Test execution tools are often used for regression testing, where tests are run that have been run before, such as in continuous integration. One of the most significant benefits of using this type of tool is that whenever an existing system is changed (for example for a defect fix or an enhancement), the tests that were run earlier can be run again, to make sure that the changes have not disturbed the existing system.

Coverage tools (for example requirements coverage, code coverage (D))

How thoroughly have you tested? Coverage tools can help answer this question. Requirements coverage tools measure how many requirements have been exercised by a set of tests; code coverage tools (D), normally used by developers, measure how many code elements, such as statements or branches, have been exercised by a set of tests.

A coverage tool first identifies the elements or coverage items that can be counted, and where the tool can identify when a test has exercised that coverage item. At component testing level, the coverage items could be lines of code or code statements or decision outcomes (for example the True or False exit from an IF statement). At component integration level, the coverage item may be a call to a function or module. At system or acceptance level, the coverage item may be a user story, a requirement, a function or a feature.

The coverage tool counts the number of coverage items that have been executed by the test suite and reports the percentage of coverage items that have been exercised and may also identify the items that have not yet been exercised (that is, not yet tested). Additional tests can then be run to increase coverage.

Note that the coverage tools only measure the coverage of the items that they can identify. Just because your tests have achieved 100% coverage, this does not mean that your software is 100% tested! See also Chapter 4 Section 4.3.

Test harnesses (D)

Some software components cannot be tested independently, for example when they depend on receiving data from other components, or they need to send a message to a different component or system and receive a reply. Waiting until such components are integrated with the whole system is asking for trouble. It is much better to test on as small a scale as possible. In this and similar cases, the component can be tested if the data it needs can be supplied to it in another way. A driver is another component or tool that will call or invoke the component we want to test and supply it with the data it needs. A stub is a small component that interacts with the tested component in the way it expects, but just for that purpose, so it pretends to be the part that receives the message and returns a reply. Stubs may also be referred to as mock objects.

A test harness is the test environment that provides these drivers and stubs so that our component can be tested as much as possible on its own.

Unit test framework tools (D)

A unit test framework is another tool which is used by developers when testing individual components (or sets of integrated components). Unit test frameworks can be used in Agile development to automate tests in parallel with development. Both unit test frameworks and test harnesses enable the developer to test, identify and localize any defects. The framework can also act as a driver and/or as a mock object to supply any information needed by the software being tested (for example an input that would have come from a user) and also receive any information sent by the software (for example a value to be displayed on a screen).

Test harnesses or unit test frameworks may be developed in-house for particular systems.

There are a large number of xUnit tools for different programming languages, for example JUnit for Java, NUnit for .Net applications, etc. There are both commercial tools and also open source tools. Unit test framework tools are very similar to test execution tools, since they include facilities such as the ability to store test cases and monitor whether tests pass or fail, for example. The main difference is that there is no capture/playback facility and they tend to be used at a lower level, that is, for component or component integration testing, rather than for system or acceptance testing. Unit test frameworks may also provide support for measuring coverage.

Tool support for performance measurement and dynamic analysis

The tools described in this section support testing that can be carried out on a system when it is operational, that is, while it is running. This can be during testing or could be after a system is released into live operation. These tools support activities that cannot reasonably be done manually.

Performance testing tools

Performance testing tool A test tool that generates load for a designated test item and that measures and records its performance during test execution.

Performance testing tools are concerned with testing at system level to see whether or not the system will stand up to a high volume of usage. A load test checks that the system can cope with its expected number of transactions. A volume test checks that the system can cope with a large amount of data, for example many fields in a record, many records in a file, etc. A stress test is one that goes beyond the normal expected usage of the system (to see what would happen outside its design expectations), with respect to load or volume.

In performance testing, many test inputs may be sent to the software or system where the individual results may not be checked in detail. The purpose of the test is to measure characteristics, such as response times, throughput or the mean time between failures (for reliability testing). Load generation can simulate multiple users or high volumes of input data. More sophisticated tools can generate different user profiles, different types of activity, timing delays and other parameters. Adequately replicating the end-user environments or user profiles is usually key to realistic results. Performance testing tools normally provide reports based on test logs and graphs of load against response times.

Analyzing the output of a performance testing tool is not always straightforward and it requires time and expertise. If the performance is not up to the standard expected, then some analysis needs to be performed to see where the problem is and to know what can be done to improve the performance.

Monitoring tools

Monitoring tools are used to continuously keep track of the status of the system in use, in order to have the earliest warning of problems and to improve service. There are monitoring tools for servers, networks, databases, security, performance, website and internet usage, and applications.

Monitoring tools may help to identify performance problems and network problems, and give information about the use of the system, such as the number of users.

Dynamic analysis tools (D)

Dynamic analysis tools are so named because they require the code to be running. They are analysis rather than testing tools because they analyze what is happening behind the scenes while the software is running (whether being executed with test cases or being used in operation).

An analogy with a car may be useful here. If you go to look at a car to buy, you might sit in it to see if is comfortable and see what sound the doors make. This would be static analysis because the car is not being driven. If you take a test drive, then you would check that the car performs as you expect (for example, it turns right when you turn the steering wheel clockwise). This would be a test. While the car is running, if you were to check the oil pressure or the brake fluid, this would be dynamic analysis. It can only be done while the engine is running, but it is not a test case.

When your PC's response time gets slower and slower over time, but is much improved after you re-boot it, this may well be due to a memory leak, where the programs do not correctly release blocks of memory back to the operating system. Eventually the system will run out of memory completely and stop. Rebooting restores all of the memory that was lost, so the performance of the system is now restored to its normal state.

Dynamic analysis tools would typically be used by developers in component testing and component integration testing.

Tool support for specialized testing needs

In addition to the tools that support specific testing activities, there are tools that support other testing needs and more specific testing issues. Tool support is available to support these other testing needs.

Data quality assessment

Data quality is very important, and there are tools to assess it. In many IT-centric organizations, systems and 'systems of systems' manage very large volumes of complex, interrelated data. This puts data at the centre of many projects in these organizations. These tools can check data according to given validation rules, for example, checking that a particular field is numeric or of a given length. Any data that fails a check is reported for someone to look at and fix.

Data conversion and migration

When technology moves on, it often becomes necessary to have to transfer large sets of data from one type of storage to another. The data involved can vary in terms of criticality and volume. Data conversion and migration tools can review and verify data conversion and check that data has been migrated according to the migration rules. For example, a field in the new database may bc larger than the equivalent field in the old one, so the value stored may need to have extra characters or digits added to it. These tools can help ensure that the processed data is correct and complete, and that it complies to pre-defined, context-specific standards, even when the volume of data is large.

Usability testing

Tools to support usability testing can help to assess user experience in using the system, for example, surveys after using a website or mobile app. Tools can check to make sure there are no broken links on a web page. Tools can also monitor usage, such as which links are clicked most often. Video recorders and screen capture utilities can also be used to help assess usability. Major companies that sell to the public may also have a usability lab, where beta versions of software are used by volunteers from the target market; this could include video, analysis of key presses or even eye movement tracking.

Accessibility testing

Regulations now require that systems including websites are usable by people with various disabilities. For example, it should be possible to increase the font size of text. For blind users, each visual object on a screen should have alternative text associated with it which can be read by a screen reader. For example, a field with a magnifying glass on the left would have the alternative text 'Search'; an image of a horse galloping would have the text 'Galloping horse'. Alternative text is particularly important for buttons and interactive images, such as the 'Submit' button. See www.w3.org for more information about accessibility for websites.

Localization testing

This is also called internationalization. Localization is making sure that systems are understood in different countries and in different cultures. This involves translation of text for information, menu items, buttons, error messages, field names: in fact anything that someone will read on a page. Although tools can help in some ways with translations, the tools often get it wrong, particularly with colloquial expressions. Tools can be of more help in other ways, for example if the same translation is used in many different environments or platforms (such as mobile devices). This is one area where human intelligence is still needed.

Security testing

There are a number of tools that protect systems from external attack, for example firewalls, which are important for any system.

Security testing tools can be used to test security by trying to break into a system, whether or not it is protected by a security tool. The attacks may focus on the network, the support software, the application code or the underlying database.

Security testing tools can provide support in identifying viruses, detecting intrusions such as denial of service attacks, simulating various types of external attacks, probing for open ports or other externally visible points of attack, and identifying weaknesses in password files and passwords. In addition, these tools can perform security checks during operation, for example checking the integrity of files, intrusion detection and the results of test attacks.

Portability testing

Portability testing tools help to support testing on different platforms and in different environments. You may have an application that needs to perform the same functions on desktop computers, laptops, tablets and mobile phones. Although the functionality is the same, the way in which the information is displayed would be different. Portability testing tools can help to run the same tests on the different devices, even though the look and feel of each interface is different.

About tools in general

In this chapter, we have described tools according to their general functional classifications. There are also further specializations of tools within these classifications. For example, there are web-based performance testing tools as well as performance testing tools for back-office systems. There are static analysis tools for specific development platforms and programming languages, since each programming language and every platform has distinct characteristics. There are dynamic analysis tools that focus on security issues, as well as dynamic analysis tools for embedded systems.

Tool sets may be bundled for specific application areas such as web-based, embedded systems or mobile applications.

6.1.2 Benefits and risks of test automation

The reason for acquiring tools to support testing is to gain benefits, by using software to do certain tasks that are better done by a computer than by a person.

The term **test automation** is most often used to refer to tools that execute tests and compare results, that is, test execution tools. This type of tool is one which can provide great benefits, but there are also significant risks. Test automation is also much broader than just supporting execution; tools are available to support many aspects of testing.

> **Test automation** The use of software to perform or support test activities, for example, test management, test design, test execution and results checking.

Potential benefits of using tools

There are many benefits that can be gained by using tools to support testing, whatever the specific type of tool. Benefits include:

Reduction in repetitive manual work

Repetitive work is tedious to do manually. People become bored and make mistakes when doing the same task over and over. Examples of this type of repetitive work include running regression tests, entering the same test data over and over again (both of which can be done by a test execution tool), checking against coding standards (which can be done by a static analysis tool) or running a large number of tests through the system in a short time (which can be done by a performance testing tool). Tools can also help to set up or tear down test environments. Using tools to help with repetitive work can save time (as well as frustration).

Greater consistency and repeatability

People tend to do the same task in a slightly different way even when they think they are repeating something exactly. A tool will exactly reproduce what it did before, so each time it is run, the result is consistent. Examples of where this aspect is beneficial include checking to confirm the correctness of a fix to a defect (which can be done by a debugging tool or test execution tool), entering test inputs (which can be done by a test execution tool) and generating tests from requirements (which can be done by a test design tool, MBT tool or possibly a requirements management tool).

More objective assessment

If a person calculates a value from the software or defect reports, they may inadvertently omit something, or their own subjective prejudices may lead them to interpret that data incorrectly. Using a tool means that subjective bias is removed and the assessment is more repeatable and consistently calculated. Examples include assessing the structure of a component (which can be done by a static analysis tool), measuring coverage of the test item by a set of tests (coverage measurement tool), assessing system behaviour (monitoring tools) and defect statistics (test management tool or defect management tool).

Easier access to information about testing

Having lots of data does not mean that information is communicated. Information presented visually is much easier for the human mind to take in and interpret. For example, a chart or graph is a better way to show information than a long list of numbers. This is why charts and graphs in spreadsheets are so useful. Special-purpose tools give these features directly for the information they process. Examples include statistics and graphs about test progress (test execution tool or test management tool), defect rates (defect management or test management tool) and performance (performance testing tool).

In addition to these general benefits, each type of tool has specific benefits relating to the aspect of testing that the particular tool supports. These benefits are normally prominently featured in the information available for the type of tool. It is worth investigating a number of different tools to get a general view of the benefits.

Risks of using tools

Although there are significant benefits that can be achieved using tools to support testing activities, there are many organizations that have not achieved the benefits they expected.

Simply purchasing a tool is no guarantee of achieving benefits, just as buying membership in a gym does not guarantee that you will be fitter. Each type of tool requires investment of effort and time in order to achieve the potential benefits.

There are many risks that are present when tool support for testing is introduced and used, whatever the specific type of tool. Risks include:

Expectations for the tool may be unrealistic (including functionality and ease of use)

Unrealistic expectations may be one of the greatest risks to success with tools. The tools are only software and we all know that there are many problems with any kind of software! It is important to have clear objectives for what the tool can do and that those objectives are realistic. Unrealistic expectations may be both for functionality and for ease of use.

The time, cost and effort for the initial introduction of a tool may be under-estimated (including training and external expertise)

Introducing something new into an organization is seldom straightforward. Having purchased a tool, you will want to move from downloading the tool to having a number of people being able to use the tool in a way that will bring benefits. There will be technical problems to overcome, but there will also be resistance from other people – both need to be addressed in order to succeed in introducing a tool. Often forgotten are the time, cost and effort or external expertise to help get things onto the right track, and for training, not just in the use of the tool itself, but internal training after a pilot project so that everyone is using the tool and agreed internal conventions in a consistent way for maximum benefit. Simply acquiring a tool and getting it started is not enough either. When a tool is introduced, it will affect the way testing is done, so test processes and test documentation will need to change.

The time and effort needed to achieve significant and continuing benefits from the tool may be under-estimated

Think back to the last time you did something new for the very first time (learning to drive, riding a bike, skiing). Your first attempts were unlikely to be very good, but with more experience you became much better. Using a testing tool for the first time will not be your best use of the tool either. It takes time to develop ways of using the tool in order to achieve what's possible. In the excitement of acquiring a new tool, it is easy to forget about things like the need for changes in the test process as the tool is implemented. These changes should be planned from the start.

But it doesn't stop there. It is critical for continuing success that there is continuous improvement in the way the tool is used. This may involve re-factoring automation assets from time to time or changing the way those assets are organized. Fortunately, there are some short cuts (for example reading books and articles about other people's experiences and learning from them). See also Section 6.2.1 for more detail on introducing a tool into an organization.

The effort required to maintain the test assets generated by the tool may be under-estimated

Insufficient planning for maintenance of the assets that the tool produces and uses is a strong contributor to tools that end up as shelf-ware, along with the previously listed risks. Although particularly relevant for test execution tools, planning for maintenance is also a factor with other types of tool.

The tool may be relied on too much (seen as a replacement for test design or execution, or the use of automated testing where manual testing would be better)

Tools are definitely not magic! They can do very well what they have been designed to do (at least a good quality tool can), but they cannot do everything. A tool can certainly help, but it does not replace the intelligence needed to know how best to use it, and how to evaluate current and future uses of the tool. A test execution tool does not replace the need for good test design and should not be used for every test. Some tests are still better executed manually. For example, a test that takes a very long time to automate and will not be run very often is better done manually.

Version control of test assets or interoperability may be neglected

Configuration management is important for test assets, and that definitely includes automation assets. If this is neglected, it can lead to significant and unnecessary problems.

Relationships and interoperability issues between critical tools may be neglected, such as requirements management tools, configuration management tools, defect management tools, and tools from multiple vendors. Most organizations have a number of different tools, often to support different aspects of development and testing. Some organizations may have a tool suite with many different tool types bundled together, others may have a number of tools that are sourced from a variety of sources. The relationships and interoperability between the various tools can cause problems. These should be taken into account when acquiring a new tool, but when tools change, this may also cause interoperability problems to change. This is particularly important for continuous integration tools, but the problems there will become obvious quickly. Problems with integrating other tools may not be so obvious, but may store up problems for later.

The tool vendor may go out of business, retire the tool, or sell the tool to a different vendor

A commercial tool vendor may not be able to continue to support a tool that you have come to rely on. If a tool is acquired by a different organization, they may not have the same priorities. Sometimes tools that have been very popular are phased out. Open source tools also change over time and may become less suitable for you. When you choose a tool, always think about how you would cope if you had to change to a different tool, and structure your automation to cope with this, even if it seems very unlikely now.

The vendor may provide a poor response for support, upgrades and defect fixes

Commercial vendors, or those supporting open source tools, may not respond quickly or adequately to questions, problems or bugs found in the tools (yes it does happen!). Upgrades may cause problems for you because of the way that you have used the tool, but the vendor may not be interested in helping you if you are in a small minority of their customers.

An open source project may be suspended

Even open source projects can be affected. Since they are very much supported by a community, if the people involved are no longer active, it may be difficult to get help with tool problems.

A new platform or technology may not be supported by the tool

Your own applications are changing over time as well, moving onto new platforms and using new technology. If you are in the forefront of your industry, your testing tools may not yet be able to deal with these innovations.

There may be no clear ownership of the tool (for example for mentoring, updates etc.)

There should be one person who is responsible for technical aspects of the tool. This person may be an enthusiastic champion for automation in general, or they may have a more technical role and be the person who deals with licences, reporting problems, installing updates, etc. If no one takes ownership of the tool, there will be problems in the future, and the automation will begin to decay.

This list of risks is not exhaustive. Two other important factors are:

- The skill needed to create good tests.
- The skill needed to use the tools well, depending on the type of tool.

The skills of a tester are not the same as the skills of the tool user. The tester concentrates on what should be tested, what the test cases should be and how to prioritize the testing. The tool user concentrates on how best to get the tool to do its job effectively and how to give increasing benefit from tool use.

6.1.3 Special considerations for test execution and test management tools

Test execution tools

In order to know what tests to execute and how to run them, the test execution tool must have some way of knowing what to do – this is the script for the tool. But since the tool is only software, the script must be completely exact and unambiguous to the computer, which has no common sense. This means that the script is a program, written in a programming language. The scripting language may be specific to a particular tool, or it may be a more general language. Scripting languages are not used just by test execution tools, but the scripts used by the tool are stored electronically to be run when the tests are executed under the tool's control.

There are tools that can generate scripts by identifying what is on the screen rather than by capturing a manual test, but they still generate scripts to be used in execution: they are not 'script-free' or 'code-free'. This later generation of tools may use smart image-capturing technology and they can help to generate initial scripts quickly, so may be more useful than the traditional capture/replay tools. However, maintenance will still be needed on the scripts over time as the user interface evolves, for example. This will need someone to be able to work directly with the scripting language. The sales pitches for these tools may imply that this is not necessary, but this is misleading.

There are different levels of scripting. Five are described in Fewster and Graham [1999]:

- Linear scripts, which could be created manually or captured by recording a manual test.
- Structured scripts, using selection and iteration programming structures.
- Shared scripts, where a script can be called by other scripts so can be re-used: shared scripts also require a formal script library under configuration management.
- Data-driven scripts, where test data is in a file or spreadsheet to be read by a control script.
- Keyword-driven scripts, where all of the information about the test is stored in a file or spreadsheet, with a single control script that implements the tests described in the file using shared and keyword scripts.

Capturing a manual test seems like a good idea to start with, particularly if you are currently running tests manually anyway. But a captured test (a linear script) is not a good solution, for a number of reasons, including:

- The script does not know what the expected result is until you program it in. It only stores inputs that have been recorded, not test cases.
- A small change to the software may invalidate dozens or hundreds of scripts.
- The recorded script can only cope with exactly the same conditions as when it was recorded. Unexpected events (for example a file that already exists) will not be interpreted correctly by the tool.

However, there are some times when capturing test inputs (that is, recording a manual test) is useful. For example, if you are doing exploratory testing or if you are running unscripted tests with experienced business users, it can be very helpful simply to record everything that is done, as an audit trail. This serves as a form of documentation of what was tested (although analyzing it may not be easy). This audit trail can also be very useful if a failure occurs which cannot be easily reproduced. The recording of the specific failure can be played to the developer to see exactly what sequence caused the problem.

Captured test inputs can be useful in the short term, where the context remains valid. Just don't expect to replay them as regression tests (when the context of the test may be different). Captured tests may be acceptable for a few dozen tests, where the effort to update them when the software changes is not very large. Don't expect a linear scripting approach to scale to hundreds or thousands of tests.

Capturing tests does have a place, but it is not a large place in terms of automating test execution.

Data-driven testing A scripting technique that stores test input and expected results in a table or spreadsheet, so that a single control script can execute all of the tests in the table. Data-driven testing is often used to support the application of test execution tools such as capture/playback tools.

Data-driven testing uses scripts that allow the data, that is, the test inputs and expected outcomes, to be stored separately from the script. This can include situations where, instead of the tester putting hard-coded data combinations into a spreadsheet, a tool generates and supplies data in real time, based on configurable parameters. For example, a tool may generate a random user ID for accounts and can take advantage of random number seeding to ensuring repeatability in the pattern of user IDs. Whichever way data-driven testing is implemented, it has the advantage that a tester who does not know how to use a scripting language can populate a file or spreadsheet with the data for a specific test. This is particularly useful when there are a large number of data values that need to be tested using the same control script.

Keyword-driven testing (action word-driven testing) A scripting technique that uses data files to contain not only test data and expected results, but also keywords related to the application being tested. The keywords are interpreted by special supporting scripts that are called by the control script for the test.

Keyword-driven testing uses scripts that include not just data but also keywords in the data file or spreadsheet. In other words, the spreadsheet or data file contains keywords that describe the actions to be taken and the test data. Action words is another term used for keywords as described in Buwalda *et al.* [2001]. Keyword-driven (or action word) automation enables a tester (who is not a script programmer) to devise a great variety of tests, not just varied input data for essentially the same test, as in data-driven scripts. The tester needs to know what keywords are currently available to use (by someone having written a script for it) and what data the keyword is expecting, but the tester can then write tests, not just enter specific test data. The tester can also request additional keywords to be added to the available programmed set of scripts as needed. Keywords can deal with both test inputs and expected outcomes.

Someone still needs to be able to use the tool directly and be able to program in the tool's scripting language, in order to write and debug the keyword scripts that will use the data tables or keyword tables. A small number of automation specialists can support a larger number of testers, who then do not need to learn to be script programmers (unless they want to).

The data files (data-driven or keyword-driven) include the expected results for the tests. The actual results from each test run also need to be stored, at least until they are compared to the expected results and any differences are logged.

Whatever form of scripting is used, there are two important points to remember:

- Someone needs to have expertise in the scripting language of the tool.
- The expected results of a test still need to be compared to the actual result produced by the application when the (automated) test is run.

There are two types of result comparison: dynamic, which is done while the test is running, or post-execution, which is done after the test completes. Dynamic comparison is best for things like pop-ups or error messages during a test, and can help to determine the subsequent progress of the test. Post-execution comparison is best for comparing large volumes of data, for example in a database, after tests have made many changes.

Model-based testing tools include not only test execution capability, but can also generate test inputs and expected results. The tool stores a functional specification such as an activity diagram or finite state machine. This is generally specified by a system designer. The MBT tool uses the stored model to generate inputs and expected results. For example, a state diagram shows the type of input that would generate a state transition. The tool selects a sample value from the input space, and the expected result would include the end state after the transition. The generated test cases can be stored in a test management tool or run by a test execution tool. Note that there is an ISTQB qualification for MBT: Foundation Level Model-Based Testing (an extension to the Foundation level).

More information on data-driven and keyword-driven scripting can be found in Fewster and Graham [1999], Buwalda et al [2001], Janssen and Pinkster [2001], Graham and Fewster [2012] and Gamba and Graham [2018]. Note that there is an ISTQB qualification in test automation: Advanced Level Test Automation Engineer.

Test management tools
Test management tools can provide a lot of useful information, but the information as produced by the tool may not be in the form that will be most effective within your own context. Some additional work may be needed to produce interfaces to other tools or a spreadsheet in order to ensure that the information is communicated in the most effective way.

Test management tools need to interface with other tools (including spreadsheets for example) for various reasons, including:

- To produce useful information in a format that fits the needs of the organization.
- To maintain consistent traceability to requirements in a requirements management tool.
- To link with test object version information in the configuration management tool.

Tools such as application lifecycle management (ALM) tools may have aspects that are used by different people within the organization. For example, a high-level manager wants to see trends and graphs about test progress, application quality schedules and budgets, but a developer wants to see detailed information about how a defect occurred.

A report produced by a test management tool (either directly or indirectly through another tool or spreadsheet) may be a very useful report at the moment, but the same information may not be useful in three or six months. It is important to monitor the information produced to ensure it is the most relevant now.

It is important to have a defined test process before test management tools are introduced. If the testing process is working well manually, then a test management tool can help to support the process and make it more efficient. If you adopt a test management tool when your own testing processes are immature, one option is to follow the standards and processes that are assumed by the way the tool works.

This can be helpful, but it is not necessary to follow the processes specific to the tool. The best approach is to define your own processes, taking into account the tool you will be using, and then adapt the tool to provide the greatest benefit to your organization.

6.2 EFFECTIVE USE OF TOOLS

In this section, we discuss the principles and process of introducing tools into your organization. We look at the process of tool selection. We'll talk about how to carry out tool pilot projects. We'll conclude with thoughts on what makes tool introduction successful. There are no Glossary terms for this section.

Lots of tool advice is online, and good advice on automation can be found in Fewster and Graham [1999 and 2012], Gamba and Graham [2018] and Axelrod [2018].

6.2.1 Main principles for tool selection

The place to start when introducing a tool into an organization is not with the tool: it is with the organization. In order for a tool to provide benefit, it must match a need within the organization, and solve that need in a way that is both effective and efficient. The tool should help to build on the strengths of the organization and address its weaknesses. The organization needs to be ready for the changes that will come with the new tool. If the current testing practices are not good and the organization is not mature, then it is generally more cost-effective to improve testing practices rather than to try to find tools to support poor practices. Automating chaos just gives faster chaos!

Of course, we can sometimes improve our own processes in parallel with introducing a tool to support those practices. We can pick up some good ideas for improvement from the ways that the tools work. However, be aware that the tool should not take the lead, but should provide support to what your organization defines.

The following factors are important in selecting a tool:

- Assessment of the organization's maturity (for example strengths and weaknesses, readiness for change).
- Identification of the areas within the organization where tool support will help to improve testing processes.
- Understanding the technologies used by the test object(s), so that a tool will be selected that is compatible with those technologies.

- Knowledge of any build and continuous integration tools already being used within the organization, to make sure that the new tool(s) will integrate with them and be compatible.

- Evaluation of tools against clear requirements and objective criteria.

- Consideration of any free trial period for the tool (for commercial tools) to ensure that this gives adequate time to evaluate the tool.

- Evaluation of the vendor (including training, support and other commercial aspects) or support for non-commercial tools (open source).

- Identification of internal requirements for coaching and mentoring in the use of the tool.

- Evaluation of training needs for those who will use the tools directly and indirectly (for example without technical detail), taking into account testing skills and test automation skills (for those working directly with the tools).

- Consideration of pros and cons of different licencing models (for example commercial or open source).

- Estimation of a cost-benefit ratio based on a concrete and realistic business case (if required).

A final step would be to do a proof-of-concept evaluation. The purpose of this is to see whether or not the tool performs as expected, both with the software under test and with any other tools or aspects of your own infrastructure. For example, you want to find out now if your proposed tool cannot communicate with your configuration management system. You may also need to identify changes to your current infrastructure to enable the new tool(s) to be used effectively.

6.2.2 Pilot project

After selecting a tool (or tools) and a successful proof-of-concept, the next step is to have a pilot project as the first step in using the tool(s) for real. The pilot project will use the tool in earnest but on a small scale, with sufficient time to explore different ways of using the tool. Objectives should be set for the pilot in order to assess whether or not the tool can accomplish what is needed within the current organizational context.

A pilot tool project should expect to encounter problems. They should be solved in ways that can be used by everyone later on. The pilot project should experiment with different ways of using the tool. For example, different reports from a test management tool, different scripting and comparison techniques for a test execution tool or different load profiles for a performance testing tool.

The objectives for a pilot project for a newly acquired tool are:

- To gain in-depth knowledge about the tool (more detail, more ways of using it) and to understand more fully both its strengths and its weaknesses.

- To see how the tool would fit with existing processes and practices, determining how those would need to adapt and change to work well with the tool, and how to use the tool to streamline and improve existing processes.

- To decide on standard ways of using the tool that will work for all potential users (for example naming conventions for files and tests, creation of libraries, defining modularity, where different elements will be stored, how they and the tool itself will be maintained, and coding standards for test scripts).

- To assess whether or not the benefits will be achieved at reasonable cost.
- To understand (and experiment with) metrics that you want the tool(s) to collect and to report, and configuring the tool(s) to ensure that your goals for these metrics can be achieved.

6.2.3 Success factors for tools

Success is not guaranteed or automatic when acquiring a testing tool, but many organizations have succeeded. After a successful selection process and a pilot project, two other things are also important to get the greatest benefit from the tools: the way in which the tool(s) is deployed within the wider organization, and the way in which ongoing support is organized. Here are some of the factors that contribute to success:

- Rolling out the tool incrementally (after the pilot) to the rest of the organization (a gradual uptake of the tool, not trying to get the whole organization to use it at once immediately).
- Adapting and improving processes, testware and tool artefacts to get the best fit and balance between them and the use of the tool.
- Providing adequate support, training (for example for those using the tool directly), coaching (for example from external specialist automation consultants) and mentoring for tool users.
- Defining and communicating guidelines for the use of the tool, based on what was learned in the pilot (for example internal standards for automation).
- Implementing a way to gather information about the use of the tool, to enable continuous improvement as tool use spreads through more of the organization.
- Monitoring the use of the tool and the benefits achieved, and adapting the use of the tool to take account of what is learned.
- Providing continuing support for anyone using test tools, such as the test team (for example, technical expertise is needed to help non-programmer testers who use keyword-driven testing).
- Gathering lessons learned, based on information gathered from all teams who are using test tools.

Any tools also need to be integrated both technically and organizationally into the software development life cycle. This may involve separate organizations that are responsible for different aspects, such as operations and/or third-party suppliers. Failure in tool use can come from any one factor; success needs all factors to be working together.

More information and advice about experiences in using tools can be found in Graham and Fewster [2012] and Gamba and Graham [2018].

CHAPTER REVIEW

Let's review what you have learned in this chapter.

From Section 6.1.1, you should now be able to classify different types of test tools according to the test process activities that they support. You should also recognize the tools that may help developers in their testing (shown by (D) below). In addition to the list below, you should recognize that there are tools that support specific application areas and that general purpose tools can also be used to support testing. The tools you should now recognize are:

Tools that support the management of testing and tests:

- Test management tools and application lifecycle management (ALM) tools.
- Requirements management tools.
- Defect management tools.
- Configuration management tools.
- Continuous integration tools (D).

Tools that support static testing:

- Tools that support reviews.
- Static analysis tools (D).

Tools that support test design and implementation:

- Test design tools.
- Model-Based Testing (MBT) tools.
- Test data preparation tools.
- Acceptance test-driven development (ATDD) and behaviour-driven development (BDD) tools.

Tools that support test execution and logging:

- Test execution tools.
- Coverage tools, for example requirements coverage, code coverage (D).
- Test harnesses (D).
- Unit test framework tools (D).

Tools that support performance measurement and dynamic analysis:

- Performance testing tools.
- Monitoring tools.
- Dynamic analysis tools (D).

You should know the Glossary terms **performance testing tool, test execution tool**, and **test management tool**.

From Section 6.1.2, you should be able to summarize the potential benefits and potential risks of test automation.

From Section 6.1.3, you should recognize the special considerations of test execution tools and test management tools.

From these two sections, you should know the Glossary terms **data-driven testing**, **keyword-driven testing** and **test automation**.

From Section 6.2.1, you should be able to state the main principles of introducing a tool into an organization.

From Section 6.2.2, you should be able to state the objectives of a pilot project as a starting point to introduce a tool into an organization.

From Section 6.2.3, you should recognize that simply acquiring a tool is not the only factor in achieving success in using test tools; there are many other factors that are important for success.

There are no specific definitions for these three sections.

SAMPLE EXAM QUESTIONS

Question 1 Which tools help to support static testing?

a. Static analysis tools and test execution tools.

b. Review tools, static analysis tools and coverage measurement tools.

c. Dynamic analysis tools and modelling tools.

d. Review tools and static analysis tools.

Question 2 Which test activities are supported by test harnesses?

a. Test management and control.

b. Test design and implementation.

c. Test execution and logging.

d. Performance measurement and dynamic analysis.

Question 3 What are the potential benefits from using test automation?

a. Greater quality of code, reduction in the number of testers needed, better objectives for testing.

b. Greater repeatability of tests, reduction in repetitive work, objective assessment.

c. Greater responsiveness of users, reduction of tests run, objectives not necessary.

d. Greater quality of code, reduction in paperwork, fewer objections to the tests.

Question 4 Which of the following are advanced scripting techniques for test execution tools?

a. Data-driven and keyword-driven.

b. Data-driven and capture-driven.

c. Capture-driven and keyhole-driven.

d. Playback-driven and keyword-driven.

Question 5 Which of the following would NOT be done as part of selecting a tool for an organization?

a. Assess organizational maturity, strengths and weaknesses.

b. Roll out the tool to as many users as possible within the organization.

c. Evaluate the tool features against clear requirements and objective criteria.

d. Identify internal requirements for coaching and mentoring in the use of the tool.

Question 6 Which of the following is a goal for a pilot project for introducing a tool into an organization?

a. Decide which tool to acquire.

b. Decide on the main objectives and requirements for this type of tool.

c. Evaluate the tool vendor including training, support, and commercial aspects.

d. Decide on standard ways of using, managing, storing and maintaining the tool and the test assets.

Question 7 What is a success factor for the use of tools within an organization?

a. Implement a way to gather usage information from the actual use of the tool.

b. Evaluate how the tool fits with existing processes and adopt the tool's approach.

c. Roll out the tool to all of the rest of the organization at once, as quickly as possible.

d. Assess whether the benefits will be achieved at reasonable cost.

CHAPTER SEVEN

ISTQB Foundation Exam

We wrote (and re-wrote and re-wrote) this book specifically to cover the International Software Testing Qualification Board (ISTQB) Foundation Syllabus 2018. Because of this, mastery of the previous six chapters should ensure that you master the exam too. Here are some thoughts on how to make sure you show how much you know when taking the exam.

7.1 PREPARING FOR THE EXAM

7.1.1 Studying for the exam

Whether you have taken a preparatory course along with reading this book or just read the book, we have some study tips for certification candidates who intend to take an exam under one of the ISTQB-recognized National Boards or Exam Boards.

Of course, you should carefully study the Syllabus. If you encounter any statements or concepts you do not *completely* understand, refer back to this book and to any course materials used, to prepare for the exam. Exam questions often turn on *precise* understanding of a concept or the wording.

While you should study the whole Syllabus, scrutinize the learning objectives in the Syllabus one by one. Ask yourself if you have achieved that learning objective to the given level of knowledge. If not, go back and review the appropriate material in the section corresponding to that learning objective. Note that the sections in both the Syllabus and the book often have the same numbering, and this is usually the same as the learning objective in the Syllabus.

Going beyond the Syllabus, notice that a number of international standards are referred to in the Syllabus. Some exam questions may be about the standards and there will also be questions about Glossary terms, and often even experienced testers are unfamiliar with them.

We recommend that you try to answer all of the sample exam questions in this book. If you have understood the material in a chapter, you should have no trouble with the questions. Make sure you understand why the right answer is the right answer and why the wrong answers are wrong. If you cannot answer a question and don't understand why, review that section.

We also recommend that you try to do all of the exercises in the book. If you can complete them correctly, you probably understand the concepts. If you do the exercises well, you are more likely to pass the exam.

Finally, be sure to take the mock exam we have provided at the end of this chapter. If you have understood the material in the book, you should have no trouble with most, if not all, of the questions on the mock exam. Make sure you carefully review the book sections corresponding to any questions that you haven't answered correctly. When you take the mock exam, try to simulate exam conditions as much as possible. Set aside a full hour to do the exam, and make sure that you are not disturbed during the hour: no interruptions! Turn off email and leave your phone in another room.

7.1.2 The exam and the Syllabus

The ISTQB Foundation exam is designed to assess your knowledge and understanding of basic testing ideas and terms, which provides a solid starting point for your future testing efforts. These exams are not perfect. Even well-qualified candidates often fail a few questions or disagree with some answers. Study hard, so you can take the exam in a relaxed and confident way.

If you take the exam unprepared, you should expect your lack of preparation to show in your score. Since you will pay to take the exam, consider preparation time an investment in protecting your exam fee.

The ISTQB Foundation Syllabus 2018 is the current Syllabus. It replaces the 2011 version, which in turn replaced the 2007 version, which in turn replaced the 2005 version. Do not refer to the old Syllabi, as the exam covers the new Syllabus.

7.1.3 Where should you take the exam?

If you have taken an accredited training course, it is quite likely the exam will occur on the last day of the course. The exam fee may have been included in the course fee. If so, you should plan to study each evening during the course, including material that will be covered on the last day. Any topic covered in the Syllabus may be in the exam. You might even want to read this book before starting the course.

You might be taking an online course. Again, we recommend that you study the materials as you cover each section. Consider reading the book during or even before taking the course.

If you have studied on your own, without taking a course, then you will need to find a place open to the general public where the exam is offered. Many conferences around the world offer the exam this way. Otherwise the website for the testing board for your country (the National Board) should be able to help you find the right venue for a public exam.

In addition, ISTQB-recognized exam providers such as ASTQB, BCS (British Computer Society), Brightest, Cert-IT, CertInstitute, GASQ, iSQI and Kryterion (list adapted from ISTQB website at the time of publication) will provide you with ISTQB-branded certificates, as they work in close cooperation with the ISTQB and its National Boards. The ISTQB and each ISTQB-recognized National Board and Exam Board are constitutionally obliged to support a single, universally accepted, international qualification scheme. Therefore, you are free to choose ISTQB-accredited trainers, if desired, and ISTQB-accredited exam providers based on factors like convenience, competence, suitability of the training to your immediate professional and business needs and price.

7.2 TAKING THE EXAM

All the National Boards offer the same type of Foundation exam. It is a multiple choice exam that conforms to the guidelines established by the ISTQB. The exam in this book also follows the new guidelines from ISTQB for the balance of questions from the different sections/chapters. For some of us, it's been a while since we last took an exam and you may not remember all the tricks and techniques for taking a multiple choice exam. Here are a few paragraphs that will give you some ideas on how to take the exam.

7.2.1 How to approach multiple choice questions

Remember that there are two aspects to correctly answering a multiple choice exam question. First, you must understand the question and decide what the right answer is. Second, you must correctly communicate your answer by selecting the correct option from the choices listed.

Each question has one correct answer. This answer is always or most frequently true, given the stated context and conditions in the question. The other answers are intended to mislead people who do not completely understand the concept and are called 'distracters' in the examination business.

Read the question carefully and make sure you understand it before you decide on your answer. It may help to highlight or underline the keywords or concepts stated in the question. Some questions may be ambiguous or ask which is the best or worst alternative. You should choose the best answer based on what you have learned in this book. Remember that your own situation may be different from the most common situation or the ideal situation.

Some of the distracters may confuse you. In other words, you might be unsure about the correct answers to some of the questions. So make two passes through the exam. On your first pass, answer all of the questions you are sure of. Come back to the others later.

If a question will take a long time to answer, come back to it later, when you feel confident that you have enough time. Each correct answer is worth one point, whether it takes 30 seconds or 5 minutes to decide on it.

It's important to pace yourself. We suggest that you spend 45–60 seconds on each question. That way your first pass will take less than 40 minutes. You can then use the remaining time to have a one-minute break, then double-check your answers, and then finally go back to any questions you haven't answered yet.

If you use an answer sheet for the exam, they may vary slightly from one National Board or Exam Board to another. You should make sure that each answer corresponds to the correct question number. Especially if you have skipped a question; it is easy to get confused and mark the answer option above or below the question you are trying to answer.

Also, make sure you have an answer for every question. Double-check that you have selected the answer you want, as it is easy to select the wrong answer.

7.2.2 On trick questions

There are no deliberately designed trick questions in the ISTQB exams, but some can seem quite difficult if you are not completely sure of the right answer. Remember, just because it is hard to answer does not make it a trick. Here are some ideas for dealing with the tough questions.

First, read the question and each of the options very thoroughly. It is easy to read what you expect to be there rather than what is there.

If you are tempted to change your answer, do so only if you are quite sure. When you are undecided between two options, it's usually best to go with your first instinct. Remember that the correct answer is the one always or most often true. Simply because you can imagine a circumstance under which an answer might not be true does not make it wrong, just as knowing a 95-year-old cigarette smoker does not prove that cigarette smoking is not risky.

For most exams, you are allowed to write on the question paper or make notes on paper (which would need to be handed in). In addition, there is typically no penalty for the wrong answer. So feel free to guess!

While the ISTQB guidelines call for straightforward questions, some topics are difficult to cover without some amount of complexity. Be especially careful with negative questions and complex questions. If the question asks which is false (or true), mark them T or F first if you can. This will make it easier to see which is the odd one out. If the question requires matching a list of definitions, you might be able to draw lines between the definitions and the words they define. And remember to use the process of elimination to work for you whenever possible. Use what you know to eliminate wrong answers and cross them out up front to avoid mistakes.

Finally, remember that the ISTQB exam is about the theory of good practice, not what you typically do in practice. The ISTQB Syllabus was developed by an international working group of testing experts based on the good practices they have seen in the real world. In testing, good practices may lead typical practices by about 20 years' time. Some organizations are struggling to implement even basic testing principles, such as removing the misconception that "complete" testing is possible, while other organizations may already be doing most of the things discussed in the Syllabus. Still other organizations may do things well but differently from what is described in the Syllabus. So remember to apply what you have learned in this book to the exam. When an exam question calls into conflict what you have learned here and what you typically have done in the past, rely on what you have learned to answer the exam question. And then go back to your workplace and put the good ideas that you have learned into practice!

7.2.3 Last but not least

ISTQB has sample exam papers available to download, as well as the correct answers and justifications for those answers. It is well worth working through these exams as well! Search under 'Exams', 'Sample exams', and "Foundation level' for CTFL 2018 exams.

We wish you good luck with your certification exam and best of success in your career as a test professional! We stand poised on the brink of great forward progress in the field of testing and are happy that you will be a part of it.

7.3 MOCK EXAM

In the real exam, you will have 60 minutes (75 if the exam is not in your first language) to work through 40 questions of approximately the same difficulty mix and Syllabus distribution as shown in the following mock exam. After you have taken this mock exam, check your answers with the answer key. The answers to all exam questions in this book are in the section after the Glossary.

Question 1 Assume postal rates for light letters are:

$0.25 up to 10 grams.

$0.35 up to 50 grams.

$0.45 up to 75 grams.

$0.55 up to 100 grams.

Which test inputs (in grams) could be selected using equivalence partitioning?

a. 0, 9, 10, 49, 50, 74, 75, 99, 100.

b. 5, 35, 65, 95, 115.

c. 0, 1, 10, 11, 50, 51, 75, 76, 100, 101.

d. 5, 25, 35, 45, 55.

Question 2 Consider the following statements about testing and debugging and identify which are True:

1. Debugging is a testing activity.

2. Testers may be involved in debugging and component testing in Agile development.

3. Testing finds, analyzes and fixes defects.

4. Debugging executes tests to show failures caused by defects.

5. Checking whether fixes resolved the defects found is a form of testing.

a. 2 and 5.

b. 2, 3 and 4.

c. 1, 2 and 5.

d. Only 5 is True.

Question 3 Consider the following statements about the reasons to adapt life cycle models for specific projects or products:

I   Different projects have different goals.

II The life cycle model should be adapted to suit all types of development within the company for consistency.

III Different types of product have different product risks.

IV Business priorities are different depending on the context of the project or product.

V Different test environments may be necessary.

Which of the statements are true?

a. I, III and IV.

b. I, II and IV.

c. III, IV and V.

d. II, IV and V.

Question 4 Which of the following statements about use case testing are True?

1. A use case actor may be a business user; a use case subject is the system.

2. Error messages are tested in the main behavioural flow of the use case.

3. Interactions may be represented by activity diagrams.

4. Coverage cannot be measured for use case testing.

5. Interactions may change the state of the subject.

a. 1, 2 and 3.

b. 1, 4 and 5.

c. 2, 3 and 4.

d. 1, 3 and 5.

Question 5 Consider the following list of either product or project risks:

I   An incorrect calculation of fees might short-change the organization.

II A vendor might fail to deliver a system component on time.

III A defect might allow hackers to gain administrative privileges.

IV A skills gap might occur in a new technology used in the system.

V A defect-prioritization process might overload the development team.

Which of the following statements is true?

a. I is primarily a product risk and II, III, IV and V are primarily project risks.

b. II and V are primarily product risks and I, III and V are primarily project risks.

c. I and III are primarily product risks, while II, IV and V are primarily project risks.

d. III and V are primarily product risks, while I, II and IV are primarily project risks.

Question 6 Consider the following statements about regression tests:

I They may usefully be automated if they are well designed.

II They are the same as confirmation tests (re-tests).

III They are a way to reduce the risk of a change having an adverse affect elsewhere in the system.

IV They are only effective if automated.

Which pair of statements is true?

a. I and II.

b. I and III.

c. II and III.

d. II and IV.

Question 7 According to the ISTQB Glossary, what is a black-box test technique?

a. A sequence of test cases in execution order, and any associated actions that may be required to set up the initial preconditions and any wrap-up activities post-execution.

b. A procedure to derive and/or select test cases based on the tester's experience, knowledge and intuition.

c. A procedure to derive and/or select test cases based on an analysis of the specification, either functional or non-functional, of a component or system without reference to its internal structure.

d. A procedure to derive and/or select test cases based on an analysis of the internal structure of a component or system.

Question 8 Review the following portion of a defect report, which occurs after the defect ID, time and date, and author.

1. I place any item in the shopping cart.

2. I place any other (different) item in the shopping cart.

3. I remove the first item from the shopping cart, but leave the second item in the cart.

4. I click the <Checkout> button.

5. I expect the system to display the first checkout screen. Instead, it gives the pop-up error message, 'No items in shopping cart. Click <Okay> to continue shopping'.

6. I click <Okay>.

7. I expect the system to return to the main window to allow me to continue adding and removing items from the cart. Instead, the browser terminates.

8. The failure described in steps 5 and 7 occurred in each of three attempts to perform steps 1, 2, 3, 4 and 6.

Assume that no other narrative information is included in the report. Which of the following important aspects of a good defect report is missing from this report?

a. The steps to reproduce the failure.

b. The summary.

c. The check for intermittence.

d. The use of an objective tone.

Question 9 Which of the tasks below is typically done by a tester (not a test manager)?

a. Support setting up the defect management system.

b. Share testing perspectives with other project activities such as integration planning.

c. Design, set up and verify test environment(s).

d. Initiate the analysis, design, implementation and execution of tests.

Question 10 Consider the following factors:

1. The test levels and test types being considered.

2. The best practices implemented in other companies.

3. The business domain.

4. Required internal and external standards.

5. The way in which the previous system was developed.

Which of these factors may influence the test process in context?

a. 1, 2 and 5.

b. 2, 4 and 5.

c. 1, 3 and 4.

d. 1, 3 and 5.

Question 11 Of the following statements about reviews of specifications, which statement is true?

a. Reviews are not generally cost-effective as the meetings are time consuming and require preparation and follow up.

b. There is no need to prepare for or follow up on reviews.

c. Reviews must be controlled by the author.

d. Reviews are a cost-effective early static test on the system.

Question 12 Consider the following list of test process activities:

I Analysis and design.

II Test closure activities.

III Evaluating exit criteria and reporting.

IV Planning and control.

V Implementation and execution.

Which of the following places these in their logical sequence?

a. I, II, III, IV and V.

b. IV, I, V, III and II.

c. IV, I, V, II and III.

d. I, IV, V, III and II.

Question 13 Test objectives vary between projects and so should be stated in the test plan. Which one of the following test objectives might conflict with the proper tester mindset?

a. Show that the system works before we ship it.

b. Find as many defects as possible.

c. Reduce the overall level of product risk.

d. Prevent defects through early involvement.

Question 14 Which of the following is a test metric?

a. Percentage of planned functionality that has completed development.

b. Confirmation test results (pass/fail).

c. Cost of development, including time and effort.

d. Effort spent in fixing defects, not including confirmation testing or regression testing.

Question 15 If you are flying with an economy ticket, there is a possibility that you may get upgraded to business class, especially if you hold a gold card in the airline's frequent flyer programme. If you do not hold a gold card, there is a possibility that you will get bumped off the flight if it is full and you check in late. This is shown in Figure 7.1. Note that each box (i.e. statement) has been numbered.

Three tests have already been run:

Test 1: Gold card holder who gets upgraded to business class.

Test 2: Non-gold card holder who stays in economy.

Test 3: A person who is bumped from the flight.

FIGURE 7.1 Control flow diagram for flight check-in

What additional tests would be needed to achieve 100% decision coverage?

a. A gold card holder who stays in economy and a non-gold card holder who gets upgraded to business class.

b. A gold card holder and a non-gold card holder who are both upgraded to business class.

c. A gold card holder and a non-gold card holder who both stay in economy class.

d. A gold card holder who is upgraded to business class and a non-gold card holder who stays in economy class.

Question 16 Consider the following types of tools:

V Test management tools.

W Static analysis tools.

X Continuous integration tools.

Y Dynamic analysis tools.

Z Performance testing tools.

Which of the following of these tools is most likely to be used by developers?

a. W, X and Y.

b. V, Y and Z.

c. V, W and Z.

d. X, Y and Z.

Question 17 Which of the following statements about error guessing are True?

P. Error guessing uses a test charter and test session sheets.

Q. Error guessing is based on tester knowledge.

R. Error guessing always uses a checklist.

S. Error guessing is a black-box test technique.

T. Error guessing can be based on mistakes developers may make.

a. P and T.

b. Q and R.

c. Q and T.

d. Q and S.

Question 18 Which of the following is the most important difference between the metrics-based approach and the expert-based approach to test estimation?

a. The metrics-based approach is more accurate than the expert-based approach.

b. The metrics-based approach uses calculations from historical data while the expert-based approach relies on team wisdom.

c. The metrics-based approach can be used to verify an estimate created using the expert-based approach, but not vice versa.

d. The expert-based approach takes longer than the metrics-based approach.

Question 19 If the temperature falls below 18 degrees, the heating is switched on. When the temperature reaches 21 degrees, the heating is switched off. What is the minimum set of test input values to cover all valid equivalence partitions?

a. 15, 19 and 25 degrees.

b. 17, 18, 20 and 21 degrees.

c. 18, 20 and 22 degrees.

d. 16 and 26 degrees.

Question 20 According to the ISTQB Glossary, what is coverage?

a. An attribute or combination of attributes that is derived from one or more test conditions by using a test technique that enables the measurement of the thoroughness of the test execution.

b. The degree to which specified coverage items have been determined to have been exercised by a test suite, expressed as a percentage.

c. The degree to which specified tests have been run, compared to the full set of tests that could have been run.

d. The degree to which tests have been automated, compared to tests that could have been automated.

Question 21 Which of the following statements about static testing is False?

a. Reviews are applicable to web pages and user guides.

b. Static analysis is applicable to executing test scripts.

c. Static analysis can be applied to work products written in natural language (e.g. English).

d. Reviews can be applied to security requirements and project budgets.

Question 22 Which success factors are required for good tool support within an organization?

a. Acquiring the best tool and ensuring that all testers use it.

b. Adapting processes to fit with the use of the tool and monitoring tool use and benefits.

c. Setting ambitious objectives for tool benefits and aggressive deadlines for achieving them.

d. Adopting practices from other successful organizations and ensuring that initial ways of using the tool are maintained.

Question 23 Match the keyword terms to the correct definitions:

x. Something incorrect in a work product.

y. A person's mistake.

z. An event where the system does NOT perform correctly.

a. x. is a defect, y. is an error, z. is a failure.

b. x. is an error, y. is a defect, z. is a failure.

c. x. is a failure, y. is an error, z. is a defect.

d. x. is a defect, y. is a failure, z. is an error.

Question 24 Which of the following would be a typical defect found in component testing?

a. Incorrect sequencing or timing of interface calls.

b. Incorrect code and logic.

c. Business rules not implemented correctly.

d. Unhandled or improperly handled communication between components.

Question 25 Which of the following could be a root cause of a defect in financial software in which an incorrect interest rate is calculated?

a. Insufficient funds were available to pay the interest rate calculated.

b. Insufficient calculations of compound interest were included.

c. Insufficient training was given to the developers concerning compound interest calculation rules.

d. Inaccurate calculators were used to calculate the expected results.

Question 26 Assume postal rates for light letters are:

$0.25 up to 10 grams.

$0.35 up to 50 grams.

$0.45 up to 75 grams.

$0.55 up to 100 grams.

Which test inputs (in grams) would be selected using boundary value analysis?

a. 0, 9, 19, 49, 50, 74, 75, 99, 100.

b. 10, 50, 75, 100, 250, 1000.

c. 0, 1, 10, 11, 50, 51, 75, 76, 100, 101.

d. 25, 26, 35, 36, 45, 46, 55, 56.

Question 27 Consider the following decision table.

TABLE 7.1 Decision table for car rental

Conditions	Rule 1	Rule 2	Rule 3	Rule 4
Over 23?	F	T	T	T
Clean driving record?	Don't care	F	T	T
On business?	Don't care	Don't care	F	T
Actions				
Supply rental car?	F	F	T	T
Premium charge?	F	F	F	T

Given this decision table, what is the expected result for the following test cases?

TC1: A 26-year-old on business but with violations or accidents on his driving record.

TC2: A 62-year-old tourist with a clean driving record.

a. TC1: Do not supply car;
TC2: Supply car with premium charge.

b. TC1: Supply car with premium charge;
TC2: Supply car with no premium charge.

c. TC1: Do not supply car;
TC2: Supply car with no premium charge.

d. TC1: Supply car with premium charge;
TC2: Do not supply car.

Question 28 What is exploratory testing?

a. The process of anticipating or guessing where defects might occur.

b. A systematic approach to identifying specific equivalent classes of input.

c. The testing carried out by a chartered engineer.

d. Concurrent test design, test execution, test logging and learning.

Question 29 Which statement about functional, non-functional and white-box testing is True?

a. Functional testing evaluates characteristics such as reliability, security or usability; non-functional testing evaluates characteristics such as system architecture and the thoroughness of testing; white-box testing evaluates characteristics such as completeness and correctness.

b. Functional testing evaluates characteristics such as completeness and correctness; non-functional testing evaluates characteristics such as reliability, security or usability; white-box testing evaluates characteristics such as system architecture and the thoroughness of testing.

c. Functional testing evaluates characteristics such as completeness and correctness; non-functional testing evaluates characteristics such as system architecture and the thoroughness of testing; white-box testing evaluates characteristics such as reliability, security or usability.

d. Functional testing evaluates characteristics such as system architecture and the thoroughness of testing; non-functional testing evaluates characteristics such as reliability, security or usability; white-box testing evaluates characteristics such as completeness and correctness.

Question 30 A test plan is written specifically to describe a level of testing where the primary goal is establishing confidence in the system. Which of the following is a likely name for this document?

a. Master test plan.

b. System test plan.

c. Acceptance test plan.

d. Project plan.

Question 31 How do experience-based test techniques differ from black-box test techniques?

a. They depend on the tester's understanding of the way the system is structured rather than on a documented record of what the system should do.

b. They depend on an individual's domain knowledge and expertise rather than on a documented record of what the system should do.

c. They depend on a documented record of what the system should do rather than on an individual's personal view.

d. They depend on having older testers rather than younger testers.

Question 32 Which of the following statements are characteristics of static testing, and which are characteristics of dynamic testing?

1. Finds defects in work products directly.

2. Better for ensuring internal quality (e.g. standards are followed).

3. Finds defects through failures in execution.

4. Easier and cheaper to find and fix security vulnerabilities (e.g. buffer overflow).

5. Focuses on externally visible behaviours.

a. Static testing: 2 and 4, Dynamic testing: 1, 3 and 5.

b. Static testing: 3 and 5, Dynamic testing: 1, 2 and 4.

c. Static testing: 1, 2 and 4, Dynamic testing: 3 and 5.

d. Static testing: 1, 2 and 3, Dynamic testing: 4 and 5.

Question 33 System test execution on a project is planned for eight weeks. After a week of testing, a tester suggests that the test objective stated in the test plan of 'finding as many defects as possible during system test' might be more closely met by redirecting the test effort in what way?

a. By asking a selection of users what is most important for them, and testing that.

b. By testing the main workflows of the business.

c. By repeating the unit and integration tests.

d. By testing in areas where the most defects have already been found.

Question 34 Consider the following activities that might relate to configuration management:

I Identify and document the characteristics of a test item.

II Control changes to the characteristics of a test item.

III Check a test item for defects introduced by a change.

IV Record and report the status of changes to test items.

V Confirm that changes to a test item fixed a defect.

Which of the following statements is True?

a. Only I is a configuration management task.

b. All are configuration management tasks.

c. I, II and III are configuration management tasks.

d. I, II and IV are configuration management tasks.

Question 35 Consider the following state transition diagram.

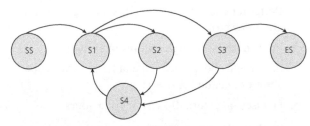

FIGURE 7.2 State transition diagram

Given this diagram, which test case below covers every valid transition?

a. SS – S1 – S2 – S4 – S1 – S3 – ES

b. SS – S1 – S2 – S3 – S4 – S3 – S4 – ES

c. SS – S1 – S2 – S4 – S1 – S3 – S4 – S1 – S3 – ES

d. SS – S1 – S4 – S2 – S1 – S3 – ES

Question 36

You are the test manager for a user acceptance test project. You have decided to use a requirements-based and risk-based test strategy. Test suites have been designed to cover all of the requirements.

Table 7.2 (below) shows the priority and the designed test suites associated with the requirements (a lower priority number means higher risk).

The table also shows the configuration of the test environment in which the requirements can be tested. Thus two different configurations, ABC and XYZ, are required to execute all test suites.

Assume that the test environment is delivered initially to the test team under the configuration ABC; XYZ will be available from the start of week 4. Each test suite will take approximately 1 week to execute.

The execution of TS4 depends on TS3 to be executed before, and the execution of TS2 depends on TS1 to be executed before.

Based only on the given information, which of the following test execution schedules would be preferred given the constraints of the test environment and the test strategy chosen?

a. TS5, TS6, TS4, TS3, TS1, TS2, TS7.

b. TS5, TS4, TS1, TS6, TS3, TS2, TS7.

c. TS5, TS6, TS1, TS3, TS4, TS2, TS7.

d. TS5, TS6, TS1, TS2, TS7, TS4, TS3.

TABLE 7.2 Priority and dependency table for Question 36

Requirement	Priority	Test Suites	Environment	Dependency
R1	4	TS1	ABC	
R2	4	TS2	ABC	TS1
R3	3	TS3	XYZ	
R4	2	TS4	XYZ	TS3
R5	1	TS5, TS6	ABC	
R6	5	TS7	ABC	

Question 37 What is the most important factor for successful performance of reviews?

a. A separate scribe during the logging meeting.

b. Trained participants and review leaders.

c. The availability of tools to support the review process.

d. A reviewed test plan.

Question 38 How is impact analysis used in maintenance testing?

a. It evaluates intended consequences and possible side effects of a change to the system, in order to plan what testing to do.

b. It evaluates the consequences of an intended change on the test environment.

c. It evaluates the ease of maintaining the system when there are changes to the system or to the tests.

d. It evaluates the existing regression tests to assess whether a planned change to the system should go ahead.

Question 39 When you sign up, you must give your first and last name, address and postcode or zip code, your mobile/cell phone number, your email address and set yourself a password.

When you log in, you must give the following details: last name, phone number and password. You are logged in until you select 'Logout' followed by answering 'Yes' to 'Are you sure?'

You can update your details once you are logged in, but you need to confirm the change by entering a code sent to your phone. You then need to log in again.

In reviewing the specification above, which of the following are potential defects likely to be found by a user perspective review?

1. Cannot log back in if not logged yourself out (e.g. when changing details).

2. Incorrect format of the code sent to the phone.

3. Buffer overflow for a postal address that is too long.

4. Cannot change the phone number, as the code is sent to the old phone.

5. When details are changed, they create a separate new record in the database.

a. 1 and 2.

b. 3 and 5.

c. 1 and 4.

d. 4 and 5.

Question 40 Which of the following is an advantage of independent testing?

a. Independent testers do NOT have to spend time communicating with the project team.

b. Developers can stop worrying about the quality of their work and focus on producing more code.

c. The others on a project can pressure the independent testers to accelerate testing at the end of the schedule.

d. Independent testers sometimes question the assumptions behind requirements, designs and implementations.

GLOSSARY

This glossary provides the complete definition set of software testing terms, as defined by ISTQB.

The glossary has been arranged in a single section of definitions ordered alphabetically. Some terms are preferred to other synonymous ones, in which case the definition of the preferred term appears, with the synonyms listed afterwards. For example, a synonym of *white-box testing* is *structural testing*.

'See also' cross-references are also used. They assist the user to quickly navigate to the right index term. 'See also' cross-references are constructed for relationships such as broader term to a narrower term and overlapping meanings between two terms.

Finally, note that the terms that are underlined are those that are specifically mentioned as keywords in the Syllabus at the beginning of Chapters 1 to 6. These are the terms that you should know for the exam.

Acceptance criteria   The criteria that a component or system must satisfy in order to be accepted by a user, customer or other authorized entity.

Acceptance testing   Formal testing with respect to user needs, requirements, and business processes conducted to determine whether or not a system satisfies the acceptance criteria and to enable the user, customers or other authorized entity to determine whether or not to accept the system. See also: *user acceptance testing.*

Accessibility   The degree to which a component or system can be used by people with the widest range of characteristics and capabilities to achieve a specified goal in a specified context of use.

Accessibility testing   Testing to determine the ease by which users with disabilities can use a component or system.

Actual result   The behavior produced/observed when a component or system is tested. Synonym: actual outcome

Ad hoc reviewing   A review technique carried out by independent reviewers informally, without a structured process.

Alpha testing   Simulated or actual operational testing conducted in the developer's test environment, by roles outside the development organization.

Anomaly   Any condition that deviates from expectation based on requirements specifications, design documents, user documents, standards, etc., or from someone's perception or experience. Anomalies may be found during, but not limited to, reviewing, testing, analysis, compilation, or use of software products or applicable documentation.

Audit   An independent examination of a work product, process or set of processes that is performed by a third party to assess compliance with specifications, standards, contractual agreements or other criteria.

Availability   The degree to which a component or system is operational and accessible when required for use.

Behavior (behaviour)   The response of a component or system to a set of input values and preconditions.

Beta testing   Simulated or actual operational testing conducted at an external site, by roles outside the development organization. Synonym: field testing

Black-box test technique   A procedure to derive and/or select test cases based on an analysis of the specification, either functional or non-functional, of a component or system without reference to its internal structure. Synonyms: black-box technique, specification-based technique, specification-based test technique

Boundary value   A minimum or maximum value of an ordered equivalence partition.

Boundary value analysis   A black-box test technique in which test cases are designed based on boundary values. See also: *boundary value.*

Burndown chart   A publicly displayed chart that depicts the outstanding effort versus time in an iteration. It shows the status and trend of completing the tasks of the iteration. The X-axis typically represents days in the sprint, while the Y-axis is the remaining effort (usually either in ideal engineering hours or story points).

Checklist-based reviewing   A review technique guided by a list of questions or required attributes.

Checklist-based testing   An experience-based test technique whereby the experienced tester uses a high-level list of items to be noted, checked, or remembered, or a set of rules or criteria against which a product has to be verified.

Code coverage   An analysis method that determines which parts of the software have been executed (covered) by the test suite and which parts have not been executed, for example, statement coverage, decision coverage or condition coverage.

Commercial off-the-shelf (COTS)   A software product that is developed for the general market, i.e. for a large number of customers, and that is delivered to many customers in identical format.
Synonym: off-the-shelf software

Compatibility   The degree to which a component or system can exchange information with other components or systems.

Complexity   The degree to which a component or system has a design and/or internal structure that is difficult to understand, maintain and verify.

Compliance   The capability of the software product to adhere to standards, conventions or regulations in laws and similar prescriptions.

Component   A minimal part of a system that can be tested in isolation.
Synonyms: module, unit

Component integration testing   Testing performed to expose defects in the interfaces and interactions between integrated components.
Synonym: link testing

Component specification   A description of a component's function in terms of its output values for specified input values under specified conditions, and required non-functional behavior (for example, resource utilization).

Component testing   The testing of individual hardware or software components.
Synonyms: module testing, unit testing

Condition   A logical expression that can be evaluated as True or False, for example, A>B.
Synonym: branch condition

Configuration   The composition of a component or system as defined by the number, nature and interconnections of its constituent parts.

Configuration item   An aggregation of work products that is designated for configuration management and treated as a single entity in the configuration management process.

Configuration management   A discipline applying technical and administrative direction and surveillance to identify and document the functional and physical characteristics of a configuration item, control changes to those characteristics, record and report change processing and implementation status, and verify compliance with specified requirements.

Configuration management tool   A tool that provides support for the identification and control of configuration items, their status over changes and versions, and the release of baselines consisting of configuration items.

Confirmation testing   Dynamic testing conducted after fixing defects with the objective to confirm that failures caused by those defects do not occur anymore.
Synonym: re-testing

Contractual acceptance testing   Acceptance testing conducted to verify whether a system satisfies its contractual requirements.

Control flow   The sequence in which operations are performed during the execution of a test item.

Cost of quality   The total costs incurred on quality activities and issues and often split into prevention costs, appraisal costs, internal failure costs and external failure costs.

Coverage   The degree to which specified coverage items have been determined to have been exercised by a test suite expressed as a percentage.
Synonym: test coverage

Coverage item   An attribute or combination of attributes that is derived from one or more test conditions by using a test technique that enables the measurement of the thoroughness of the test execution.

Coverage tool   A tool that provides objective measures of what structural elements, for example, statements, branches have been exercised by a test suite.
Synonym: coverage measurement tool

Data flow   An abstract representation of the sequence and possible changes of the state of data objects, where the state of an object is any of creation, usage or destruction.

Data-driven testing   A scripting technique that stores test input and expected results in a table or spreadsheet, so that a single control script can execute all of the tests in the table. Data-driven testing is often used to support the application of test execution tools such as capture/playback tools. See also: *keyword-driven testing*.

Debugging   The process of finding, analyzing and removing the causes of failures in software.

Decision   A type of statement in which a choice between two or more possible outcomes controls which set of actions will result.

Decision coverage   The coverage of decision outcomes.

Decision outcome   The result of a decision that determines the next statement to be executed.

Decision table   A table used to show sets of conditions and the actions resulting from them. Synonym: cause-effect decision table

Decision table testing   A black-box test technique in which test cases are designed to execute the combinations of inputs and/or stimuli (causes) shown in a decision table. See also: *decision table*.

Decision testing   A white-box test technique in which test cases are designed to execute decision outcomes.

Defect   An imperfection or deficiency in a work product where it does not meet its requirements or specifications. Synonyms: bug, fault

Defect density   The number of defects per unit size of a work product. Synonym: fault density

Defect management   The process of recognizing and recording defects, classifying them, investigating them, taking action to resolve them and disposing of them when resolved.

Defect management tool   A tool that facilitates the recording and status tracking of defects. Synonyms: bug tracking tool, defect tracking tool

Defect report   Documentation of the occurrence, nature and status of a defect. See also: *incident report*. Synonym: bug report

Driver   A software component or test tool that replaces a component that takes care of the control and/or the calling of a component or system. Synonym: test driver

Dynamic analysis   The process of evaluating behavior, for example, memory performance, CPU usage, of a system or component during execution.

Dynamic analysis tool   A tool that provides run-time information on the state of the software code. These tools are most commonly used to identify unassigned pointers, check pointer arithmetic and to monitor the allocation, use and de-allocation of memory and to flag memory leaks.

Dynamic testing   Testing that involves the execution of the software of a component or system.

Effectiveness   Extent to which correct and complete goals are achieved. See also: *efficiency*.

Efficiency   Resources expended in relation to the extent with which users achieve specified goals. See also: *effectiveness*.

Entry criteria   The set of conditions for officially starting a defined task. Synonym: definition of ready

Equivalence partition   A portion of the value domain of a data element related to the test object for which all values are expected to be treated the same based on the specification. Synonym: equivalence class

Equivalence partitioning   A black-box test technique in which test cases are designed to exercise equivalence partitions by using one representative member of each partition. Synonym: partition testing

Error   A human action that produces an incorrect result. Synonym: mistake

Error guessing   A test technique in which tests are derived on the basis of the tester's knowledge of past failures, or general knowledge of failure modes.

Executable statement   A statement which, when compiled, is translated into object code, and which will be executed procedurally when the program is running and may perform an action on data.

Exercised   A program element is said to be exercised by a test case when the input value causes the execution of that element, such as a statement, decision or other structural element.

Exhaustive testing   A test approach in which the test suite comprises all combinations of input values and preconditions. Synonym: complete testing

Exit criteria   The set of conditions for officially completing a defined task.
Synonyms: completion criteria, test completion criteria, definition of done

Expected result   The predicted observable behavior of a component or system executing under specified conditions, based on its specification or another source.
Synonyms: expected outcome, predicted outcome

Experience-based test technique   A procedure to derive and/or select test cases based on the tester's experience, knowledge and intuition.
Synonym: experience-based technique

Experience-based testing   Testing based on the tester's experience, knowledge and intuition.

Exploratory testing   An approach to testing whereby the testers dynamically design and execute tests based on their knowledge, exploration of the test item and the results of previous tests.

Extreme Programming (XP)   A software engineering methodology used within Agile software development where core practices are programming in pairs, doing extensive code review, unit testing of all code, and simplicity and clarity in code. See also: *Agile software development*.

Facilitator   The leader and main person responsible for an inspection or review process. See also: *moderator*.

Fail   A test is deemed to fail if its actual result does not match its expected result.

Failure   An event in which a component or system does not perform a required function within specified limits.

Failure rate   The ratio of the number of failures of a given category to a given unit of measure.

Feature   An attribute of a component or system specified or implied by requirements documentation (for example, reliability, usability or design constraints).
Synonym: software feature

Finding   A result of an evaluation that identifies some important issue, problem or opportunity.

Formal review   A form of review that follows a defined process with a formally documented output.

Functional integration   An integration approach that combines the components or systems for the purpose of getting a basic functionality working early. See also: *integration testing*.

Functional requirement   A requirement that specifies a function that a component or system must be able to perform.

Functional suitability   The degree to which a component or system provides functions that meet stated and implied needs when used under specified conditions.
Synonym: functionality

Functional testing   Testing conducted to evaluate the compliance of a component or system with functional requirements. See also: *black-box test technique*.

GUI   Acronym for Graphical User Interface.

High-level test case   A test case without concrete values for input data and expected results. See also: *low-level test case*.
Synonyms: abstract test case, logical test case

IDEAL   An organizational improvement model that serves as a roadmap for initiating, planning and implementing improvement actions. The IDEAL model is named for the five phases it describes: initiating, diagnosing, establishing, acting and learning.

Impact analysis   The identification of all work products affected by a change, including an estimate of the resources needed to accomplish the change.

Incident report   Documentation of the occurrence, nature and status of an incident.
Synonyms: deviation report, software test incident report, test incident report. See also: *defect report*

Incremental development model   A development life cycle model in which the project scope is generally determined early in the project life cycle, but time and cost estimates are routinely modified as the project team understanding of the product increases. The product is developed through a series of repeated cycles, each delivering an increment which successively adds to the functionality of the product. See also: *iterative development model*.

Independence of testing   Separation of responsibilities, which encourages the accomplishment of objective testing.

Informal group review   An informal review performed by three or more persons. See also: *informal review.*

Informal review   A type of review without a formal (documented) procedure.

Input   Data received by a component or system from an external source.

Inspection   A type of formal review to identify issues in a work product, which provides measurement to improve the review process and the software development process.

Installation guide   Supplied instructions on any suitable media, which guides the installer through the installation process. This may be a manual guide, step-by-step procedure, installation wizard or any other similar process description.

Integration   The process of combining components or systems into larger assemblies.

Integration testing   Testing performed to expose defects in the interfaces and in the interactions between integrated components or systems. See also: *component integration testing, system integration testing.*

Interoperability   The degree to which two or more components or systems can exchange information and use the information that has been exchanged.

Interoperability testing   Testing to determine the interoperability of a software product. See also: *functionality testing.*
Synonym: compatibility testing

Iterative development model   A development life cycle where a project is broken into a usually large number of iterations. An iteration is a complete development loop resulting in a release (internal or external) of an executable product, a subset of the final product under development, which grows from iteration to iteration to become the final product.

Keyword-driven testing   A scripting technique that uses data files to contain not only test data and expected results but also keywords related to the application being tested. The keywords are interpreted by special supporting scripts that are called by the control script for the test. See also: *data-driven testing.*
Synonym: action word-driven testing

Life cycle model   A description of the processes, workflows and activities used in the development, delivery, maintenance and retirement of a system. See also: *software life cycle.*

Load testing   A type of performance testing conducted to evaluate the behavior of a component or system under varying loads, usually between anticipated conditions of low, typical and peak usage. See also: *performance testing, stress testing.*

Low-level test case   A test case with concrete values for input data and expected results. See also: *high-level test case.*
Synonym: concrete test case

Maintainability   The degree to which a component or system can be modified by the intended maintainers.

Maintenance   The process of modifying a component or system after delivery to correct defects, improve quality attributes or adapt to a changed environment.

Maintenance testing   Testing the changes to an operational system or the impact of a changed environment to an operational system.

Master test plan   A test plan that is used to coordinate multiple test levels or test types. See also: *test plan.*

Maturity   (1) The capability of an organization with respect to the effectiveness and efficiency of its processes and work practices. (2) The degree to which a component or system meets needs for reliability under normal operation.

Measure   The number or category assigned to an attribute of an entity by making a measurement.

Measurement   The process of assigning a number or category to an entity to describe an attribute of that entity.

Memory leak   A memory access failure due to a defect in a program's dynamic store allocation logic that causes it to fail to release memory after it has finished using it, eventually causing the program and/or other concurrent processes to fail due to lack of memory.

Metric   A measurement scale and the method used for measurement.

Milestone   A point in time in a project at which defined (intermediate) deliverables and results should be ready.

Model-based testing (MBT)   Testing based on or involving models.

Moderator   A neutral person who conducts a usability test session. See also: *facilitator*.
Synonym: inspection leader

Monitoring tool   A software tool or hardware device that runs concurrently with the component or system under test and supervises, records and/or analyzes the behavior of the component or system. See also: *dynamic analysis tool*.

Non-functional requirement   A requirement that describes how well the component or system will do what it is intended to do.

Non-functional testing   Testing conducted to evaluate the compliance of a component or system with non-functional requirements.

Operational acceptance testing   Operational testing in the acceptance test phase, typically performed in a (simulated) operational environment by operations and/or systems administration staff focusing on operational aspects, for example, recoverability, resource-behavior, installability and technical compliance.
See also: *operational testing*.
Synonym: production acceptance testing

Operational environment   Hardware and software products installed at users' or customers' sites where the component or system under test will be used. The software may include operating systems, database management systems and other applications.

Output   Data transmitted by a component or system to an external destination.

Pass   A test is deemed to pass if its actual result matches its expected result.

Path   A sequence of events, for example, executable statements, of a component or system from an entry point to an exit point.
Synonym: control flow path

Peer review   A form of review of work products performed by others qualified to do the same work.

Performance efficiency   The degree to which a component or system uses time, resources and capacity when accomplishing its designated functions.
Synonyms: time behavior, performance

Performance indicator   A high-level metric of effectiveness and/or efficiency used to guide and control progressive development, for example, lead-time slip for software development.
Synonym: key performance indicator

Performance testing   Testing to determine the performance of a software product.

Performance testing tool   A test tool that generates load for a designated test item and that measures and records its performance during test execution.

Perspective-based reading   A review technique whereby reviewers evaluate the work product from different viewpoints. See also: *role-based reviewing*.

Planning poker   A consensus-based estimation technique, mostly used to estimate effort or relative size of user stories in Agile software development. It is a variation of the Wideband Delphi method using a deck of cards with values representing the units in which the team estimates. See also: *Agile software development, Wideband Delphi*.

Portability   The ease with which the software product can be transferred from one hardware or software environment to another.

Portability testing   Testing to determine the portability of a software product.
Synonym: configuration testing

Postcondition   The expected state of a test item and its environment at the end of test case execution.

Precondition   The required state of a test item and its environment prior to test case execution.

Priority   The level of (business) importance assigned to an item, for example, a defect.

Probe effect   The effect on the component or system by the measurement instrument when the component or system is being measured, for example, by a performance testing tool or monitor. For example, performance may be slightly worse when performance testing tools are being used.

Problem   An unknown underlying cause of one or more incidents.

Process   A set of interrelated activities, which transform inputs into outputs.

Process improvement   A program of activities designed to improve the performance and maturity of the organization's processes, and the result of such a program.

Product risk   A risk impacting the quality of a product. See also: *risk*.

Project   A project is a unique set of coordinated and controlled activities with start and finish dates undertaken to achieve an objective conforming to specific requirements, including the constraints of time, cost and resources.

Project risk   A risk that impacts project success. See also: *risk*.

Quality   The degree to which a component, system or process meets specified requirements and/or user/customer needs and expectations.

Quality assurance   Part of quality management focused on providing confidence that quality requirements will be fulfilled.

Quality characteristic   A category of product attributes that bears on quality.
Synonyms: software product characteristic, software quality characteristic, quality attribute

Quality control   The operational techniques and activities, part of quality management, that are focused on fulfilling quality requirements.

Quality management   Coordinated activities to direct and control an organization with regard to quality. Direction and control with regard to quality generally includes the establishment of the quality policy and quality objectives, quality planning, quality control, quality assurance and quality improvement.

Quality risk   A product risk related to a quality characteristic. See also: *quality characteristic, product risk*.

Rational Unified Process (RUP)   A proprietary adaptable iterative software development process framework consisting of four project life cycle phases: inception, elaboration, construction and transition.

Regression   A degradation in the quality of a component or system due to a change.

Regression testing   Testing of a previously tested component or system following modification to ensure that defects have not been introduced or have been uncovered in unchanged areas of the software as a result of the changes made.

Regulatory acceptance testing   Acceptance testing conducted to verify whether a system conforms to relevant laws, policies and regulations.

Reliability   The degree to which a component or system performs specified functions under specified conditions for a specified period of time.

Reliability growth model   A model that shows the growth in reliability over time during continuous testing of a component or system as a result of the removal of defects that result in reliability failures.

Requirement   A provision that contains criteria to be fulfilled.

Requirements management tool   A tool that supports the recording of requirements, requirements attributes (for example, priority, knowledge responsible) and annotation, and facilitates traceability through layers of requirements and requirements change management. Some requirements management tools also provide facilities for static analysis, such as consistency checking and violations to pre-defined requirements rules.

Result   The consequence/outcome of the execution of a test. It includes outputs to screens, changes to data, reports and communication messages sent out. See also: *actual result, expected result*.
Synonyms: outcome, test outcome, test result

Retrospective meeting   A meeting at the end of a project during which the project team members evaluate the project and learn lessons that can be applied to the next project.
Synonym: post-project meeting

Review   A type of static testing during which a work product or process is evaluated by one or more individuals to detect issues and to provide improvements.

Review plan   A document describing the approach, resources and schedule of intended review activities. It identifies, amongst others: documents and code to be reviewed, review types to be used, participants, as well as entry and exit criteria to be applied in case of formal reviews, and the rationale for their choice. It is a record of the review planning process.

Reviewer   A participant in a review, who identifies issues in the work product.
Synonyms: checker, inspector

Risk   A factor that could result in future negative consequences.

Risk analysis   The overall process of risk identification and risk assessment.

Risk-based testing   Testing in which the management, selection, prioritization and use of testing activities and resources are based on corresponding risk types and risk levels.

Risk level   The qualitative or quantitative measure of a risk defined by impact and likelihood. Synonym: risk exposure

Risk management   The coordinated activities to direct and control an organization with regard to risk.

Risk mitigation   The process through which decisions are reached and protective measures are implemented for reducing or maintaining risks to specified levels. Synonym: risk control

Risk type   A set of risks grouped by one or more common factors. Synonym: risk category

Robustness   The degree to which a component or system can function correctly in the presence of invalid inputs or stressful environmental conditions. See also: *error-tolerance, fault-tolerance.*

Role-based reviewing   A review technique where reviewers evaluate a work product from the perspective of different stakeholder roles.

Root cause   A source of a defect such that if it is removed, the occurrence of the defect type is decreased or removed.

Root cause analysis   An analysis technique aimed at identifying the root causes of defects. By directing corrective measures at root causes, it is hoped that the likelihood of defect recurrence will be minimized. Synonym: causal analysis

Safety   The capability that a system will not, under defined conditions, lead to a state in which human life, health, property or the environment is endangered.

Scenario-based reviewing   A review technique where the review is guided by determining the ability of the work product to address specific scenarios.

Scribe   A person who records information during the review meetings. Synonym: recorder

Scrum   An iterative incremental framework for managing projects commonly used with Agile software development. See also: *Agile software development.*

Security   The degree to which a component or system protects information and data so that persons or other components or systems have the degree of access appropriate to their types and levels of authorization.

Security testing   Testing to determine the security of the software product. See also: *functionality testing.*

Sequential development model   A type of development life cycle model in which a complete system is developed in a linear way of several discrete and successive phases with no overlap between them.

Session-based testing   An approach to testing in which test activities are planned as uninterrupted sessions of test design and execution, often used in conjunction with exploratory testing.

Severity   The degree of impact that a defect has on the development or operation of a component or system.

Simulation   The representation of selected behavioral characteristics of one physical or abstract system by another system.

Simulator   A device, computer program or system used during testing, which behaves or operates like a given system when provided with a set of controlled inputs. See also: *emulator.*

Software   Computer programs, procedures and possibly associated documentation and data pertaining to the operation of a computer system.

Software development life cycle   The activities performed at each stage in software development, and how they relate to one another logically and chronologically.

Software life cycle   The period of time that begins when a software product is conceived and ends when the software is no longer available for use. The software life cycle typically includes a concept phase, requirements phase, design phase, implementation phase, test phase, installation and checkout phase, operation and maintenance phase and sometimes, retirement phase. Note these phases may overlap or be performed iteratively.

Software quality   The totality of functionality and features of a software product that bear on its ability to satisfy stated or implied needs. See also: *quality.*

Specification   A document that specifies, ideally in a complete, precise and verifiable manner, the requirements, design, behavior, or other characteristics of a component or system, and, often, the procedures for determining whether these provisions have been satisfied.

Stability   The degree to which a component or system can be effectively and efficiently modified without introducing defects or degrading existing product quality.

Standard   Formal, possibly mandatory, set of requirements developed and used to prescribe consistent approaches to the way of working or to provide guidelines (for example, ISO/IEC standards, IEEE standards and organizational standards).

State diagram   A diagram that depicts the states that a component or system can assume, and shows the events or circumstances that cause and/or result from a change from one state to another.
Synonym: state transition diagram

State transition   A transition between two states of a component or system.

State transition testing   A black-box test technique using a state transition diagram or state table to derive test cases to evaluate whether the test item successfully executes valid transitions and blocks invalid transitions. See also: *N-switch testing*.
Synonym: finite state testing

Statement   An entity in a programming language, which is typically the smallest indivisible unit of execution.
Synonym: source statement

Statement coverage   The percentage of executable statements that have been exercised by a test suite.

Statement testing   A white-box test technique in which test cases are designed to execute statements.

Static analysis   The process of evaluating a component or system without executing it, based on its form, structure, content or documentation.

Static testing   Testing a work product without code being executed.

Structural coverage   Coverage measures based on the internal structure of a component or system.

Stub   A skeletal or special purpose implementation of a software component, used to develop or test a component that calls or is otherwise dependent on it. It replaces a called component.

System   A collection of interacting elements organized to accomplish a specific function or set of functions.

System integration testing   Testing the combination and interaction of systems.

System testing   Testing an integrated system to verify that it meets specified requirements.

System under test (SUT)   A type of test object that is a system.

Technical review   A formal review type by a team of technically-qualified personnel that examines the suitability of a work product for its intended use and identifies discrepancies from specifications and standards.

Test   A set of one or more test cases.

Test analysis   The activity that identifies test conditions by analyzing the test basis.

Test approach   The implementation of the test strategy for a specific project.

Test automation   The use of software to perform or support test activities, for example, test management, test design, test execution and results checking.

Test basis   The body of knowledge used as the basis for test analysis and design.

Test case   A set of preconditions, inputs, actions (where applicable), expected results and postconditions, developed based on test conditions.

Test case specification   Documentation of a set of one or more test cases.

Test charter   Documentation of test activities in session-based exploratory testing. See also: *exploratory testing*.
Synonym: charter

Test completion   The activity that makes test assets available for later use, leaves test environments in a satisfactory condition and communicates the results of testing to relevant stakeholders.

Test condition   An aspect of the test basis that is relevant in order to achieve specific test objectives.

Test control   A test management task that deals with developing and applying a set of corrective actions to get a test project on track when monitoring shows a deviation from what was planned.
See also: *test management*.

Test cycle   Execution of the test process against a single identifiable release of the test object.

Test data   Data created or selected to satisfy the execution preconditions and inputs to execute one or more test cases.

Test data preparation tool A type of test tool that enables data to be selected from existing databases or created, generated, manipulated and edited for use in testing.
Synonym: test generator

Test design The activity of deriving and specifying test cases from test conditions.

Test design tool A tool that supports the test design activity by generating test inputs from a specification that may be held in a CASE tool repository, e.g., requirements management tool, from specified test conditions held in the tool itself, or from code.

Test environment An environment containing hardware, instrumentation, simulators, software tools and other support elements needed to conduct a test.
Synonyms: test bed, test rig

Test estimation The calculated approximation of a result related to various aspects of testing (for example, effort spent, completion date, costs involved, number of test cases, etc.), which is usable even if input data may be incomplete, uncertain or noisy.

Test execution The process of running a test on the component or system under test, producing actual result(s).

Test execution schedule A schedule for the execution of test suites within a test cycle.

Test execution tool A test tool that executes tests against a designated test item and evaluates the outcomes against expected results and postconditions.

Test harness A test environment comprised of stubs and drivers needed to execute a test.

Test implementation The activity that prepares the testware needed for test execution based on test analysis and design.

Test infrastructure The organizational artefacts needed to perform testing, consisting of test environments, test tools, office environment and procedures.

Test input The data received from an external source by the test object during test execution. The external source can be hardware, software or human.

Test item A part of a test object used in the test process.
See also: *test object*

Test leader On large projects, the person who reports to the test manager and is responsible for project management of a particular test level or a particular set of testing activities. See also: *test manager*.
Synonym: lead tester

Test level A specific instantiation of a test process.
Synonym: test stage

Test management The planning, scheduling, estimating, monitoring, reporting, control and completion of test activities.

Test management tool A tool that provides support to the test management and control part of a test process. It often has several capabilities, such as testware management, scheduling of tests, the logging of results, progress tracking, incident management and test reporting.

Test manager The person responsible for project management of testing activities and resources, and evaluation of a test object. The individual who directs, controls, administers, plans and regulates the evaluation of a test object.

Test monitoring A test management activity that involves checking the status of testing activities, identifying any variances from the planned or expected status and reporting status to stakeholders. See also: *test management*.

Test object The component or system to be tested. See also: *test item*.

Test objective A reason or purpose for designing and executing a test.

Test oracle A source to determine expected results to compare with the actual result of the system under test.
Synonym: oracle

Test plan Documentation describing the test objectives to be achieved and the means and the schedule for achieving them, organized to coordinate testing activities.

Test planning The activity of establishing or updating a test plan.

Test policy A high-level document describing the principles, approach and major objectives of the organization regarding testing.
Synonym: organizational test policy

Test procedure A sequence of test cases in execution order, and any associated actions that may be required to set up the initial preconditions and any wrap-up activities post execution.
See also: *test script*.

Test process   The set of interrelated activities comprising of test planning, test monitoring and control, test analysis, test design, test implementation, test execution and test completion.

Test process improvement   A program of activities designed to improve the performance and maturity of the organization's test processes and the results of such a program.

Test progress report   A test report produced at regular intervals about the progress of test activities against a baseline, risks, and alternatives requiring a decision.
Synonym: test status report

Test report   Documentation summarizing test activities and results.

Test reporting   Collecting and analyzing data from testing activities and subsequently consolidating the data in a report to inform stakeholders. See also: *test process.*

Test schedule   A list of activities, tasks or events of the test process, identifying their intended start and finish dates and/or times, and interdependencies.

Test script   A sequence of instructions for the execution of a test. See also: *test procedure.*

Test session   An uninterrupted period of time spent in executing tests. In exploratory testing, each test session is focused on a charter, but testers can also explore new opportunities or issues during a session. The tester creates and executes on the fly and records their progress. See also: *exploratory testing.*

Test strategy   Documentation that expresses the generic requirements for testing one or more projects run within an organization, providing detail on how testing is to be performed, and is aligned with the test policy.
Synonym: organizational test strategy

Test suite   A set of test cases or test procedures to be executed in a specific test cycle.
Synonyms: test case suite, test set

Test summary report   A test report that provides an evaluation of the corresponding test items against exit criteria.
Synonym: test report

Test technique   A procedure used to derive and/or select test cases.
Synonyms: test case design technique, test specification technique, test technique, test design technique

Test tool   A software product that supports one or more test activities, such as planning and control, specification, building initial files and data, test execution and test analysis.

Test type   A group of test activities based on specific test objectives aimed at specific characteristics of a component or system.

Testability   The degree of effectiveness and efficiency with which tests can be designed and executed for a component or system.

Testable requirement   A requirements that is stated in terms that permit establishment of test designs (and subsequently test cases) and execution of tests to determine whether the requirement has been met.

Tester   A skilled professional who is involved in the testing of a component or system.

Testing   The process consisting of all life cycle activities, both static and dynamic, concerned with planning, preparation and evaluation of software products and related work products to determine that they satisfy specified requirements, to demonstrate that they are fit for purpose and to detect defects.

Testware   Work products produced during the test process for use in planning, designing, executing, evaluating and reporting on testing.

Traceability   The degree to which a relationship can be established between two or more work products.

Understandability   The capability of the software product to enable the user to understand whether the software is suitable, and how it can be used for particular tasks and conditions of use. See also: *usability.*

Unit test framework   A tool that provides an environment for unit or component testing in which a component can be tested in isolation or with suitable stubs and drivers. It also provides other support for the developer, such as debugging capabilities.

Unreachable code   Code that cannot be reached and therefore is impossible to execute.
Synonym: dead code

Usability   The degree to which a component or system can be used by specified users to achieve specified goals in a specified context of use.

Usability testing   Testing to evaluate the degree to which the system can be used by specified users with effectiveness, efficiency and satisfaction in a specified context of use.

Use case   A sequence of transactions in a dialogue between an actor and a component or system with a tangible result, where an actor can be a user or anything that can exchange information with the system.

Use case testing   A black-box test technique in which test cases are designed to execute scenarios of use cases.
Synonyms: scenario testing, user scenario testing

User acceptance testing   Acceptance testing conducted in a real or simulated operational environment by intended users focusing on their needs, requirements and business processes.
See also: *acceptance testing.*

User interface   All components of a system that provide information and controls for the user to accomplish specific tasks with the system.

User story   A high-level user or business requirement commonly used in Agile software development, typically consisting of one sentence in the everyday or business language capturing what functionality a user needs and the reason behind this, any non-functional criteria and also includes acceptance criteria. See also: *Agile software development, requirement.*

V-model   A sequential development life cycle model describing a one-for-one relationship between major phases of software development from business requirements specification to delivery, and corresponding test levels from acceptance testing to component testing.

Validation   Confirmation by examination and through provision of objective evidence that the requirements for a specific intended use or application have been fulfilled.

Variable   An element of storage in a computer that is accessible by a software program by referring to it by a name.

Verification   Confirmation by examination and through provision of objective evidence that specified requirements have been fulfilled.

Walkthrough   A type of review in which an author leads members of the review through a work product and the members ask questions and make comments about possible issues. See also: *peer review.*
Synonym: structured walkthrough

White-box test technique   A procedure to derive and/or select test cases based on an analysis of the internal structure of a component or system.
Synonyms: structural test technique, structure-based test technique, structure-based technique, white-box technique

White-box testing   Testing based on an analysis of the internal structure of the component or system.
Synonyms: clear-box testing, code-based testing, glass-box testing, logic-coverage testing, logic-driven testing, structural testing, structure-based testing

Wideband Delphi   An expert-based test estimation technique that aims at making an accurate estimation using the collective wisdom of the team members.

ANSWERS TO SAMPLE EXAM QUESTIONS

This section contains the answers and the learning objectives for the sample questions in each chapter and for the full mock exam in Chapter 7.

If you get any of the questions wrong or if you were not sure about the answer, then the learning objective tells you which part of the Syllabus to go back to in order to help you understand why the correct answer is the right one. The learning objectives are listed at the beginning of each section. For example, if you got Question 3 in Chapter 1 wrong, then go to Chapter 1 and read Learning Objective 1.2.2. Then re-read the section in the chapter which deals with that topic.

CHAPTER 1 FUNDAMENTALS OF TESTING

Question	Answer	Learning objective
1	a	1.2.1
2	b	Keywords
3	c	1.2.2
4	a	1.1.1
5	a	1.3.1
6	c	1.4.4
7	b	1.5.1
8	d	1.4.3

CHAPTER 2 TESTING THROUGHOUT THE SOFTWARE DEVELOPMENT LIFE CYCLE

Question	Answer	Learning objective
1	d	2.1.1
2	d	2.2.1
3	b	Keywords
4	b	2.4.1
5	c	2.3.1
6	d	2.3.3
7	c	2.3.3
8	b	2.3.1
9	a	2.2.1

CHAPTER 3 **STATIC TECHNIQUES**

Question	Answer	Learning objective
1	d	3.1.1
2	a	3.2.1
3	d	3.1.3
4	a	3.2.3
5	d	3.2.2
6	b	3.2.3
7	a	3.2.5
8	c	3.2.4
9	c	3.2.4

CHAPTER 4 **TEST TECHNIQUES**

Question	Answer	Learning objective
1	d	4.4.3
2	a	4.2.2
3	c	4.3.3
4	a	4.1.1
5	b	4.1.1
6	c	4.2.3
7	d	4.2.4
8	b	4.2.1
9	b	4.2
10	c	4.3
11	a	4.2.5
12	c	4.3
13	a	4.4
14	c	4.3.1
15	d	4.3
16	b	4.1.1
17	a	4.2.4

CHAPTER 5 TEST MANAGEMENT

Question	Answer	Learning objective
1	b	5.1.1
2	d	5.1.2
3	b	Keywords
4	a	5.2.1
5	c	5.2.5
6	c	5.2.2
7	d	5.2.3
8	a	Keywords
9	c	5.3.1
10	b	5.3.2
11	a	5.6.1
12	c	5.4.1
13	d	5.5.2
14	b	5.5.1
15	a	5.5.2
16	a	5.5.3
17	b	5.2.6
18	d	5.6.1
19	c	5.2.4
20	a	5.2.3

CHAPTER 6 TOOL SUPPORT FOR TESTING

Question	Answer	Learning objective
1	d	6.1.1
2	c	6.1.1
3	b	6.1.2
4	a	6.1.3
5	b	6.2.1
6	d	6.2.2
7	a	6.2.3

CHAPTER 7 MOCK EXAM

Question	Answer	Learning objective
1	b	4.2.1
2	a	1.1.2
3	a	2.1.2
4	d	4.2.5
5	c	5.5.2
6	b	2.3.3
7	c	Chapter 4 Keywords
8	b	5.6.1
9	c	5.1.2
10	c	1.4.1
11	d	3.2.1
12	b	1.4.2
13	a	1.5.2
14	b	5.3.1
15	a	4.3.2
16	a	6.1.1
17	c	4.4.1
18	b	5.2.6
19	a	4.2.1
20	b	Chapters 1/4 Keyword
21	b	3.1.1
22	b	6.2.3
23	a	1.2.3
24	b	2.2.1
25	c	1.2.4
26	c	4.2.2
27	c	4.2.3
28	d	4.4.2
29	b	2.3.1
30	c	5.2.1
31	b	4.1.1
32	c	3.1.3
33	d	1.1.1
34	d	5.4.1
35	c	4.2.4
36	c	5.2.4
37	b	3.2.5
38	a	2.4.2
39	c	3.2.4
40	d	5.1.1

REFERENCES

Key:
<u>In Syllabus</u>
Extra to Syllabus

CHAPTER 1 FUNDAMENTALS OF TESTING

<u>Beizer, B. (1990) *Software Testing Techniques* (2nd edition), Van Nostrand Reinhold: Boston, MA</u>
Black, R. (2004) *Critical Testing Processes*, Addison Wesley: Reading, MA
<u>Black, R. (2009) *Managing the Testing Process* (3rd edition), John Wiley & Sons: New York, NY</u>
<u>Gilb, T. and Graham, D. (1993) *Software Inspection*, Addison Wesley: Reading, MA</u>
<u>ISO/IEC/IEEE 29119-1 (2013) *Software and systems engineering – Software testing – Part 1: Concepts and definitions*</u>
<u>ISO/IEC/IEEE 29119-2 (2013) *Software and systems engineering – Software testing – Part 2: Test processes*</u>
<u>ISO/IEC/IEEE 29119-3 (2013) *Software and systems engineering – Software testing – Part 3: Test documentation*</u>
Jones, C. (2008) *Estimating Software Costs* (3rd edition), McGraw Hill Education: New York, NY
<u>Myers, G., Badgett, T., and Sandler, C. (2012) *The Art of Software Testing* (3rd edition), John Wiley & Sons: New York, NY</u>
<u>Weinberg, G. (2008) *Perfect Software and Other Illusions about Testing*, Dorset House: New York, NY</u>

CHAPTER 2 TESTING THROUGHOUT THE SOFTWARE DEVELOPMENT LIFE CYCLE

Berard, Edward V. (1993) *Essays on Object-oriented Software Engineering* (Volume 1), Prentice Hall: Englewood Cliffs, NJ
<u>Black, R. (2017) *Agile Testing Foundations*, BCS Learning & Development Ltd: Swindon, UK</u>
Boehm, B. (1986) 'A Spiral Model of Software Development and Enhancement', *ACM SIGSOFT Software Engineering Notes*, ACM, 11(4):14–25, August 1986
<u>Crispin, L. and Gregory, J. (2008) *Agile Testing*, Pearson Education: Boston, MA</u>
<u>Gregory, J. and Crispin, L. (2015) *More Agile Testing*, Pearson Education: Boston, MA</u>
<u>ISO/IEC 25010 (2011) *Systems and software engineering – Systems and Software Quality Requirements and Evaluation (SQuaRE) System and Software Quality Models*</u>

CHAPTER 3 STATIC TECHNIQUES

<u>Gilb, T. and Graham, D. (1993) *Software Inspection*, Addison-Wesley: London</u>
<u>ISO/IEC 20246 (2017) *Software and system engineering – Work product reviews*</u>
<u>Kramer, A. and Legeard, B. (2016) *Model-Based Testing Essentials: Guide to the ISTQB Certified Model-Based Tester: Foundation Level*, John Wiley & Sons: New York, NY</u>
Mars.jpl.nasa.gov (1999) *Mars climate orbiter failure board releases report, numerous NASA actions underway in response.* [Online] Available at: https://mars.jpl.nasa.gov/msp98/news/mco991110.html [Accessed 02 April 2019]
<u>Sauer, C. (2000) 'The Effectiveness of Software Development Technical Reviews: A Behaviorally Motivated Program of Research', *IEEE Transactions on Software Engineering*, 26(1):1–14</u>
<u>Shull, F., Rus, I. and Basili, V. (2000), 'How Perspective-Based Reading can Improve Requirement Inspections', *IEEE Computer*, 33(7):73–79</u>
van Veenendaal, E. (1999) 'Practical Quality Assurance for Embedded Software', in *Software Quality Professional*, Vol. 1, no. 3, American Society for Quality, June 1999
<u>van Veenendaal, E. (ed.) (2004) *The Testing Practitioner* (Chapters 8–10), UTN Publisher: The Netherlands</u>
van Veenendaal, E. and van der Zwan, M. (2000) 'GQM Based Inspections', in *Proceedings of the 11th European Software Control and Metrics Conference (ESCOM)*, Munich, May 2000
<u>Wiegers, K. (2002) *Peer Reviews in Software*, Pearson Education: Boston, MA</u>

CHAPTER 4 TEST TECHNIQUES

Beizer, B. (1990) *Software Testing Techniques* (2nd edition), Van Nostrand Reinhold: Boston, MA
Black, R. (2007) *Pragmatic Software Testing*, John Wiley & Sons: New York, NY
Broekman, B. and Notenboom, E. (2003) *Testing Embedded Software*, Addison Wesley: London
Copeland, L. (2004) *A Practitioner's Guide to Software Test Design*, Artech House: Norwood, MA
Craig, R. D. and Jaskiel, S. P. (2002) *Systematic Software Testing*, Artech House: Norwood, MA
Gilb, T. (1988) *Principles of Software Engineering Management*, Addison Wesley: Reading, MA
Hetzel, B. (1988) *The Complete Guide to Software Testing* (2nd edition), QED Information Sciences: Wellesley, MA
ISO/IEC/IEEE 29119-4 (2015) *Software and system engineering - Software testing - Part 4: Test techniques*
Jacobson, I. (1992) *Object-Oriented Software Engineering: A Use Case Driven Approach*, Addison Wesley: Reading, MA
Jorgensen, P. (2014) *Software Testing: A Craftsman's Approach* (4e), CRC Press: Boca Raton FL
Kaner, C., Bach, J., and Petticord, B. (2002) *Lessons Learned in Software Testing*, John Wiley & Sons: New York, NY
Kaner, C., Padmanabhan, S., and Hoffman, D. (2013) *The Domain Testing Workbook*, Context-driven Press: Orlando, FL
Marick, B. (1994) *The Craft of Software Testing*, Prentice Hall: New York, NY
Myers, G., Badgett, T., and Sandler, C., (2012) *The Art of Software Testing* (3rd edition), John Wiley & Sons: New York, NY
Pol, M., Teunissen, R., and van Veenendaal, E. (2001) *Software Testing: A Guide to the TMap Approach*, Addison Wesley: Harlow, UK
UML 2.5: Omg.org (2017) *About the Unified Modeling Language Specification Version 2.5.1*. [Online] Available at: http://www.omg.org/spec/UML/2.5.1/ [Accessed 02 April 2019]
Whittaker, J. A. (2003) *How to Break Software: A Practical Guide to Testing*, Addison Wesley: Reading, MA

CHAPTER 5 TEST MANAGEMENT

Beizer, B. (1990) *Software Testing Techniques* (2nd edition), Van Nostrand Reinhold: Boston, MA
Black, R. (2004) *Critical Testing Processes*, Addison Wesley: Reading, MA
Black, R. (2009) *Managing the Testing Process* (3rd edition), John Wiley & Sons: New York, NY
Brooks, F. (1995) *The Mythical Man-Month and Other Essays on Software Engineering*, Addison Wesley: New York, NY
Craig, R. D. and Jaskiel, S. P. (2002) *Systematic Software Testing*, Artech House: Norwood, MA
Hetzel, W. (1988) *Complete Guide to Software Testing*, QED: Wellesley, MA
ISO/IEC/IEEE 29119-3 (2013) *Software and systems engineering – Software testing – Part 3: Test documentation*
ISO/IEC 25010 (2011) *Systems and software engineering – Systems and software Quality Requirements and Evaluation (SQuaRE) System and software quality models*
Kaner, C., Bach, J., and Petticord, B. (2002) *Lessons Learned in Software Testing*, John Wiley & Sons: New York, NY
Pol, M., Teunissen, R., and van Veenendaal, E. (2002) *Software Testing: A Guide to the TMap Approach*, Addison Wesley: Reading, MA
van Veenendaal, E. and Wells, B. (2012) *Test Maturity Model integration TMMi: (Guidelines for Test Process Improvement)*, UTN Publishers: Den Bosch, The Netherlands
Whittaker, J. (2002) *How to Break Software: A Practical Guide to Testing*, Addison Wesley: Reading, MA
Whittaker, J. and Thompson, H.H. (2003) *How to Break Software Security*, Addison Wesley: Reading, MA

CHAPTER 6 TOOL SUPPORT FOR TESTING

Adzic, G. (2011) *Specification by Example*, Manning Publications Co: Shelter Island, NY
Axelrod, A. (2018) *Complete Guide to Test Automation: Techniques, Practices and Patterns for Building and Maintaining Effective Software Projects*: apress: New York, NY
Buwalda, H., Janssen, D., and Pinkster, I. (2001) *Integrated Test Design and Automation*, Addison Wesley: Reading, MA
Fewster, M. and Graham, D. (1999) *Software Test Automation*, Addison Wesley: Reading, MA
Gamba, S. and Graham, D. (2018) *A Journey Through Test Automation Patterns*, amazon
Graham, D. and Fewster, M. (2012) *Experiences of Test Automation*, Pearson Education: Boston, MA

AUTHORS

DOROTHY GRAHAM

Dorothy Graham (Dot) has been involved in software testing for roughly 50 years, since 1970, when her first job (for Bell Labs in the US) was as a programmer in a testing group, and her task was to write two testing tools (test execution and comparison). After emigrating to the UK (with her British husband), she worked for Ferranti Computer Systems, developing software for UK Police forces. She then joined the National Computing Centre as a trainer and courseware developer, and later became an independent consultant.

At that time, software testing was not a respected profession; in fact, in the early 1990s, many thought of testing at best as a necessary evil (if they thought of testing at all!). There were few people who specialized in testing, and it was seen as a second-class activity, and not well thought of. There was a general perception that testing was easy, that anyone could do it, and that you were rather strange if you liked it. It was then that Dot decided to specialize in testing, seeing great scope for improvement in testing activities in industry, not only in imparting fundamental knowledge about testing (basic principles and techniques) but also in improving the view testers had of themselves, and the perceptions of testers in their companies. She developed training courses in testing, and began Grove Consultants, named after her house in Macclesfield, UK. One of her most popular talks at the time was called *Test is a four-letter word*, reflecting the prevailing culture about testing.

It was into this context that the initiative to create a qualification for testers was born. Although not the initiator, Dot was involved from the first meetings and the earliest working groups that developed the first Foundation Syllabus, donating many hours of time to help progress this effort. This work was carried out with support from ISEB (Information Systems Examination Board) of the British Computer Society, and the testing qualification was modelled on ISEB's successful qualifications in Project Management and Information Systems Infrastructure. One of the aims at this time was to give people a common vocabulary to talk about testing, since people seemed to be using many different terms for the same thing.

Grove Consultants (Dorothy Graham and Mark Fewster at that time) gave the first course based on the ISEB Foundation Syllabus in October 1998 and the first Foundation Certificates in Software Testing were awarded. In her 20 years with them, Grove went on to be highly respected for the quality of their training material, particularly for ISTQB courses. Grove continues to licence high-quality ISTQB training material to organizations wishing to provide training without expending a significant effort in course development (www.grove.co.uk).

The success of the Foundation qualification took everyone by surprise. There seemed to be a hunger for a qualification that gave testers more respect, both for themselves and from their employers. It also gave testers a common vocabulary and more confidence in their work. The Foundation qualification had met its main objective of 'removing the bottom layer of ignorance' about software testing.

Work then began on extending the ISEB qualification to a more advanced level (which became the ISEB Practitioner qualification) and also to extending it to other countries, as news of the qualification spread in the international community. Dot was a facilitator at the meeting that formed ISTQB in 2001 in Sollentuna, Sweden. She has not been actively involved in the ISTQB Advanced levels.

Dorothy's other activities over the years include being Programme Chair for the first European testing conference (EuroSTAR 1993); she was Programme Chair again in 2009. During the 1990s, she started and later co-authored *The CAST Report*, a summary of commercial testing tools (in the days before the internet!). In addition to all editions of this book on Foundations of Software Testing, she was co-author of four other books: *Software Inspection* (1993) with Tom Gilb, *Software Test Automation* (1998) and *Experiences of Software Test Automation* (2012), both with Mark Fewster, and *A Journey Through Test Automation Patterns* (2018) with Seretta Gamba.

Her book with Seretta is the story of a team using the test automation patterns wiki, TestAutomationPatterns.org. This wiki, developed by Seretta and Dot, provides solutions that have worked for others for a number of issues and problems in test automation. The issues and patterns are organized into four sections: Process, Management, Design and Execution. The wiki was first published in 2013 and is a popular source of advice about test automation.

During her career, Dot has spoken at numerous testing conferences and events worldwide. She was awarded the second European Excellence Award in Software Testing in 1999 and was awarded the first ISTQB Excellence Award in Software Testing in 2012.

Her main non-testing activities include singing (choirs, madrigal groups and solos) and enjoyable holidays with her husband, Roger. They have two children, Sarah (married to Tim) and James.

Dorothy can be contacted on LinkedIn and www.DorothyGraham.co.uk.

REX BLACK

With over 35 years of software and systems engineering experience, Rex Black is President of RBCS (www.rbcs-us.com), a leader in software, hardware and systems testing. For 25 years, RBCS has delivered consulting, training and expert services for software and hardware testing. Employing the industry's most experienced and recognized consultants, RBCS builds and improves testing groups, trains teams and provides testing experts for hundreds of clients worldwide. Ranging from Fortune 100 companies to start-ups, RBCS clients save time and money through improved product development, decreased tech support calls, improved corporate reputation and more. As the leader of RBCS, Rex is the most prolific author practising in the field of software testing today. More about RBCS is shown after Rex's biography.

Rex's popular first book, *Managing the Testing Process*, has sold over 100,000 copies around the world, including Japanese, Chinese, and Indian releases and is now in its third edition. In addition to *Managing the Testing Process* and *Foundations of Software Testing*, Rex has written 12 other books on testing, including *Advanced Software Testing: Volume I, Advanced Software Testing: Volume II, Advanced Software Testing: Volume III, Critical Testing Processes, Pragmatic Software Testing, Agile Testing Foundations, Mobile Testing, Expert Test Manager* and *Fundamentos de Prueba de Software*. These works have also sold tens of thousands of copies, including Hebrew, Indian, Chinese, Japanese and Russian editions. He has written over 30 articles; presented hundreds of papers, workshops, and seminars; and given about 50 keynotes and other speeches at conferences and events around the world.

Rex is the past President of the International Software Testing Qualifications Board and the past President of the American Software Testing Qualifications Board. He remains involved in the ISTQB, having served as Project Manager of the Foundation 2018 Syllabus effort and as Chair of the Agile Working Group.

Rex is married to his college girlfriend, Laurel Becker. They met in 1987 at the University of California, Los Angeles. They have two children, Emma and Charlotte, and three dogs, Kibo, Mmink and Roscoe. They live in Bulverde, Texas and Lake Tahoe, California.

COMPANY PROFILE: RBCS, INC.

Rex Black Consulting Services (RBCS) is a premier international testing consultancy specializing in consulting, training and expert services. Led by one of the most recognized and published industry leaders, Rex Black, RBCS is an established company you can trust to show you results, with the track record to prove it.

Since 1994, RBCS has been both a pioneer and leader in quality hardware and software testing. Through its training, consulting and expert services, RBCS has helped hundreds of companies improve their test practices and achieve quality results. RBCS is based in the US, and works with partners around the world.

RBCS utilizes deep industry experience to solve testing problems and improve testing processes. It helps clients reduce risk and save money through higher-quality products and services. The consultancy's goal is to help clients avoid the costs associated with poor product quality (such as tech support calls, loss of business, customer dissatisfaction, lawsuits and reputation damage) by helping them understand and solve testing and performance issues and build better testing teams. Whether it's customizing a program to fit your company's needs, or providing the hands-on experience and resources that will allow your testing team to grow professionally, RBCS helps companies produce better products and increase ROI. RBCS pours its resources into ensuring our clients become successful.

Employing the industry's most experienced and recognized consultants, RBCS builds and improves testing groups, trains teams and provides testing experts for hundreds of clients worldwide. RBCS's principals include published, international experts in the area of hardware and software testing. Their skilled test managers and engineers all hold International Software Testing Qualifications Board (ISTQB) certifications and are highly trained.

RBCS believes in the value of real-life experience and leadership which is why the RBCS team is always striving to improve and perfect the testing process. Every trainer and consultant is ISTQB certified and encouraged to write articles and books, share leading ideas through presentations, and continuously research new ideas. In addition, as past President of the ISTQB and the American Software Testing Qualifications Board (ASTQB), Rex Black has more than 35 years of software and systems engineering experience and strongly leads the company with the most recent, proven testing methodologies and strategies.

RBCS' client-centred approach helps companies deliver better quality products and reduce costs by improving their test practices. The difference? RBCS's recognized industry experts started their careers in our customers' shoes; they have the real-world knowledge required to deliver the best services with proven practices.

From Fortune 100 to small and mid-size organizations, RBCS works with a variety of companies, in industries such as technology, finance, communications, retail, government and education.

RBCS offers customized consulting services that will not only help you solve your testing challenges, but provide you with the tools and framework for managing a successful testing organization. Our consulting methodology is based on successful, peer-reviewed publications with a customized approach that focuses on the individual needs of each client. Plus we have a long list of happy, referenceable customers around the globe that have benefited from RBCS expertise.

RBCS, Inc.
31,520 Beck Road
Bulverde, TX 78163
USA
www.rbcs-us.com
email: info@rbcs-us.com
Web: www.rbcs-us.com
LinkedIn: www.linkedin.com/in/rex-black
YouTube: www.youtube.com/user/RBCSINC
Facebook: www.fb.me/TestingImprovedbyRBCS
Twitter: @RBCS

ERIK VAN VEENENDAAL

Erik van Veenendaal is an internationally recognized testing expert, author of a number of books and has published a large number of papers within the profession. He is currently working as an independent consultant and as the Chief Executive Officer (CEO) of the TMMi Foundation.

Dr Erik van Veenendaal CISA graduated at the University of Tilburg in Business Economics. He has been working as a practitioner and manager in the IT industry since 1987. After a career in software development, he moved to the area of software quality, where he specializes in software testing.

As a test manager and test consultant he has been involved in a great number and variety of projects. He has implemented structured testing and reviews and inspections, and as a consultant has contributed to many test process improvement projects. He worked for Sogeti as manager of operations and was one the core developers of the TMap testing methodology. He is the author of numerous papers and a number of books on testing and software, including the best sellers *The Testing Practitioner, The Little TMMi, Foundations of Software Testing* and *Testing according to TMap*.

Erik van Veenendaal founded Improve Quality Services BV, a company that provides consultancy and training services in the areas of testing, requirements engineering and quality management. He has been the company director for over 12 years. Within this period Improve Quality Services became a leading testing company in

The Netherlands focused on innovative and high-quality testing services. Customers were especially to be found in the areas of embedded software (e.g., Philips, Océ en Assembléon) and in the finance domain (e.g., Rabobank, ING and Triodos Bank). Improve Quality Services was market leader for test training in The Netherlands both in terms of quantity and quality.

Nowadays Erik is living in Bonaire (Caribbean Netherlands) and is occupied as an independent consultant doing consultancy and training in the areas of testing (especially based on ISTQB Syllabi) and requirements engineering. He also publishes and delivers keynote presentations on a regular basis. In addition, he is actively involved in the TMMi Foundation, International Software Testing Qualifications Board and the IREB requirements engineering organization.

Erik, being one the initiators to found the TESTNET organization, is now an honorary member of TESTNET (the Dutch Special Interest Group in Software Testing). Erik was the first person to receive the ISEB Practitioner certificate with distinction and is also a Certified Information Systems Auditor (CISA). Erik has also been a senior lecturer at the Eindhoven University of Technology, Faculty of Technology Management for almost ten years.

Since its foundation in 2002, Erik has been strongly involved in the International Software Testing Qualifications Board (ISTQB). From 2005 till 2009 he was the vice-president of the ISTQB organization and he is the founder of the local Belgium and The Netherlands board; the Belgium Netherlands Testing Qualifications Board (BNTQB). For many years, he was the editor of the ISTQB *Standard Glossary of Terms used in Software Testing* and chair for the ISTQB Expert level working party. Today, he is the president of the Curaçao Testing Qualifications Board (CTQB). For his major contribution to the field of testing, Erik received the European Testing Excellence Award in December 2007 and the ISTQB International Testing Excellence Award in October 2015.

Erik can be contacted via email at erik@erikvanveenendaal.nl and through his website www.erikvanveenendaal.nl.

INDEX